Cultural Capital Doesn't Pay the Rent

A Queer Memoir

Jessica Lawless

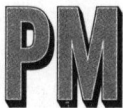

Cultural Capital Doesn't Pay the Rent: A Queer Memoir
© 2026 Jessica Lawless
This edition © 2026 PM Press

ISBN: 979-8-88744-168-9 (paperback)
ISBN: 979-8-88744-169-6 (ebook)
Library of Congress Control Number: 2025943654

Cover design by Courtney Davis
Interior design by briandesign
The ornamental flowers used to mark section breaks are Carolina Jessamine, a poisonous flower. They are inspired by the bell hooks section of the 1991 RE/Search Publications journal *Angry Women*.

10 9 8 7 6 5 4 3 2 1

PM Press
PO Box 23912
Oakland, CA 94623
www.pmpress.org

Printed in the USA.

Praise for *Cultural Capital Doesn't Pay the Rent*

"Granular in detail and expansive in scope, *Cultural Capital Doesn't Pay the Rent* bursts with the possibilities of self-actualization, mutual aid, and collective struggle. Resisting the redemptive arc to tell the truth about surviving domestic violence, the myth of upward mobility in academia, and the limitations of union organizing, Lawless offers not only a scathing critique of misogyny in all its forms but also an abolitionist analysis grounded in a quest for accountability and a desire to transform everything. I dare you to read this book without sobbing."
—Mattilda Bernstein Sycamore, author of *Touching the Art*

"In a voice all her own, Jessica Lawless takes readers on a journey that so many of us will recognize, through all the failing institutions of the past several decades: the family, the workplace, the activist movements promising to save us. She writes of her life with unflinching honesty, sparing herself least of all, through punk rock and queer community, in feminist self-defense work and art practice and finally labor unions. She offers no easy answers but dares to dream of movements that are built on a different set of values: an abolitionist feminist labor movement, one that challenges us once and for all to find meaning in our connections rather than our work."
—Sarah Jaffe, author of *From the Ashes* and *Work Won't Love You Back*

"Raw, brilliant, and uncompromising. Jessica Lawless captures the brutal reality of coming of age as a queer, working-class feminist in the wreckage of the American Dream. From the punk clubs of Seattle to the adjunct trenches of academia to the belly of the labor movement, Lawless traces a path through three decades of survival, resistance, and heartbreak with the fierce intelligence of someone who's lived every contradiction of late-stage capitalism. This is memoir at its most essential—no nostalgia, no easy answers, just the hard-won wisdom of a hardworking human who refused to be broken by a world designed to destroy us. Both deeply personal and urgently political."
—Ariel Gore, author of *We Were Witches*

"*Cultural Capital Doesn't Pay the Rent* is at once memoir and call to action; a history of violence and a love letter to queers and artists and freaks; a classic story of American poverty and an exceptional anticapitalist analysis from an organizer who dreams of something better for us all. Through her immersive storytelling, Jessica Lawless offers us a rich archive of a radical past that holds necessary wisdom for anyone who wants a better world."
—Raechel Anne Jolie, author of *Rust Belt Femme*

"In *Cultural Capital Doesn't Pay the Rent*, Jess's experiences in art and activist communities take us on a journey of how political the personal is. Jess's vulnerability about the violence they have survived offers so much insight into the ways the precarity of capitalism exacerbates the risk of violence. This is a stick-and-poke tattoo of a book: DIY, angry, messy, beautiful, fun, painful at times—and totally worth it. After reading it you will forever be a little bit different. A little punker, a little more beautiful."
—Katie Tastrom, author of *A People's Guide to Abolition and Disability Justice*

"Unable to withstand the sexist rambling of a know-it-all ponytail dude (an unfortunate character we've all run into at least once in our lives), Jessica Lawless finally snapped: 'I got up and left class, remembering that leaving is an act of self-defense.' This sharp, defiant humor cuts through a raw narrative chronicling a lifetime of violence, sexism, and the collapse of a system hell-bent on crushing its own people. Like a classic punk rock album, *Cultural Capital Doesn't Pay the Rent* is unflinching, profane, brilliant, hilarious, and terrifying all at once. If this book is a punk ballad, Lawless is its snarling frontwoman, screaming mercilessly into the fray. Read this book at full volume."
—Josh Fernandez, author of *The Hands That Crafted the Bomb: The Making of a Lifelong Antifascist*

"The do-it-ourselves ethos in this book is contagious. Lawless brings the lessons of a lifetime of organizing and creative cultural interventions to us right on time. You'll remember it the same way you do the first song that made you want to change the world."
—James Tracy, coauthor of *Hillbilly Nationalists, Urban Race Rebels, and Black Power*

for Mia, Marc, and Miranda
and for Minnie Bruce

Just to wake up tells me, hell, I must be brave.
—Mia Zapata

Contents

Author's Note

Memoir is a creative practice. As an artist, a writer, a ruminator, I was compelled to piece together the fragments and traces of my dreams and nightmares into a story. It's a collage process. The materials glued down on the page are memories I recorded in journals, notes I took at meetings, commentary I wrote in zines, art I made, videos I produced, photos I took starting when cameras used film and you had to cross your fingers and hope the moment of time captured was the right one but days later, when you got the pictures back, the wrong moment sometimes turned out to be even better. Some of the memories took shape in conversations with other people; some of them loomed so large for so long that the ice-solid shape only melted into words when I finally chipped away at it. The point is: This book isn't a documentary. It's not a researched autobiography, or a piece of journalism. It's memory shaped into narrative. I'm more concerned with beats and poetic flow than potentially offending someone with different memories or someone who has, over time, become a stranger. If you were there, you might notice sometimes names are changed and sometimes they aren't. There's an internal logic for when I choose to protect the guilty, when I choose not to, and when I left a trail of breadcrumbs that isn't hard to follow. And yes, absolutely, I'm as guilty as anyone. But I promise you, dear reader, that everything in this book is truth. If reading this leaves you feeling like I'm full of shit, please write your own memoir. I truly would love to read it.

PART ONE

SUBCULTURAL

[CHICAGO AND

SEATTLE]

CHAPTER ONE

Gasp

"You sound mature," the woman on the other end of the phone said, and I immediately felt my perimenopausal breasts droop slightly farther into my thickening belly. "I mean," she continued, "you have a lot of experience and knowledge. How would you feel taking an entry-level position?"

Sitting on the edge of the desk in my studio, I glanced at the framed poster on the wall across from me—a contorted depiction of President George W. Bush with the word *THIEF* in thick block letters above his head. I'd bought it a decade earlier from the artist Robbie Conal at a performance art exhibit in an industrial warehouse in Santa Monica. I shifted my gaze toward the floor-to-ceiling wall of windows displaying the ever-stunning northern New Mexico landscape. My partner, Von, and I were renting a house down the road from the community college where he worked as a cook and I worked as an adjunct professor. We were an economic collapse and a lifetime away from the Los Angeles art scene in which we were once young and fabulous queers.

Entry-level was a corporate term I didn't associate with my decades of earning a paycheck to pay rent while I made art and did activism. Nevertheless, I thought carefully as I answered the question. I really needed and even wanted this job organizing adjunct faculty unions. "As an adjunct professor, I don't have any upward movement," I said. "I have no idea if I'll have a job next semester. It's lower than entry-level."

Feeling the momentum of telling someone about my shitty state of employment, I kept talking. "There's no standard. Right now, I'm paid just over two thousand dollars a course. I'm making sixteen thousand dollars a year teaching six college classes. When I lived in Los Angeles, I taught at two different schools. I was paid thirty-eight hundred a class at one and eight thousand a class at the other." Talking fast, forgetting to breathe, I turned back toward Robbie's poster, a more contained frame to hold my thoughts than the endless cholla cacti dropping prickly needles onto the desert floor. "An entry-level position would be a step up."

There was an audible gasp. I still think about that gasp. I was being interviewed by a seasoned union organizer. She probably believed education was a path to middle-class stability, she probably had worked her way up a straightforward career ladder, she probably had employer-provided health care benefits and an income that allowed for savings. She probably had a retirement plan.

I felt like a loser, interviewing for an entry-level position at forty-six years old. Instead of learning about pensions or IRAs, I was looking for work, again. In the past few days, I had interviewed for a job with Planned Parenthood that paid a nonnegotiable thirteen dollars an hour, as well as an education position at a rape crisis center for eleven dollars an hour where a friend fifteen years younger than me would be my boss. I'd had an interview for an admissions specialist at a for-profit art school that went really well, but it turned out to be a call-center position conning potential students into taking out $30,000 in loans. The interview was conversational and engaging, and I got a call the next day. Instead of a job offer, I was told how much she enjoyed meeting me but that she thought I should be in a more advanced job, that I'd be too bored in the call center. I was glad not to be faced with the ethical dilemma of taking that job, but I didn't need someone else deciding what I was willing to do for a paycheck with health care.

I heard the union interviewer's clipped East Coast accent again. It had softened. "It's been very interesting speaking with you, Jessica. I appreciate your time and will be in touch in the next few days." I clicked off the phone and watched a cloud formation pull apart as rays of sun pierced through its center. The rain bursting inside sprinkled down while the other half of the cloud grew brighter. Frost glistened on the clumps of thirsty chamisa dancing across the open field between my house and the corral where my landlord's horse and donkey huddled together to stay warm. I watched them instead of making the post-interview notes the career counselor at the community college had suggested in an ego-bruising meeting I'd had with her for help updating my resume.

This interview was for an organizer-in-training position with the Service Employees International Union. Organizers-in-training are usually in their early twenties, with or without college degrees, applying for their first professional jobs. I had an undergraduate degree in visual arts, a master's in cultural studies, and a Master of Fine Arts—a terminal degree, or the highest degree in a field—in studio art. I had taught visual culture and studio art courses as a graduate student at the University of California, Irvine. I had taught as an adjunct professor in the American studies department at California State University, Fullerton. I had taught undergraduate and graduate courses focused on gender, race, and class in media studies and women's studies at the Claremont Colleges, and media arts and humanities at Santa Fe Community College. I had presented at professional academic conferences, at social justice conferences, in classrooms, and in activist spaces across the country. I had publications in peer-reviewed and popular journals and online activist and literary sites, along with a chapter in a book on contemporary video art practices. I had shown artwork internationally in galleries and film festivals. This litany of fancy-ass accomplishments doesn't include the self-defense organization I cofounded in Seattle after a friend was raped and murdered, the art I made individually and in collectives that had been part of queer, feminist, BIPOC activism for almost three decades, and the various jobs I had had since I was fourteen. My resume didn't include my vast range of life experiences, such as kicking the worst of my drug use and drinking, getting out of violent relationships, being homeless, and being off and on government assistance. There wasn't a bullet point to demonstrate how all of that shaped my ability to code-switch across racial, gender, and class lines and to make deep and authentic connections with people different from me.

During the interview with the union, I managed to do something I had failed to do in all my other recent interviews. I couldn't name it, but I could feel it in that gasp. I felt a tiny bit of the weight of lost dreams lift off my chest. I felt a tiny bit of hope.

❧❧❧

My first job was working for a friend of my mom's. No, my first job was babysitting, which I hated. That was back in the late 1970s, when people left their babies with stoned twelve-year-olds. When I was fourteen, my mom convinced a friend of hers working on a dissertation to pay me to go to the Evanston Public Library in the suburb just north of Chicago where we lived and scroll through microfiche film of old Hawaiian newspapers and write down mentions of a queen she was researching. At the time, my mom worked as a freelance editor. She said her clients, male doctoral candidates in the business school at Northwestern University, were terrible writers. She said she practically wrote the dissertations for them, that she should get the PhD. She told me she would have gone to graduate school if she had known that she had options other than to get married and have kids. "Good girls from White Folks Bay, Wisconsin, went to college for an MRS," my mom told me, her clever quip about growing up in the predominantly white Milwaukee suburb of Whitefish Bay covering up regret.

Before she married my dad, my mom worked for the Wisconsin Democratic Party. After my parents divorced, my mom was a resentful secretary in an architecture firm run by men. The part of herself she held on to was her passion for folk dancing. That's how she met my stepfather; they were in the same performance troupe. After they got married, she set up her editing business and worked from home. My stepfather had an MBA and celebrated paying off his student loans and his metallic-blue 1965 Ford Mustang the same year he came into our family. He worked for telecommunication start-up companies that formed after AT&T was forced to break up its monopoly. Always in management-level positions, he jumped around to different companies until he left the corporate world to build a folk-dance education empire with my mother. He also brought in money by dabbling in financial advising and renting out the top floor of the colossal house my dad had bought before the divorce. It was a middle-class household run by artist-hustlers, pieced together with gum and duct tape.

College was assumed. All my parents had gone. My older brother did too. I went to visit him once at the University of Wisconsin. I still remember the crowds of students feeling dangerous and overwhelming, like something terrible could happen and no one would pay attention. I decided college wasn't for me.

Neither was being an unhappy, resentful secretary. I ditched out on my required typing class for as many art classes as possible. It was easy to disappear in my public high school. My freshman class had a thousand students, though only six hundred made it to graduation. We were split up into three tracks. One for college (mostly white kids), one for work (mostly kids of color), one for not evidently college or work (mostly forgotten kids not easily categorized). I was in that last group. I worked as much as I could all through high school. First for my mom's friend who was writing her dissertation, then for another of my mom's friends with an at-home mail-order business. Once I could work legally, I got a job at the neighborhood hobby and craft store, where the girls took care of the craft section and the boys took care of the hobby section. I finished classes by noon my senior year so that every afternoon I could go to one of my three jobs: the craft store, a concession stand at Northwestern University, and as a studio assistant to a ceramic jewelry artist. I was sure that earning money and making art were the paving stones for a path into my own life.

I planned to drive slowly across the country after high school, seeking a world resembling Andy Warhol's Factory. I was infatuated with the music, the drugs, and the queerness I didn't yet fully understand. I would work at truck-stop diners when I needed money, an employment goal that came from a young adult novel I had read in junior high. In the book, two girls accidentally kill one girl's abusive stepfather and, to cover up his death, put his decaying body on ice in the back of the family station wagon and drive across the country to California.

California was my dad's dream, the place he imagined being if he felt he had a choice to do something other than get married, have children, and have a secure government job to provide for everyone. He told me he had dreamed about riding a motorcycle to San Francisco and owning a bookstore. San Francisco was where one of his girlfriends lived, the one who eventually became his third wife.

On one of our Sunday visits, a two-hour excursion to our favorite diner to drink orange sodas and eat french fries sprinkled with seasoned salt, I shared my post-graduation plan with my dad. "What car are you going to drive?" my dad asked, his nasally Queens accent rising sharply.

"I don't know. I'll figure something out."

"If you don't go to college, you'll always be a fuckup." His Hungarian intonations cracked distinctively on his already sharp vowels. "I know it doesn't matter what I say. You're going to do what you want," he said, drawing from his well-worn script that never explained why what I wanted to do was so wrong. The conversation ended with a comment blaming my mom for being too soft on me and a heavy, loud sigh.

My dad lived in Chicago, an hour's ride on the El away from my mom's house in Evanston. My relationship with him happened in sporadic chunks of time depending on his mood. Sometimes he canceled our plans, sometimes I canceled after we had a fight on the phone. When we did get together, we fought and ate, or we fought and then joked around while bowling, or he took me to an art museum and explained why what I liked was wrong. He never taught me the things he wanted me to know. He just let me know how I had failed his unstated expectations.

I thought having a job and earning my own way was what I was supposed to be doing. It was the message I got growing up in the house with my mom and stepdad. My dad's messages were confusing. He was of the first generation that could secure assimilation into the middle class and whiteness through education. That was the weight behind the unspoken expectations: I was supposed to carry on blending in and following the rules. Every message was about not drawing attention to what made us different—accented English, hard-to-pronounce names, unfamiliar religious practices, curvy noses and bellies, loud voices, a willingness to fight, ancestors killed in pogroms and genocide—even though we all wore the pain of not being like everyone else on our sleeves. My dad taught me that blending in poorly was better than taking chances on not passing as white. My mom taught me that we lived in the Jewish diaspora, that we were a tribal culture others hated, and that culture was the most important thing, more important than believing in punishing gods. They both taught me that we weren't from here, but there wasn't anywhere to go back to.

My parents both blamed their mothers for being too mean, too tough, too broken, and too fragile. "Personality traits skip a generation," my mom told me when I was old enough to learn that just being myself was a problem. In a scrapbook she kept called "Baby's First Seven Years," in the section for two-year-old memories, she wrote, "Jess is the toughest one in the family." There weren't a lot of entries by the time I was five. That was the year my parents separated.

"Maybe you're like our grandmother," my brother said to me more than once throughout my life. He meant our father's mother, who we had met only a few times. We were told she was difficult, crazy. Family lore said she was to blame for her brother's suicide. Family lore didn't account for their immediate family members who had stayed in Hungary and been killed in Nazi concentration camps. No one ever talked about what it might have felt like to be the ones who were still alive, the ones who left.

My father told me that when he was a kid, he couldn't sleep at night because of his parents' loud fights. He left Queens and went to college in Michigan because his uncle had said, "Go. Go as far away as you can," to escape the violence in his house. I could never understand why my dad didn't see the pattern he was handing down. The most important thing to me when I graduated from high school was getting as far away as possible from the violence in my house.

The list of the violence in my house I couldn't make until now:

1. My stepdad drank too much and expressed a prurient interest in my body, making me uncomfortable in my skin.
2. My best friend's sister's boyfriend, a Vietnam vet, supplied us with LSD and weed in trade for sex. We were twelve.
3. The man who moved into the house next door when I was fourteen put a train set and life-sized Candy Land game pieces in his front yard. He knew my mom and stepdad taught a folk-dance class at the parks and rec center on Monday nights and would call the house while they were gone to try to get me to have sex with him.
4. My brother punched me in the face one of the times our mom and stepdad were out of town performing with their folk-dance troupe. He was angry over something shitty I'd said that no one can remember. I was sixteen; he was twenty.
5. My high school boyfriend bruised and battered my teenage body and psyche.

My bruised body and broken sense of self were why I wasn't ready to go to college. I didn't understand that at the time.

"You can't break down over your body all the time!" my mother said with exasperation when I was in tears over a girl's casual—not mean—remark about my "thick" upper arms. "You will never make it in a dorm with other girls!" Dorms with girls sounded awful.

My upper arm was the part of my body my high school boyfriend, Luke, first bruised. We were at a party, sitting on a couch, drinking what we called Guyana—a mix of the liquor everyone stole from their parents combined with a generic red fruit punch. We were already too jaded to respect death, to respect the mass cult murder-suicide that had happened in Guyana four years earlier at Jonestown. I saw Luke's soft brown eyes go flat. He grabbed my arm discreetly, squeezing more tightly when I told him to stop. Then it was over. His eyes filled with tears. He put his head in my lap. We kept drinking. The next day I had finger-shaped bruises on my upper arm. I chose a long-sleeved shirt to wear to school on that humid spring day and skipped gym class.

The violence mostly happened in public, since we lived in our parents' homes. It mostly happened in rooms full of other almost-adults, but really only kids, who were drinking and smoking and avoiding going to homes filled with violence.

I don't remember Luke's fist coming at me that night at our friends' third-floor walk-up apartment. I do remember us sitting on the edge of a bed covered in coats. I had a drink in my hand, most likely a Tab and Bacardi 151. I probably had a Marlboro Red in my other hand.

I remember talking about our boss at Dyche Stadium on Northwestern University's campus, where Luke managed the concession stands and I worked selling nachos, hot dogs, and popcorn during women's volleyball games.

"You were flirting with him!"

I turned to see who Luke was yelling at.

"You were flirting with him!" Luke leaped up from the bed, above me but bent over, yelling in my face. "I saw you. You were flirting with him!"

"What the fuck are you talking about?" I felt my pupils widen and my eyes flatten with anger.

This memory is still incredibly cinematic in my mind: the long shot of the people in the bedroom receding, the depth of field blurring the details, Luke and me coming into sharp focus. The boy-man in front of me becoming an archetype of pure male rage reflected in the mirror on top of the dresser. My body on the floor, felled by his fist cracking into my face. A purely visceral memory transformed into visual remnants backed up by witnesses I no longer know.

Someone stepped forward to help me up. Confused, I started lashing out, punching and kicking the body closest to me.

"Don't hit me," the person trying to help me said.

Those are the words I didn't say out loud when Luke had hit me. No one said them to Luke. Something between rage and shame settled into my bones and latched onto my psyche, a demon I sometimes still hold too close. I froze. I couldn't break free from the layer of ice descending over me, locking me onto the outside edge of friendship, love, and human warmth for way too many years after that night.

I ran down the three flights of stairs to my car, forgetting my coat, pained by the bitter cold hitting my body. I only think I remember this. I do remember being inside the yellow Nova. I do remember Luke jumping onto the car, trying to keep me from driving away. I know he kicked out the driver's side mirror, because my stepdad was mad at me about it.

I don't remember driving home. I remember opening the back door even though I don't remember unlocking it. I took my platform heels off in the mudroom and pushed through the door to the kitchen, cringing at the squeak in its hinges. I floated across the kitchen and up the stairs until I saw my mother's shadow at the top of the landing. I remember this clearly. I remember feeling caught, clinging to the banister for balance while I looked upward, toward her. And I remember our exchange ten minutes after I'd fled the party.

"It's 3:30 a.m.," my mom said.

"I know," I said, from a few steps below.

"What happened to your face?" she asked.

Without missing a beat, I tapped into the ancient covenant made by battered women subconsciously protecting their abusers: "I fell into a door."

My mom remembers going to the bathroom and throwing up. But she didn't tell me that until many years later, when both our chests had loosened enough for air to push out the pained words of distrust between us, a bruise Luke inflicted on both of us that has never fully healed.

❦

Going to school with that black eye was horrible. I had to dodge looks of pity in the hallway and whispers behind my back. Going to work was worse, especially at the ceramic jewelry studio. At that time, the studio was in the basement of my boss's house. She, her sister-in-law, and I sat at a table rolling out clay beads. They both seethed, telling me they'd never liked Luke. I felt dumb. Then the phone rang. It was the police asking to speak to me. My mom had called the cops.

For her, calling them meant doing something to protect me. For me, dealing with the cops shined a spotlight more brightly on my shame. I had to leave work early and walk the five blocks home feeling afraid. Afraid I wouldn't remember the details of the lies I had invented to form a thin thread of self-preservation against too many rumors and too many other people's feelings.

I wanted my mom to get ice for the black eye distorting my face, to hug me, to tell me why she had left my dad, why she didn't trust her mom. I wanted my mom to make soup for me. These weren't things she could do.

From the distance of the present, I wish she would have called Luke's mom instead of the cops. She knew his parents. He was the younger brother of my brother's best friend. I wish my brother had intervened. But no one had taught him to do that for me. All these years later, I still need to remind myself there was no language for teenage dating violence in 1982. No one knew what to do about something there were no words for. Luke's violence became my problem to figure out on my own.

Luke's violence was layered. Our friend group was diverse—Black, white, Latinx, Asian, Christian, Jewish, and Buddhist. Middle and working class, probably also wealthy and poor. Queer, not only straight, something else that wasn't secret but that we had no words for. Except slurs. Luke was multiracial but didn't talk about it. His father was Irish Catholic, his mother—I still don't know. I texted my brother recently to ask if he knew. He didn't. It's stunning to me that racial identity never came up in the fifty years of friendship he's had with Luke's brother. And, I suppose, maybe it's not stunning.

There were four brothers. My brother's best friend and the youngest were fair-skinned with wavy red hair. They looked white. Luke and his oldest brother had brown skin, dark eyes, and wiry curls. They didn't look white. Once, in a photography class, a Black classmate asked how I knew Prince when they saw a picture of Luke. He was so pretty and so full of self-hatred. When he was fourteen, he went to the infamous Nazi march in Skokie, a suburb just west of Evanston where a large community of Jewish Nazi genocide survivors lived. Luke and his multiracial crew of friends idiotically waved swastikas.

A couple of years before Luke and I started dating, I was hanging out with him and his crew getting stoned. I was excited to be with them in his bedroom, to be part of a world of kids who didn't give a fuck about rules and parents. Some boy with piercing blue eyes directed his gaze at me and pointed to a swastika drawn on the wall. "You're Jewish, right? What do you think about that." It wasn't a question. I didn't know what to say. I felt danger. But I was more afraid of the possibility of not being accepted by this group. Until then, I'd had friends but wasn't part of a group. I was an outsider bullied for being a fat kid. Then I found drugs. And bulimia. And other teenage outsiders already holding too much pain. Luke told me to ignore the question about the swastika, that he was embarrassed it was still on his wall. I felt protected.

I had noticed how he protected his then-girlfriend when he'd wait for her outside our middle school, even though he was already in high school. When the bell rang, he'd be there smoking and pacing in the cold, waving hello with a big grin to people he knew. I felt cool when he waved to me. I'd watch him hug and kiss and wrap his arm around his girlfriend when she came out the door. I wanted to be his girlfriend. What I mean is, I wanted to be her, the girl I knew from smoking together in the bathroom. I wanted to have her confidence to show up alone at a movie like I saw her do when my best friend and I snuck out to go to a midnight showing of *The Rocky Horror Picture Show*. I wanted to project the *fuck off* attitude she projected when she came back from visiting her family in Texas, pregnant. Luke wasn't the father but he protected her when her body showed other people's secrets. I wanted someone to protect my body, which was keeping other people's secrets. So when Luke snapped at the blue-eyed nazi kid about the swastika and said, "Don't ask her about that," and then turned to me and said, "I don't like talking about that time. I don't think that way anymore," I was all in.

Three years later, Luke punched a hole in the living room wall of my mom's house and knocked me down so hard when I tried to stop him that he broke my arm. My stepdad covered up the hole with a wall hanging instead of fixing the damage Luke had made. When I OD'd at a concert and was rushed by ambulance to have my stomach pumped, Luke destroyed the hospital waiting room. He said a doctor told him I had died. My dad witnessed the destruction. I had called him to pick me up when the hospital wouldn't release me on my own as a minor. I don't remember my dad saying anything about Luke's behavior on the drive to drop me at my mom's house. All I remember is feeling like everyone was mad at me and knowing that I had to go to school the next day, like nothing was out of the ordinary.

Luke and I broke up for the last time after my senior prom. I graduated from high school but didn't drive across the country to California. The world had become too unsafe to explore it alone. I started to work full-time at the ceramic jewelry studio and moved out of my mom's house into an apartment building a block away from the Granville El stop in Chicago called "Artists in Residence." My dad hated the building, hated the neighborhood, hated that I didn't go to the college I had applied to only to appease him during my senior year. He developed a relentless plan: *Get Jess to College.* To mitigate his belief in my eternal fucked-upness, I enrolled in classes at a commuter art school. But I fucked up and ended up dropping out. Then my dad learned about Antioch College in Yellow Springs, Ohio, from a colleague whose fucked-up kid went there. I would fit in, my dad said. It was a college for misfits who wore dark trench coats like my friends and I did, he said.

Antioch gave credit for life and work experience in addition to academics, attracting other students like me who weren't college-bound right after high school. Internships called "co-ops" were required every year alongside classroom learning. The college's motto was "Be ashamed to die until you have won some victory for humanity," a quote by its first president, Horace Mann. What I liked the best about Antioch was that it was a quarter the size of my high school, a manageable, less dangerous size. My dad and I reached an agreement. I'd grudgingly go to college; he'd grudgingly accept that I wasn't going to what he considered a "good school."

In Yellow Springs, I worked at HaHa's, the locally owned pizzeria. I got the job through Sarah, a new friend I'd met smoking outside the campus cafeteria. My dinner shift at HaHa's started just as the theme song to NPR's evening news program came on the radio. When I had a co-op working for a sculptor, I'd arrive at the studio and grab the buffing tools just as NPR's morning news show came on the radio. Concerned the dulcet tones of progressive newscasts were concocting the wrong messages about work and art, Sarah had my back. She'd quickly switch off NPR and put on a witchy mixtape leading off with Grace Jones or Laurie Anderson.

Antioch was in the middle of southern Ohio farmlands, and it's where I found a punk rock, Warhol Factory–like group of pissed-off, creative young people. We drank, did drugs, and had sex with each other. We bonded in joyous mosh pits, sweatily dancing to each other's bands. The local band that glued everything together was the Gits. The lead singer, Mia, sang with the bluesy depths of Bessie Smith and the punk poetry of Patti Smith. I loved her lyrics and her stage presence. She was raw and genuine on and off the stage, openhearted in her alcohol-infused angst.

We didn't quite get each other at first. I was raw and genuine, but angry, accidentally shooting out my protective layer of sharp quills even when people were kind to me. But since Mia and Sarah were best friends and Sarah and I were becoming best friends, Mia and I decided to make a sculpture together to forge our own friendship. She had drawn a chicken on a sheet of rusted steel; her nickname was "Chicken" because of her skinny, knock-kneed legs. I helped her cut it out. I can still feel the pain of trying to cut through the too-thick metal with too-small shears.

Tired and frustrated, we took a break. Mia had a key to get into the locked art building, and we climbed the stairs to the studios on the top floor of the airplane hangar–like structure. In Mia's studio, she handed me a bottle of whiskey as she clicked on the cassette in her paint-covered tape deck sitting in the middle of her collection of oil paints. Patti Smith's album *Horses* came on, the same tape I played repeatedly on my own paint-covered tape deck, three studios over. Mia sang along to "Free Money."

"This is the first song I heard you sing. It was at that open mic," I said.

"Do you sing?" Mia asked me.

"No, I suck. But I think it'd be fun to try."

"Come by the practice space. I can give you some lessons."

I would take Mia up on that when I screamed my vocal cords raw during another cathartic quarter fronting Birth Control, an all-female punk band. Mia would share her healing ginger root tea and breathing exercises to help me get through the one and only performance of our three-song set.

We turned off the studio lights and carried the second bottle of whiskey outside to finish the metal sculpture. My hands hurt too much to keep cutting. I lay in the grass, looking at the stars and listening to Mia swear. Finally, she said, "Okay, you asshole, you're done." A rusty chicken with dangerously sharp edges lay in front of her. Using a cement trowel, we scraped a trench into the ground, then buried the chicken's feet down in the dirt. From far away it looked like it was walking across the grass. Toasting with the last of the whiskey, we then walked up Corry Street to our favorite bar. Mia bought me a rum and diet soda.

"I know you like this crap better than whiskey," she said, putting her arm around my shoulder, anointing me with her warmth.

✿❦✿❦✿

At Antioch, I learned art was connection. It was the secret to finding other people who thought differently and weren't afraid of pissing off everyone else. It became my way to be heard and seen, to communicate my rage to and at the world. Karen Shirley, my favorite professor, was a severe Midwestern woman whose dark hair was always pulled into a tight bun on top of her head. Her face was a maze of deep, beautiful smoker's lines. Karen worked in clay, influenced by ancient Japanese tea rituals and contemporary art theory. I loved sitting in her small office inside the ceramics studio smoking Marlboros together and talking about the books crowding her shelves.

"I want to make it look cracked," I said to Karen about a three-foot-tall hand-coiled clay vessel I was making, inspired by the Patti Smith song "Poppies" and its line about women being vessels.

"No. Don't make it *look like*," Karen said.

Her terse, succinct communication helped me understand how to go deeper than the surface, how to stop making art that *looked like* something and start making art that *felt like* something. I coiled and burnished the piece for days, forming it into a full, thick vessel. I fired it in a metal garbage can filled with sawdust, a precarious method that could have shattered the piece at any point in the forty-eight-hour process. After it had been transformed by fire, I pulled the vessel from the garbage can and set it on a table outside the clay studio. With welding goggles on, I climbed up on the table and whacked the piece with a hammer until it crumbled and split down one side, but not all the way down. I could physically feel the cracks in the clay reflecting the cracks I felt in my heart. I could feel myself becoming an artist.

Amid endless cornfields, Karen taught cutting-edge theory that eventually became known as postmodernism and cultural studies. She taught Marxist and feminist art history that challenged "imperialist, white supremacist, capitalist patriarchy," as I learned to call it from reading bell hooks. I learned about Gloria Anzaldúa, Cherríe Moraga, Lorna Simpson, Betye Saar, Adrian Piper, Robert Mapplethorpe, Andres Serrano, Kathy Acker, Lydia Lunch, Barbara Kruger, Jenny Holzer, the Guerrilla Girls, Group Material, ACT UP, Félix González-Torres. My world was rocked.

Art was a discipline. Art was a way of learning. Art had a history. Art was political. Art could change society.

Sarah and I collaborated on our senior art show, mounting a joint gallery exhibit on the first floor of the art building. My mom, stepdad, and dad all came to Yellow Springs for it. It was the first time since I was a kid that

I had a meal with both of my parents. It was also the last time. My dad didn't come to my graduation, expressing his disdain for the education I got at Antioch—yearslong commentary that continues to this day. No, it doesn't matter that he's the one who found the school and paid for part of the degree, or that I went there to please him and meet his demand that I get an education.

Graduating from Antioch was an accomplishment, especially considering how many students simply left after four years on campus, whether they had earned a degree or not. I may not have had a whole lot of historical dates or algebraic formulas memorized, but I was an independent, critically thinking, relatively functional grown person. At the time, working a minimum-wage job to pay the rent was possible, so my after-graduation plan began and ended with being an artist. I just didn't know where I wanted to live. Some of my college friends were moving to Minneapolis to help organize a new chapter of the burgeoning Green Party, but electoral politics wasn't the type of activism I was interested in. The Gits were headed to Seattle, where a music scene was taking off, but Birth Control wasn't continuing as a band and who the hell knew where Seattle was. Sarah and some other friends were going to Chicago, but I definitely didn't want to go back there.

Talking on the phone with my mom about my lack of a plan, she said, "Jess, come home. You know the city. And you can take care of the cats when we go out of town."

I stretched the phone cord as far as it would go to light a cigarette on the front porch of my rented house next to the cemetery on the outskirts of town. *Maybe it'd be nice to be home*, I thought while pulling more tar and smoke into my lungs.

A couple of months later, Sarah and I drove a U-Haul from Yellow Springs to the house in Evanston I'd sworn I'd never live in again. I was taking care of the cats while my mom and stepfather were in Hungary with their folk-dance troupe. Other friends who'd just graduated, who were done and moving to Chicago or just passing through, planned to meet at the house to hang out together before splitting off for the next thing. It turned out to be about eight people.

Within a few days, we'd managed to litter every surface of the living room and kitchen with beer cans and bottom-shelf vodka bottles. A fifth of whiskey sat next to the TV, where Sarah and Mia spent most of the day watching horror films. When *Dawn of the Dead* ended for the third time, Sarah said, "I want to finish reading *Cujo*." Mia and I headed to the kitchen to make drinks.

"Do you want to figure out those Patti lyrics now?" she asked.

We sat on the living room floor with a tape deck and a cassette of *Easter*. Mia took a red felt-tip marker out of her pencil case stuffed full of drawing tools. We pressed play and rewind for an hour until we were sure that the red words Mia scrawled into my spiral notebook were the correct lyrics to "Because the Night."

Two weeks later, Sarah and Mia hitchhiked to Minneapolis for a last adventure together before Mia went out to Seattle to meet the rest of her band and Sarah had to start the job she'd found in an artist's studio. I was looking for an apartment with Danielle and Eugene, two other art students who, I'm pretty sure, had graduated. We scoured rental listings in the *Chicago Reader* looking for places we could afford near the El, since none of us had a car. We found a three-bedroom apartment in Wicker Park right next to the Damen El stop on Milwaukee Avenue for $500 a month. Milwaukee Avenue was full of shuttered furniture stores, dive bars, and botanicas. Thanks to my working-class, Puerto Rican neighbors, there was also a uniform store that stocked smaller-sized men's steel-toed boots that fit me without having to wear extra pairs of socks.

Our Ukrainian landlord, another working-class population in the neighborhood, lived on the bottom floor of our three-flat walk-up. He made a lot of antisemitic jokes that we did our best to ignore, since we paid rent in cash and didn't have to prove we were employed. He also mumbled racist comments at people of color walking by the building as he picked grapes from the vines growing over the wrought-iron fence. His son sold drugs from the stoop, telling us how the neighborhood wasn't what it used to be, how suburban assholes were buying buildings for too much money, trying to push out the hardworking Ukrainians. Wicker Park was an experiential lesson in gentrification in 1989.

While Danielle and I were walking home from a gallery opening across the river one night, the streets were desolate. It was long after bar time, and the buses and El had inconsistent stops. Some asshole hanging out the passenger side of a car yelled crass, sexist shit at us. Used to it, we kept chatting while I flipped him off nonchalantly. The car screeched to a halt in the middle of the street and did two U-turns until it was dangerously close. A full bottle of beer smashed against the empty storefront in front of us. I turned toward the car, ready for a fight. Danielle had more sense and pulled me into a foyer for protection. We ducked down and covered our heads as several more bottles crashed against the brick and cement. Luckily none of them hit us. Covered in the spray of beer and glass, I was pissed as fuck at the misogyny, while taking in the message that I shouldn't assume this was my neighborhood.

I got work installing museum exhibitions through a friend of a friend of my brother's. She helped me get hired on my first gig, and after that I went from gig to gig, working at different museums. I picked up extra work on the cleaning crew for openings and special events. I saw a Basquiat for the first time when I hung it for an art auction and then helped hold it on the stage while rich people waved numbered paddles to place their bids on the painting.

I was on my way to install a show at the Museum of Contemporary Art when a poster wheat-pasted to a streetlamp made me laugh out loud. A blurry photo of a fetus specimen in a jar had a caption above it that said, "For all you folks who consider a fetus more valuable than a woman ..." Several suggestions for what they could do with a fetus were scattered around the image: "Cry on a fetal shoulder," "Try to get a fetus to work for minimum wage," and "Fuck a fetus." I felt less alone trying to ignore the men making crude comments about my body while I waited for my bus.

Over the next few weeks, I saw more and more stickers and posters along my routes to work, and while in bars, and when stopping in taquerias for vegetarian chimichangas. My favorite was "Get Angry ... Piss on Patriarchy." The most educational was "Misogyny. Look it up. Stamp it out." That's how I learned to spell *misogyny*. I loved the simplicity of "This is sexist crap: Don't buy it" stuck onto bus stop advertisements with airbrushed bodies of sickly thin women. Sister Serpents, a feminist art collective that modeled themselves after the Guerrilla Girls, were behind the public art. When they advertised a public meeting in the *Reader*, I went to it and immediately signed up to be a collective member.

Collective meetings were steeped in the feminist debates of the era. One of the most formative for me was the heated, hours-long meeting over our role as a leftist feminist collective in the campaign against the Chicago Police Department's torturous treatment of Black and Brown men in custody. The deadly racism of my hometown butting up against some socialist feminists' separatist beliefs taught me that gender oppression was more complex than individual experience. My individual experience with cops as a battered teenager who had been taught I was both white and not white put me in alignment with the one woman of color and the few antiracist white women in the collective who were pointing to the intersection of racism and sexism. Our side lost, and some members left the collective. I stayed, knowing I still had a lot to learn.

At other meetings, people passed around copies of the radical feminist publication *Off Our Backs*. I regularly confused it with the lesbian erotica magazine *On Our Backs* and was chastised by my sisters for that mistake. I liked *On Our Backs*. It was sexy and ironic and had excellent photography of inspiring outfits. Worried that I was misunderstanding the feminist perspective on sex and not wanting to be a dupe of the patriarchy, I joined some collective members at a porn shop protest. I didn't tell them about shopping for sex toys at similar shops with Lisa, my best friend from high school, or how much I enjoyed being fucked with large, lifelike dildos. At the protest, Sister Serpents stood side by side with born-again Christians whose brimstone and vigor scared the shit out of me to the point that I had to step away. I watched women chase cars through the parking lot, calling men pedophiles and rapists while Christians holding huge placards with antiwoman, antisemitic, and antigay biblical quotes cheered them on. I didn't go to the next protest. It was at a queer leather bar, "freeing" women consensually cage dancing with the headlining band.

Late-night, collective wheat-pasting missions posting art we had made was more my cup of tea. So was making our zine, *Madwoman*, with Helena, a bitingly funny collective member with an alluring British accent. We distributed the zine as part of the anticapitalist Mail Art movement, where for the price of a postage stamp, people all over the globe traded art and zines autonomously, outside of the elite, gatekeeping practices of the art world.

We put together a Sister Serpents art show at an alternative art space in Andersonville, a neighborhood on Chicago's north side. At the packed opening, a DJ pumped music in between spoken-word performances. A woman I didn't quite recognize came up to me to say hello. Shit. It was Erin, who had dated Luke after he and I broke up for good. The gallery suddenly felt claustrophobic. I had been able to create a new Chicago for myself after college, never running into anyone I knew from high school. Seeing Erin collapsed too much together. I froze.

"I really like your art," Erin said.

I didn't know what to do with her warm gesture.

I noticed that her hair was cut short.

"Luke's an asshole," she said.

"Did he hit you?" I asked.

"What do you think?"

The sounds of the gallery blared while we looked at each other in silence.

"Okay," Erin said. "See you."

Asking Erin about Luke's violence so directly made me realize I was always on edge. I couldn't ignore, but wasn't ready to confront, the violence I'd run away from six years earlier. It's why I was always annoyed when my mom asked me to take the two-hour ride on public transportation to her house. I didn't want to be pulled back into places I didn't trust.

Penelope, who was friends with Eugene and had been in Birth Control, came to visit us in Chicago. She had moved to New York and was working as a truck driver for an art installation company. She wanted to drive out to Seattle, where she had been living before New York, to get her deposit back from her former landlord. I wanted to visit Mia, who had called me a couple of times to tell me about the music and art and the people she was meeting. So when the fancy art world went on summer hiatus and there wasn't work, Penelope and I rented a car and drove out west. It was the trip I had wanted to do since I had read that young adult novel. With no dead stepdad in the back, and unlimited mileage, the car only cost us ninety-nine dollars. We traded off driving, stopping to camp when we got tired. In the mornings, we'd freshen our black eyeliner in the rearview mirror while making coffee over a campfire. When the grime got to be too much, we pulled into truck stops with extra-large bathroom stalls and took turns changing into clean knee-length cut-off black shorts and band T-shirts. We called our friends from the telephones at the restaurant tables, giving them updates on our travels while eating a cornucopia of fried foods.

Once we got to Seattle, Penelope staked out her landlord while Mia and I walked through the incessant rain, touring her favorite bars in Queen Anne. I got drunk at the diner in Belltown where Mia worked, waiting for her to get off shift. The handsomest, butchest butch I'd ever met served me the strongest vodka tonics I'd ever drunk. I would listen to the butch's stories about their boat and truck and gun, sort of giggling, sort of rolling my eyes, but having a really good time. In the evenings, Mia and I met up with Penelope and other friends to see bands at the Vogue and the OK Hotel. Seattle was cool. I decided to complete the mission I had inherited from my father and move there, getting as far away as I could get from the violence of my childhood.

Isolated in the farthest northwest corner of the country, Seattle felt more like a small town than a city. The pace and culture reminded me more of Yellow Springs than Chicago. Not just because Antioch people were everywhere. The Gits, or another band full of my college friends, played shows so often that going to work with a hangover was as common as being wet from the rain. Demonstrations against the Gulf War happened as regularly as bands played in clubs. I found the anticapitalists and anarchists at the first protest I attended. They were clustered around a huge banner exclaiming "Seattle General Strike, 1919–1990." Left Bank Books, the collectively run anarchist bookstore in town, was an anchor. My usual outfit comprised steel-toed work boots and a "Fuck Bush" sweatshirt, garnering invites to organizing meetings and community dinners. When stickers, flyers, or zines were needed, I printed them under the radar at my new job at a locally owned print and copy shop on Capitol Hill near the community college.

One day the bartender from the Comet Tavern, the bar where I hung out with my band friends, came into the shop to make flyers for a Vietnam Veterans Against the War teach-in. She was wearing olive-drab coveralls and steel-toed work shoes. Her caramel-brown hair, instead of pulled back like at the bar, hung loose and shimmered down to her waist. It was as striking as her toughness. When she pulled out her wallet to pay, I said, "Don't worry about it."

"What do you mean?" she asked, raising up to her full five feet nine and one-half inches, scanning the room for a trap.

No one else was in the store, though it wouldn't have mattered. The store manager openly skimmed cash from the register because, as he explained, he was from a socialist country and didn't understand how a job didn't pay enough to cover basic needs like health care. He believed the company owed all of us more than we were paid and encouraged me and my coworkers to follow his example, which I did. Without guilt. Because, fuck the Man.

The bartender looked like she wanted to say something else and also like she was about to run out the door. She was catlike. I liked her.

"What's your name?" I asked.

"What's yours?" she answered.

"I'm Jessica. Antiwar copies are free."

"Mich," she said, finally getting it. "Thank you. Will you be at the Federal Building later?"

I nodded yes. We waved goodbye.

At the Federal Building, I found Mich pumping her fist in furious agreement with the former Vietnam veteran speaking. I waved to my Left Bank Books friends but stayed next to Mich. We chanted, "One, two, three, four. We don't want your fucking war!" Intriguingly hardcore without being punk, she yelled in anger to the sky one minute, whispered conspiratorial commentary on US imperialism into my ear the next, then stomped off to convince the riot-shield-wielding cops to quit their jobs. When the war ended, Mich and I both joined a planning committee for an anarchist-led antifascist march. We worked together, using intel we had from Portland anarchists to create a route between the different apartment buildings neo-Nazis from Portland had recently moved into. At some point, we discovered we had each worn tuxedos to our high school proms, attending the dance with boyfriends who were violent. We forged a closeness, learning how to name some of the shame held over similar histories.

In addition to planning the march, I participated in direct actions taking over abandoned buildings for no-to-low-income housing. Zoë, who I had met at an antiwar demonstration at Westlake Mall when she handed me a five-gallon plastic canister to drum, was also involved in the building takeovers. She volunteered at Left Bank Books and did labor support. When I asked how she liked working for unions, Zoë laughed giddily and said, no, she did doula support. I told her about Sister Serpents, and then she and I, with a group of other women, formed Lilith's Revenge. During late-night wheat-pasting and stenciling sessions making art against the Christian Right and their attempt to overturn *Roe v. Wade*, Zoë and I bonded by making snarky comments about lesbians who thought, because we were bi, we brought boy germs into the dyke community. It was a sort of coming out, claiming a queer identity in community. For me, being out about my sexuality wasn't as fraught as being out about sexual and gendered violence. No one, including me, questioned my sexuality the same way my experiences of violence were questioned. In Seattle, I was finding friends and communities to connect on all of it.

Everyone I met was consciously creating new, radical worlds. Most people lived in collective households: the Rat House, where the Gits lived with other musicians; King Street, where Left Bank Books folks lived; the Slut Hut, where Zoë and other queer friends lived. Roommates were critical, intimate relationships, sometimes sex partners, but more importantly partners in survival in the way others might rely on family members or monogamous partners. We shared bills, cars, groceries, and pets. We planned meals together, created systems for household chores, and grew abundant vegetable gardens whose harvests got distributed among other collective households and unhoused neighbors. As roommates, we hosted political organizing meetings, started bands, held art shows, and put together fundraisers for emergency medical needs. The fullness of how my new city held me made it possible to temporarily cut off communications with my Chicago family. Setting that boundary was a way to figure out who I was outside of their story about me.

I decided to volunteer at a domestic violence shelter. I signed up for the forty-hour training at New Beginnings, an organization with a stated feminist mission. The first session connected some of the misfiring synapses in my brain. I told the trainer I was pretty sure I had been in an abusive relationship in high school, a fact I tried on for size in a context where I was both believed and offered support toward healing. She gave me the number for a feminist therapist who taught in the counseling program at the Antioch extension college in Seattle. That felt safe. I called her and made an appointment. Her name was Marie-France. She was soft and round, both motherly and sisterly but without the sharp edges I associated with family. She had a sliding scale for client referrals from New Beginnings that went down to just five dollars a session. She said that there had to be some payment for the labor she performed, that emotional support was devalued as feminized work. She said paying five dollars instead of zero was a way to take responsibility in my relationship to her, and in my healing relationship to myself. Both had value, she said. If we weren't in a capitalist economy, there could be other ways to show value, she said. And she said that five dollars was clearly not about profit, it was about making a commitment to each other through shared values. I still feel her softness and firm boundaries influencing me today.

I was able to call what happened with Luke domestic violence, which helped me realize a relationship I'd had at Antioch had also been abusive. D'Cazzoni, who everyone called by his last name, was Italian and from New York. We dated for a couple of years. He bristled with dissatisfaction and entitlement but could flash a smile that made time stand still. People actually stopped him on the street to comment on his looks. He'd grin widely, lean cockily, and then spew out racist, misogynist, and antisemitic phrases in Italian that he'd learned from his grandfather. His admirer, not understanding his words, would coo with appreciation over the performance. There isn't one time I can remember him being caught by an Italian speaker, at least in Ohio. There are plenty of times I remember losing patience with his dickishness—to others, a seemingly out-of-the-blue response. D'Cazzoni would shrug his shoulders and open his palms in feigned innocence, conspiratorially pulling his admirer further into his soft brown eyes while throwing me under the bus. *She's jealous*, he'd say. *She's on her period*, he'd say. *Women*, he'd say.

People were so willing to see my anger against his beauty.

D'Cazzoni was a heroin addict. I was ready for heroin. Oh man, was I ready. The blissful liquid sensation that took over my thought processes quieted the ever-present anxious ruminations. It calmed my hypervigilant nervous system. I floated into stillness as the empty, aching hole beneath my sternum filled. Bulimia had prepared me for puking as a way to a reward, so that part of the high never dissuaded me. High, I could feel D'Cazzoni loving me for loving the thing he loved. High, I could love myself. Nothing but heroin has ever given me hours of sustained freedom from the weight of trauma. I still ache from the loss of that fraught remedy.

Each time I broke up with D'Cazzoni, he'd show up with the little packets of China White dope I loved, offering me the escape route I was always seeking. When he had me back in his bed, he'd crush any beauty, touching my body without permission when he thought I was passed out. I could feel him feeling his own guilt and shame as I pretended to be sleeping. Sometimes I'd unfreeze, roll over, and kick him off me. I never called it rape. I didn't know that's what it was.

I was finally done the day D'Cazzoni got to our media studies class late, sat down next to me in the back row of the lecture hall, and whispered, "Good morning, baby. Sorry I didn't come home last night." He saw it in my eyes. He saw it in my posture as I rose from my seat. It made him jump up and bolt through the lecture hall door. I chased after him until we got to the construction site where the new dorms were being built. He bent over to catch his breath, then pulled out a smoke from the inside pocket of his black trench coat. I picked up a sawed-off two-by-four. As he straightened up, I swung. He jumped back. I kept swinging it, creating distance between us. He ran off yelling. I felt calm. Not as calm as being high, but still.

That story followed me to Seattle, where some of my male Antioch friends laughed about it. They laughed about how I stomped my engineer boots onstage during the Birth Control performance, singing about wanting to be left alone unless I was drunk in the bar. *Screw you*, I thought. I still had Mia and other female friends from Antioch. And I had Mich and Zoë, I had my Lilith's Revenge friends, my Left Bank Books friends. I had activism, art, queerness, therapy, and new understandings of my former experiences. My anger and pain weren't a joke, they were mine.

✿❀✿❀✿

Bryce was funny, an anarchist who was the son of a cop. He grew up in Seattle in an Irish and Indigenous family. We met at an art build for the antifascist march, making fake blood to throw on Nazis. When I was with him, I felt silly in a good way, laughing and smiling at stupid shit. We drank a lot of whiskey and vodka while making art, painting wall-sized canvases with oil paints that we'd drip blood into from the geometric patterns we'd cut into our forearms, hoping to leave scars as a forever mark of our relationship. It was love and angst with no definition, because people weren't property and property was theft.

Bryce and I moved into a collective household together, as roommates. The semi-squat was a house that belonged to the family of a friend from the Comet. There was an estate battle over the property, which had two houses on it, one too dangerous to enter, another too iffy to put on the rental market. That's the one we lived in. We had an agreement with the owners to fix old plumbing, faulty electricity, and crumbling Sheetrock for $100 a month rent and a promise of long-term housing. Unfortunately, the houses had been neglected for too long, and none of our repair work made a difference. Fortunately, we didn't have to pay rent most of the time. The Bunker, as my former-soldier-turned-anarchist roommate called our house, became a central hangout for our other squatter friends. We made vegan meals from dumpster-dived delicacies and food bank staples while planning for a postrevolutionary world with nearly impossible community standards we'd spend hours arguing over. It was mostly fun.

Bryce and I rode an emotional roller coaster where it was the two of us against the world when it wasn't the two of us against each other: He could fall into drunken emotional wormholes fighting the demons of his childhood abuse. I'd bring him to the emergency room when he was bleeding and broken from punching new holes in the exposed lath of our squat. He'd pull me out of darkness, including the heroin den I found my way to during a brief but spectacular relapse that resulted in lost friends and lost employment.

When Bryce and the Bunker felt like too much, I'd escape to the Comet to drink with Antioch friends and talk politics with Mich while she served pints. Or I'd ride my bike to the Slut Hut, where we'd watch queer porn, have tattoo parties with a homemade tattoo gun, play with BDSM needles in platonic configurations, or create witchy papier-mâché body-casting rituals. Life felt balanced.

CHAPTER TWO

3:30 a.m. and $330 a Month plus Food Stamps

I was at a collective meeting for the anarchist café I was going to open with friends from Left Bank Books and King Street. We had just reached consensus to name the space the Black Cat Café when the phone rang. It was for me. Which was strange, because we were meeting at someone else's house.

I put the receiver to my ear. "You should come home," Bryce said on the phone.

When I asked why, he said, "Just come home."

The tone of his voice was unnerving. So was the fact that he was calling me. We were usually together, and if we weren't, we weren't looking around for the other, since our relationship was chaotically anarchistic, *No gods, no masters* and all. Something was clearly wrong. I left the meeting and walked the few blocks to the Bunker. I turned down the alley toward the back door of our house—the front door didn't open and close properly. I was doing some version of a prayer that my cat, Zar Bar, wasn't dead. That's when I heard the Gits' first album blasting and knew whatever was going on had to do with Antioch. I sighed, feeling relief that Zar was alive.

Bryce turned down the music and handed me a pint bottle of whiskey. I took a swig as I sat down on one of our ragged dumpster-dived chairs. Waiting.

"Danielle called," Bryce told me.

Danielle, my Chicago roommate who lived in Oakland now and hated Bryce. I couldn't imagine what she would have to say to him.

"Mia's dead."

Relief left my body.

SEATTLE POST-INTELLIGENCER

July 7, 1993

Woman's body found in street

The body of an unidentified woman in her 20s was found in the 100 block of 24th Avenue South shortly before 3:30 a.m. yesterday.

SEATTLE POST-INTELLIGENCER

July 8, 1993

Central Area—The woman's body that was found Wednesday morning in a Central Area street has been tentatively identified as Mia Zapata, a vocalist in a local punk rock group, The Gits.

There aren't words to convey the feeling that I knew she had been raped before that part of the crime was made public. It still feels impossible to tell you how I felt about Mia's death when it happened.

There wasn't a suspect, no identified perpetrator.

Men who loved her, dated her, slept with her, went to her shows, were in bands that opened or headlined for the Gits, drank at the Comet, knew her in some way, all voluntarily gave DNA samples to the Seattle police.

Her bandmates organized fundraisers to hire a private detective. Nirvana played at one of the first shows, before Kurt Cobain killed himself.

Unsolved Mysteries, *48 Hours*, and countless other shows recreated Mia's death over and over and over.

No shows were made about her life.

Mia's dying body was discovered at the same time of morning that I'd run away from Luke the night he gave me a black eye. I couldn't process this fact at the time. It lived as an expanding knot inside that unfathomable shock of violence.

Writing this now, I still feel overwhelmed. And intensely sad. Repetitive trauma enmeshed with unadulterated grief hurts across time and space.

The night Mia was killed, she had been grief-drinking for her friend Stefanie Sargent, the guitarist in 7 Year Bitch who had died from a heroin overdose a year earlier. Ten days after Mia died, Ray Skilton, the bass player in the band Christdriver, was killed while riding his bicycle over to his girlfriend's house. Mia and Ray had both left the Comet before they were killed. Violence had shattered the foundation of my new home.

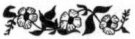

After Mia's funeral—after her wake, where I saw Ray, and then after Ray died and after his funeral—Steve, the Gits' drummer, my Antioch friend, called to tell me there was a meeting to "do something." I crawled through my tunnel of grief to join thirty other people meeting at another Antioch friend's house. We sat in a circle on her living room floor and made the decision to organize a week of concerts, art exhibits, self-defense classes, and antiviolence education. I left the Black Cat Café collective to give 100 percent to this new collective project intended to hold our community's grief, rage, fear, and vengeance. With each meeting, the group got smaller and smaller, until we were nine women determined to live despite looming death. We called the collective Home Alive, because we wanted to get home and be home, alive.

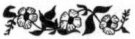

The Bunker was falling into even more disrepair. The owners determined it wasn't safe and said we needed to move out right away. Bryce decided to move in with Ray's roommates, into Ray's room. It was painted black, like Bryce's bedroom at the Bunker. There was another bedroom in Ray's house that could be cleaned out and rented to me. Or I could move into an Antioch household that came together after the Rat House was sold. I could live in Mia's old bedroom. That was just too much, so I moved with Bryce into Ray's grieving household.

Three months later, at 3:30 a.m. on Halloween night, I stood at the bottom of the nine partially broken wooden stairs leading up to the rickety porch of our new-to-us house. Bryce appeared in the front doorway, looking possessed. His dirty brown dreadlocks whipped around as he looked at me and ran back inside. Our fight had started hours earlier. We had been sitting in his truck outside the Off Ramp, waiting for our friends' band to start. Bryce told me a woman he had slept with was pregnant. She said he was the father, but Bryce said he didn't believe her because he had only slept with her once. I felt the veil of believing in him drop away into a truth I had been avoiding. He felt it too. I opened the door and left his truck in silence. He yelled at me to yell at him. I just wanted to get away from feeling disappointed and betrayed. I went into the club and ordered a vodka tonic. Then another. Then another. I danced in the middle of the mosh pit while our friends' band ground out music that matched my mood. I saw Bryce watching me, tracking me. When the band stopped, he walked over to me.

"Let's go home," he said.

I didn't want to be with him. I said I was going to a party at a friend's house and walked up the steep Denny Way hill to 10th Avenue on Capitol Hill, talking to myself all the way. Bryce showed up at the party. I tried to hook up with one of my crushes to avoid going home. Bryce intervened. I drank more vodka and tried to hook up with anyone who wasn't Bryce while Bryce shadowed me.

After a while, Bryce said, again, "Let's go home."

I thought he sounded gentle, caring. But maybe he also sounded mocking. I said I'd walk, and then I remembered Mia had walked home the night she was killed.

"C'mon," Bryce said. He took advantage of my hesitation and walked me out to his truck. He also offered my crush a ride home.

I was so drunk. I held back tears watching my crush walk into her house.

"I know you're mad at me," Bryce said.

"No shit," I replied. We didn't talk the rest of the drive.

At home, Bryce opened the refrigerator, took out a beer, and handed me a bottle of cold vodka. "I know you hate me and want me dead," he said.

I was leaning on the oven across from the fridge and looking past him, looking at the back door and thinking about escaping the fight I was too tired to have. Suddenly he was in front of me holding the butcher knife that had been lying on the small kitchen island in the middle of the room.

I covered my face. He grabbed my hands, trying to make me hold the knife while yelling, "Kill me, kill me!"

I grabbed the knife from him and threw it across the kitchen. The distraction was enough for me to push past him and out the back door into the yard.

Bryce followed. He ran over to the bush where our roommate had buried a litter of kittens who had died from malnutrition. Bryce took a rake and clawed back the dirt grave. He screamed about death, reciting lyrics from Neurosis, his favorite band. My cat, Zar, ran out from under the bush, wide-eyed and scared. Bryce looked shocked to see Zar. I went back into the house, following Zar to our room. I lay on the bed, petting him, trying to calm us both. I apologized for being a horrible parent. Bryce was back inside, rummaging through his room. I kissed Zar and tiptoed out the front door, down the nine rickety steps. I looked at the halfway house for recent parolees across the street, then behind me to the barbed wire topping the chain-link fence surrounding the juvenile detention center across the other street. I stood still, trying to figure out which direction I'd find safety.

Bryce appeared at the top of the stairs. He ran back inside. I stayed still. He appeared again. He was holding the huge console TV from the living room in his arms. I almost laughed. He looked like one of R. Crumb's *Keep on Truckin'* figures. Big boots, long arms, a tiny little head with a spray of knotted locks: a punk rock cyborg charging down the stairs.

I felt the familiar slow motion of chaos turning into calm. I settled into a fighting stance, a skill I'd recently learned in one of the first classes Home Alive offered. I put my right leg slightly behind my left, widened my stance, bent my knees, and readied one arm in front of my chest, the other in front of my face.

Bryce ran past me, screaming, "Arrrrrrrgggggghhhhhh!" Then he smashed the TV in the middle of the street.

"Arrrrrrrgggggghhhhhh!" he screamed again as he ran back toward the house and up the porch stairs.

Still in my fighting stance, I trained my eyes on him while my peripheral vision caught the shower of glass and plastic TV parts still ricocheting off the damp cement. I took a few deep breaths, another act of self-defense I had just learned. Oxygen moving into my brain, I tried to decide if I should go back in the house or not. Then Bryce appeared at the top of the porch with his gun.

He'd bought the assault rifle on sale at a gas station in Idaho, just across the Washington state border. He said it was for the war against the fascist state our anarchist community believed was imminent.

Boom!

A thick gel ran through my veins and washed over my skull. No amount of deep breathing cleared my thoughts. Fortunately, I had just finished reading a book of self-defense success stories by women who had fought their way out of sexual and physical assault. A voice in my head hollered: *Run in a zigzag, Jessica. Run in a zigzag!*

Boom!

I ran around the side of the house, zigzagging.

I squatted down low and kept moving toward the backyard. Bryce came running out the back door. I stayed low. *Should I run in the opposite direction or keep moving forward?* The self-defense I was learning gave scenarios for stranger attacks, not freaking-out, anarcho-revolutionary, polyamorous lovers.

Bryce jumped into his truck and parked fifty feet in front of me. I stayed close to the side of the house in case he planned to drive up on the lawn and run me over. He didn't. He punched the gas and sped off up the hill on the street behind our house.

Later, he said he took off because a cop had driven by and he was scared he'd be arrested. I remember cars driving by. If one was a cop, then a man shooting an assault rifle at a woman in our neighborhood wasn't worthy of a stop.

I had thirteen dollars in my pocket and didn't own a car. No buses were running. The streets were a safer place to be than my house.

I walked in the direction he had driven, figuring I was safer behind him. I sat at a bus stop where, a week earlier, a man had asked me, "How much for a blow job?" I stood up. I sat down. I stood up. I glanced around and saw a pay phone. Reaching into my pockets, all I felt was the two fives and three singles folded up. No change. I sat down, wanting a drink, realizing I wasn't drunk anymore.

Mich, I thought. She'd just be getting home from her closing shift. I dialed zero, then Mich's number. The operator came on the line.

"I'd like to make a collect call," I said.

"Whom do I say is calling?" she said in that flat, unaccented voice.

"Jessica." I heard the click and buzz of the telephone line.

Mich picked up.

"I have a collect call from Jessica. Do you accept the charges?"

"I accept," Mich replied. The operator clicked off.

"What's going on?" Mich asked me.

I started crying.

"Come over. Call a cab. I'll pay for it."

Mich didn't tell me then, but she kicked someone out of her bed to care for me that night. Thousands of miles from our families of origin, she was able to do what we both wished our families could have done when we were teenagers.

The cab company didn't accept collect calls, so I had to walk back home to use the phone. When I got there, all the lights were on and voices were coming from upstairs. I walked halfway up the stairs and saw Bryce kneeling in front of our roommates, handing over his gun like an offering. My female roommate looked over at me. I couldn't read anything in her eyes. She looked back at Bryce and stayed by her boyfriend's side. No one said a word to me. It felt like lines had been drawn.

I called Orange Cab from the living room phone and then went to my bedroom to get a coat.

"Zar ... my fluffy muffin." He was sitting on the black lace camisole and L7 T-shirt I had tossed on the bed while deciding what to wear earlier that evening.

I whispered, "Zar Bar ..."

His golden eyes were wide, his pupils black discs.

"Oh, sweet kitty." I scooped him up and hugged him to my chest. "I'm sorry. I'm sorry. I have to go, but I'll come back tomorrow. I'm sorry I have to leave you here."

He rubbed his chin against mine. I started crying again.

I put Zar back on the bed, trying not to throw up.

I wasn't working when this fight happened. The copy shop, losing money, had closed. I got a job at the dyke-owned pizza place on 15th, which I then lost when I had that relapse. I tried selling 'shrooms and weed with my ex-roommate, the former-soldier-turned-anarchist, but we ended up losing money due to issues with keeping the products stocked. Some of my anarchist friends advised me to go on public assistance, on a program called "General Assistance–Unemployable." It was an antistate intervention to use the welfare system to fund anarchist mutual aid projects like Food Not Bombs and Books to Prisoners. Living on welfare instead of working a conventional job and paying rent was an intentional fuck-you to the Reagan/Bush war against poor people and the manufactured, racist "welfare queen" stereotype.

I ended up on welfare as a desperate queer queen as much as, and maybe a bit more than, an ideological choice. I relied on the emergency room at Harborview, known as the poor people's hospital. Between Harborview and the Country Doctor, a feminist community clinic founded by Black Panther–adjacent antiwar activists, I was able to get care for my inflammatory bowel disease, a chronic illness I'd been diagnosed with at fourteen. During an emergency room visit at Harborview that Bryce drove me to, when I was bleeding from my ass, unable to eat, losing weight unintentionally, and doubled over in pain, the ER doctor told me I had colon cancer. I told her that I just needed my meds. When my scans came back showing IBD and not cancer, she told me I was lucky because cancer was imminent, having my disease as long as I had. She then class-shamed me by doctor-splaining why I should get health care instead of relying on the ER. I started crying, overwhelmed. Her response was to order a psych evaluation instead of prescribing my meds and letting me leave. I met with an impassive psychiatrist, continuing to cry as he asked intrusive questions about my life I didn't want to answer. I was deemed uncompliant and unable to hold down a job. I got my meds and a meeting with a social worker, who filled out paperwork I was told to bring to the unemployment office in the Central District the following day, which I did. I felt extremely conscious of my purple hair and tattoos while being interrogated about being twenty-seven, needing welfare, and not having any children. I left having been approved for $330 a month plus food stamps. None of it felt liberatory, or like a better world.

Bryce went to stay with his parents the day after he shot off the gun. I stayed with Mich the night of the fight but then went back home so Zar Bar wasn't alone. Back in the house, with Bryce gone, I noticed things that surprised me I'd been able to ignore. Like that my roommates weren't able to get home from work in time to take their two large dogs out, so there was dog shit all over the house. Or that the five other cats in addition to Zar, who had his food and litter box in our room, had only one always-overflowing litter box in the kitchen pantry, making the kitchen nearly impossible to use. Sitting on the threadbare, dumpster-dived couch staring at the empty space that had previously been occupied by the TV, I realized I was absentmindedly playing with bullet casings scattered in the crevices of the cushions. This is where Bryce and my roommates cleaned their guns while getting stoned and watching *The Simpsons*. This wasn't a collective household; it was a drunk punk house. It wasn't a safe place for me and Zar to be. We had to get out.

Leaving wasn't simple. I had less than $200 in my credit union account, no credit cards, no parents or siblings to rely on. I had Mich, who said I could share her bed in her studio apartment, but pets weren't allowed so Zar couldn't come with me. Also, I couldn't sleep when I was in a bed with another person. And I was too embarrassed to tell anyone else about what happened.

I decided to call the housing program at the YWCA, where I had a free, low-income membership.

"Were there weapons involved?" the woman on the other end of the phone asked me.

"Yes."

"Call New Beginnings."

That didn't seem right. Abusive relationships were in my past. I tapped on a bullet casing. I looked at the peeling paint on the walls, the dried dog shit in the corner. The smell of bong water and cat piss filtered through my denial.

I didn't call New Beginnings right away. It took a few days. Then I called the volunteer coordinator I knew from doing the forty-hour program there. I told her my situation and asked, "Do you think I should call over to the shelter?"

"Yes, Jessica, you should."

Her matter-of-fact reply shook me.

It was completely different from the rumors floating through my anarchist community, which were getting back to me. My soldier-turned-anarchist ex-roommate and others who stockpiled weapons thought I was overreacting. They thought that my emotional state—not Bryce's—would expose our revolutionary armed community to the state. They questioned the actuality of any danger posed to me by Bryce's actions. It seemed the fact that I was alive proved he didn't intend to kill me. I wasn't dead, so they seemed to think my life hadn't been threatened.

Now there was someone from the Y saying I was in so much danger I couldn't stay there, and someone from New Beginnings not questioning my story. Instead of feeling like I needed to defend myself, I realized I needed to protect myself.

I called the New Beginnings shelter. It was a short conversation. The person who answered firmly suggested I leave my house as soon as possible and reserved a bed for me. I later learned it was one of the less than one hundred beds for women in emergency domestic violence situations in all of King County. She gave me the address of a café in the University District and said to call from the pay phone out front when I got there, that's when I'd get the shelter address.

"I have a meeting until eight tonight," I said. Home Alive was holding our first open meeting for new people to join the collective.

"That's okay," the shelter advocate said. "The café is open until ten. We'll be waiting for you."

I shoved my olive-drab army pants into my large backpack along with three black T-shirts, a pullover black Gits hoodie, a pair of black leggings, my short black jersey skirt, a few pairs of underwear, two bras, and some socks. I was told not to worry about toiletries, but I still grabbed my curl cream and special conditioner for my hair texture. I packed my black eyeliner, sharpener, sketchbook, and journal into the front pocket of my backpack. I used a red bandanna to wrap a picture of Nina Simone raising her fist, a picture of Zar giving me love eyes, and a braid of Mia's hair I kept on my altar, a gift from her roommate who had helped her cut her hair in a short shag just a few months ago.

I laced my tall combat boots up over my black leggings and tied my ankle-high boots to the outside of the backpack. It was pouring rain outside, so I put on my olive-green bomber jacket over my zip-up black hoodie and pulled the hood up onto my head. I gathered Zar and a few of his toys, put him in a cardboard box with holes cut into the sides, and went out to catch the bus. My first stop before the Home Alive meeting was dropping Zar off with my friend Katie. She had moved out of the Slut Hut into an apartment on Capitol Hill with her cat, Shakti. They were going to take care of Zar until I had a home again. "I'm sorry I'm the worst parent ever," I whispered to him on the bus.

The things I decided I needed for a thirty-day shelter stay sat inconspicuously at my feet during the Home Alive meeting. Carrying a backpack with the necessities for getting from work to an organizing meeting and then to a café, a bar, or an unplanned hookup wasn't unusual. I even forgot about my next stop for a bit while I took notes with thick, smelly markers on the sheets of white chart paper taped to the walls, capturing ideas for how to create collective safety.

After the meeting, Mich walked with me to the bus stop for the 43 to the U-District. She was the only person who knew where I was going. Before heading in the opposite direction, to her shift at the Comet, she hugged me. We didn't usually hug.

I stared out the bus window watching the rain, trying not to worry about Zar. I got to the café at 8:45, ten hours after I had called the shelter. I used the pay phone out front, dialing the number that I had written down on a scrap of paper. The person on the other end of the phone gave me directions. I walked to a large house with a wooden door and knocked. I was welcomed in and given a tour along with an overview of the community rules. Then I was brought to a small room, where I'd live for the next thirty days. I said hello to my bunkmate, who had the blanket pulled up over her head, took off my boots, climbed onto the top bunk, and felt a heavy layer of fear encompass me. Loneliness welled in my lungs. It hurt to breathe.

❦

I had to attend a mandatory domestic violence support group. I lied about my drug use to the staff but was easily pegged for bulimic, so they added a mandatory eating disorder twelve-step group as a condition of my stay. They also gave me the assignment to continue using my YWCA membership.

The small, basement-level, windowless gym anchored my days. I hung out there for hours riding the elliptical bikes and lifting weights, wishing I didn't hate my body so much. Still, the Y felt safe. Eighty-year-old women gossiped naked in the locker room after their water aerobics classes, modeling how not to give a fuck about wrinkles and rolls. I'd sit near them, hoping to absorb their attitude, hoping it would help me stop puking and that I'd be willing to put on a bathing suit and swim.

When my stay at the shelter ended, friends at one of the collective households who were appropriately horrified by Bryce's actions offered me a free room until I could find housing. I kept riding my bike to the Y daily. Lulu, the trainer, taught me different strength-building routines while telling me absurd stories about her attempts to break up with her boyfriend, who she called the Prince of Darkness with the same upstate New York accent as Lydia Lunch, who I adored. Lulu made me laugh and feel less ashamed. It felt conspiratorial, like private feminist performances motivating me to pull my shit back together. The rest of the staff at the gym were equally in my corner, tracking my healing. "You're a different person than when you first started coming here," the assistant manager said one day. "You should apply for the opening we have."

I got the job.

I staffed the front desk, checking in members, scheduling free mammograms and affordable massages, and helping other women apply for the low-income scholarship. Lulu helped me design an exercise class to teach using the self-defense techniques I was learning through Home Alive. One of the massage therapists helped me get a second job at her second job with a house-cleaning service. I saved and was able to move in with Katie when she and Shakti needed a new roommate. I was so relieved not to have to uproot Zar again.

CHAPTER THREE

Exquisitely Fierce Women

Home Alive collective meetings lasted hours. We were nine exquisitely fierce women trying not to feel helpless. We'd move through laughter, tension, tears, appreciation, annoyance, exhaustion, and exhilaration while debating decisions and processing the horror of Mia's death. We decided to organize a week of art and music with free self-defense classes taught by an instructor from Los Angeles. We chose him because one of the collective members had taken classes with him down there. Pretty quickly, we were contacted by women telling us he had sexually harassed them in his classes. We didn't easily reach consensus on what to do. Several of us thought the accusations were enough to cancel his classes. Others thought there needed to be legal-type proof or it would be discriminatory to assume his guilt through hearsay.

We were still contending with Clarence Thomas's confirmation hearings for his Supreme Court nomination and Anita Hill's testimony that she had been sexually harassed by him. It was still new to talk about sexual harassment so openly. Kimberle Crenshaw was using this case, among others, to develop the concept of "intersectionality," but our activist world was far outside of academia, and it would be decades before intersectionality was embraced and then bastardized and demonized by both the left and the right. I knew that women who experienced violence weren't believed by their communities, families, cops, and government. I knew that Mia had been raped but that we were told not to talk about it by the cops. I knew that race, class, and sexual orientation were important differences, but I was still learning how to incorporate that into my own identity as well as into organizing. I didn't yet know how to apply those ideas to the similarities and differences we had as young female artists, musicians, and outsiders confronting the intense violence disrupting our world.

We were also up against the idea of a "feminist backlash" and being in a "post-feminist" era. Supposedly, the 1970s feminist movement had succeeded. Title IX, the civil rights law, had allowed more girls to participate on school sports teams, and a similar law allowed women to attend military academies. Women were earning more bachelor's degrees than men, as well as an equal number of graduate degrees, and could supposedly have it all, meaning marriage, kids, and a career. Admittedly, these concerns seemed like archaic desires from my mom's era. I wasn't going to rely on a man for anything, especially not my economic well-being— an unquestioned reality of every female I knew, including in Home Alive. We didn't talk about this collectively or think collectively of our organizing as feminist. The term hadn't yet been reclaimed as something generationally relatable. Regardless, Home Alive struggled through the feminist debates of the early 1990s. After a series of emotionally exhausting and divisive collective meetings, we finally decided not to bring the Los Angeles self-defense instructor to town.

Seated in a circle in the living room of the Slut Hut during another early Home Alive meeting, the question came up about whether Bryce had pointed his gun at me or not. For some reason, the two-by-four I had swung at D'Cazzoni also came up. I can't remember why. It was just part of my experience with domestic violence that my behaviors were on trial. When this happened, despite therapy, I became feral. My fight-or-flight response pulsed through me; I jumped up from my chair. I'm sure I told the person to fuck off, possibly even spewing rumors I'd heard about her life. She must have jumped up from her chair too, because I have a clear snapshot in my mind of her wearing a skirt and engineer boots, the two of us standing boots-to-boots, ready to go to blows. The image is a little endearing with the distance of time, though it wasn't fun for anyone in the room. We were readying ourselves for a fight I'm sure neither of us wanted to go through with. Fortunately, another collective member was able to shake off her shock and break us apart. We never went through any formal process to address the incident, to contextualize the violent reactions we had toward each other or how they impacted the collective. Though exposing interpersonal violence was a key aspect of the antiauthoritarian, anticapitalist, feminist politics Home Alive was creating, we simply weren't ready to look at ourselves and the ways we hurt each other.

We never discussed the impact of Bryce's violence on our organizing, even when we were making decisions about offering gun safety classes.

Several mentors taught weapons de-escalation techniques, which is what gun safety got folded into. I knew that I didn't freeze when Bryce shot his rifle because I had learned that guns were more often used for intimidation than murder during sexual assaults. And I had learned that guns kept for home defense ended up being used exponentially more often in domestic violence situations. I didn't want to own a gun. I didn't even want to continue wearing my necklace with the miniature toy gun I'd gotten from the gumball machine at Fred Meyer. At the same time, I wasn't against offering gun safety classes. Feminist knowledge about firearms in a self-defense context had helped me protect myself in the face of becoming a statistic brought to life. What I was against was offering a National Rifle Association gun safety class. I didn't care that it was led by a woman, even a "badass" woman, as she was described by the collective members proposing the NRA collaboration.

We couldn't reach consensus. Hours and hours of heated debate resulted in a standoff between those of us insisting on a coherent leftist position for the collective and those insisting it was paternalistic to cut off available options to participants because of our own political position. I was so pissed, by which I mean I was so hurt because I felt like Bryce's actions were being protected by the collective members I disagreed with. I went rogue and set up a second gun safety class without bringing it to the collective. It was taught by Mike Dixon, whose older brothers had started the Seattle Black Panther chapter, and included domestic violence safety planning.

❦❧❦❧

"Come over tonight," Zoë said when I stopped by the café where she worked for an iced soy chai before my shift at the YWCA. "We're having a fire ritual. The We'Moon calendar is all about transforming anger this week."

When I got off work, I rode my bike up Madison to the new Slut Hut in the Central District. "Did you bring something to burn?" Zoë asked as I laid my bike down by the table with a punch bowl full of a bright-red alcoholic concoction labeled "Moon Juice." I pulled my bike bag over my shoulder and reached into the side pocket for Bryce's drawing to show her. Zoë showed me a photo of her stepfather. We laid them in the pile of items representing abusers that would be ripped up and burned in a ritual led by Trish.

Billy Filly, one of Zoë's roommates, grinned at us. She held up her two middle fingers and yelled, "Fuck men!" We returned the gesture.

A group of San Francisco dykes huddled together on a driftwood bench, rolling cigarettes from a pouch of loose tobacco. They were friends of Tribe 8, a queercore band who had stayed at the Slut Hut when they were in town for a show a few nights earlier. San Francisco butches titillated and intimidated me with their hard edges covered in layers of flannel over cargo cutoffs and untied combat boots. San Francisco femmes intimidated me even more. I felt like a little kid playing dress-up in my army pants and plain black thrift-store camisole next to their leopard-print slips and leather biker jackets, their bright-red patches of long hair around razored undercuts, and their perfectly applied matching red lipstick.

Maura, another Home Alive collective member, was trying to get the attention of Mooch, the butchest San Francisco dyke. Maura had a mini basketball hoop strapped to her crotch, unsubtly rotating her hips to flip a Ping-Pong ball hanging from a string into the hoop. Mooch suddenly yelled, "I'm not anybody's daughter!" Then, burping loudly, ze smashed an Olympia beer can against hir forehead. Blood trickled down hir face.

"Stop!" Otter yelled. "You're bleeding." Mooch was HIV positive. Otter pulled ze's red bandanna from ze's back left pocket and handed it to Mooch. I walked over to the semicircle of tree stumps around the firepit where Mich sat smoking, observing. I sat next to her, the everything of queerness stirring sensations of safety, of belonging.

❀❁✿❀

"Are your women-only classes open to all women?" It was 1994. The confusing question was left on the Home Alive voicemail by a person named Alexis. Her voice didn't sound like what I thought a woman's voice should sound like. My first response was defensiveness, sure a man was fucking with us.

We were part of the Seattle music scene, which was predominantly male and extremely macho. Many of the all-female bands were feminist, but not necessarily activist like the Riot Grrrl bands ninety miles south in Olympia. Riot Grrrl bands would demand men go to the back of the space so women could mosh without being groped. That worked okay in a college town, but not in Seattle, even though moshing at the mostly testosterone-fueled shows meant fighting off dudes grabbing at my tits and ass when all I wanted to do was to slam my body up against other people in a shared joyous rage. Men were exhausting. L7 shows, and Babes in Toyland shows, and 7 Year Bitch shows were always more enjoyable, more queer, and women-people didn't feel confined to the edges of the pit. Even more liberating was when Tribe 8's frontperson would saw off their strapped-on dildo and throw it out to the audience. My desire bloomed for male-identified people who could detach their dicks.

Alexis's challenge to what we meant when we called ourselves *women* felt like a challenge to my newfound safety in queerness. What I didn't yet understand was that she was making herself safer by inviting Home Alive into more inclusive ideas about gender and sexuality, moving us away from the remaining dregs of radical lesbian-feminist separatism.

I was having a hard time understanding Alexis through the noisy fear and anger in my head. Some dyke friends had recently been queer-bashed by straight men when they were buying smokes at a gas station on Capitol Hill, not far from where Mia had last been seen. Lorena Bobbitt was on our minds, recently having been all over the national news for cutting off her abusive husband's dick. Certain dyke spaces, like sex parties and music festivals, had a "dick in the drawer" policy, where one could enter if their dick could be put in a drawer. Everything was about dicks.

I thought it made sense to offer self-defense training to transgender women who would then teach classes to other trans women. I believed learning self-defense was important for creating community and safety, but my strategies were steeped in 1990s identity politics that had much too narrow definitions of gender.

The exclusionary "dick in the drawer" policy was being challenged at the Michigan Womyn's Music Festival, a battleground for expanding the concept of gender through trans inclusion. Alexis, who was a community educator with a trans rights organization, had intentionally targeted Home Alive because we were a politically gendered part of the music scene. When we returned her call, she offered to facilitate a Trans 101 workshop. We agreed, and I offered to host at the comfortable, old Craftsman-style house on the backside of Capitol Hill that Katie and I had moved into with some other friends. My roommates helped me form a circular seating area in the den off the living room using kitchen chairs and giant throw pillows. I set up a table with hummus, chips, carrots, and mini chocolate bars. Zoë brought fresh-pressed carrot juice, Maura brought three bottles of cheap wine left over from an event at her loft the night before, Mich brought a bag of apples, and other collective members brought more dips and chips.

Alexis kicked ass. Surrounded by the built-in bookcases filled with my and my roommates' combined book collection, she and her trans man cofacilitator effectively used an easel and chart paper to gracefully navigate our ignorance. I was able to realize that what I had heard in her original voicemail wasn't her gender but the emotional toll it took for her to confront us. The workshop made gender a deliciously exciting concept, one I haven't stopped thinking about since. And as I stole glances at the trans-masc cofacilitator, another puzzle piece clicked into place for me about desire.

CHAPTER FOUR

Community Care

Home Alive's two femme mentors did a gender awareness exercise in their women-only classes. The class would gather together on one side of the room and, when the facilitator called out a variety of possible experiences, if we identified with the statement we'd walk to the other side of the room.

"If you grew up in a house your family owned, cross to the other side of the room."

"If your parents are still married . . ."

"If you identify as a person of color . . ."

"If you identify as a . . ."

The group, divided in two, observed each other across the space. We were reminded to breathe, to not hold our breath, and then we'd join back together.

"If you had to go hungry as a kid . . ."

"If you have health care through your job . . ."

"If you identify as Jewish . . ."

"If you have ever been in jail, go to the other side of the room."

I froze. I'd been to jail. My arrest had to do with being poor; it was not a planned arrest at a demonstration. I had class pride around that fact, but still, I hesitated. I was in the closest thing I had to a professional setting. I glanced cautiously at the group and noticed another woman looking like how I felt. With an imperceptible nod, we both stepped out from the group and walked across the room together.

On the other side, I heard her let out an audible sigh as I too exhaled. I lifted my gaze and looked across the room at the rest of the group looking at us. The woman I stood next to wore gray sweatpants with white sneakers and a blue-and-green flannel shirt over a yellow University of Washington T-shirt. Her black hair was in long dreadlocks tied back with a red, black, and green headscarf. I had eggplant-colored hair messily gathered on top of my head. I wore black leggings tucked into black engineer boots and a white V-neck men's undershirt with the Home Alive logo crookedly silk-screened onto it. We walked back to the group with our arms hooked together.

The exercise always ended with the statement "If you identify as a woman, walk to the other side of the room," intending to rebuild a sense of solidarity and closure. One time, a different time than when the jail question was asked, I hesitated at the woman question and didn't immediately walk across the room with the group.

"Jessica, come on," one of the queer femme mentors said. I thought I heard exasperation on her part. I was pretty sure that "woman," without qualification, wasn't exactly fitting me anymore, but I walked across the room by myself, not wanting to be a problem.

An ex-cop offered Home Alive his free women's self-defense presentation. Those of us opposed to working with cops didn't have an alternative to offer, since local women's self-defense organizations were priced for Microsoft workers living in the ugly new condos being built around the city. We didn't have money, so we reached a consensus to try free.

The cop was, of course, a disaster. He advised us to wear long coats if we had on short skirts and not to wait alone at bus stops after dark. He couldn't answer our question about what to do in the winter, when it got dark at 4 p.m. He didn't have an answer for what to do if we took buses because we didn't own a car and couldn't afford a cab. He only shook his head when we asked him what to do if it was dark when our work shift at the bar or strip club ended, or when our band set ended at 3 a.m. He told us not to worry about fighting fair, that kicking an attacker in the balls was our best defense. We asked what to do if the attacker was our partner. And what to do if our partner didn't have balls. The cop didn't have answers. We reached consensus on not adding him to our resource list.

The next person who offered us free instruction was a dyke martial artist from a feminist dojo. Much better. We agreed to keeping it on the down-low because the dojo had a policy of not giving away women's knowledge and labor for free. The nine of us could each invite one other person. We met in secret for six weeks in an empty warehouse near

Piecora's Pizza, where Mia had last worked. I loved the training. It created boundaries for my willingness to fight and gave focus to my anger. I felt powerful. Simply shifting my legs into a stance that gave me balance, that allowed me to strike or pivot and run, gave my disassociated psyche an embodied place to land. I learned how to pull my elbow to my waist and twist my whole forearm to get out of being grabbed by the wrist. I learned target points on another person's body and how to break out of being choked. We practiced punching and kicking small, handheld punching bags. I felt strong using my palm and elbow to strike, holding my hand up and using the force of my internal will to stop someone from coming too close. I practiced not losing my voice to fear but instead taking a breath and then yelling loudly, from deep in my belly.

Feminist self-defense included consciousness-raising. At some point during the class, we'd sit in a circle and chat. Our instructor taught us that even though most self-defense techniques for women were based on protecting oneself from the psychopathic stranger in the bushes, those types of attacks only made up about 1 percent of assaults. We learned that nearly 80 percent of sexual assaults against women were by someone known and trusted, usually of the same race, and that sexual violence against women was about power and control, not desire and attraction. When the teacher said, "Go ahead, take what you've learned and teach your friends," I volunteered to be one of the first Home Alive instructors. I wanted all women to feel this sense of liberation.

❦❧❦

My recurring nightmares began to change. I fought my way out of the feeling of being under heavy restraint and through the sense of being in an underwater cave that sometimes woke me up in a state of panic and disorientation. In one dream that had always led to me being alone and surrounded by several male attackers on a playground with a scream stuck in my throat, I instead dreamed I was speeding away from the playground on my bicycle, yelling. Other collective members had similar experiences, as did people taking our classes. So as part of the Home Alive curriculum, along with teaching basic strikes and target points and then practicing on handheld punching bags with partners, we designed a section on exploring our shifting subconscious. Instead of thinking about what we were doing as a form of 1970s feminist consciousness-raising, we considered what we did antiauthoritarian education, a form of self and community care. We knew we were healing from a shared trauma that kicked up our own traumas.

We came up with role-playing scenarios that fit our lives. We'd practice standing, walking, and waiting for a bus in postures that communicated "Don't fuck with me." We practiced loading imaginary amps into a band van parked behind a club and listening to our gut to be able to stop a person we didn't trust from getting too close. With a lot of discomfort and laughter, we worked with a partner to come up with ways to tell a potential hookup we didn't want to have sex, that we had changed our minds or realized we were too intoxicated. And we role-played having safe-sex discussions with one-night stands and partners.

Classes would begin by asking people to share a moment from their week that could be interpreted as a self-defense success: saying no to another date with a person who felt unsafe, throwing an elbow to the sternum of the guy who grabbed our ass in a mosh pit, or telling a coworker to take a couple of steps back. We'd end class sitting in a circle on the floor and committing out loud to an act of care:

"This week I'll write in my journal."

"I'll cook dinner for myself two times this week."

"I'll meet you at the bus stop so we can go home together after work."

"I'll save my tips so I can always have twenty dollars in my pocket for a cab at bar time."

"I'll take a bath with lavender and sage I picked from my friend's yard."

"I'll call you if I have suicidal thoughts."

"I'll exchange numbers with my neighbors so we don't have to call the police if we feel afraid."

Mia's unsolved murder had an impact well beyond her immediate friends. Bands and art galleries held fundraisers to help keep Home Alive classes on a sliding scale from zero to five dollars. Grocery stores and small businesses put donation jars by the register to collect change. Local media reported on Home Alive regularly, especially the weekly paper, *The Stranger*. National media stories on Seattle, about the depressed kids with brightly colored hair making angry music while playing Russian roulette with heroin, ran sidebars on Home Alive. The collective was an intimate project to deal with a communal loss, and it was also an enticing activist project coming out of the new music scene.

Of course, we didn't talk about what we were doing then the way I'm looking back at it now. We just did it. Some of us developed the self-defense curriculum and taught classes; others focused on fundraising and financial accountability, or promoting the classes and fundraising events. The more visible we became, the more volunteers showed up to help. The positive support forced us to figure out how to become an organization with internal communication systems, class registration and space rental policies, and volunteer orientations. We couldn't remain a small, DIY, make-it-up-as-we-went-along project.

CHAPTER FIVE

Inside the Machine

The idea for a fundraising CD was brought to the collective by a guy who produced singles for local bands. I remember him being genuine, and a little creepy, though most men seemed a little creepy to me then, so maybe he wasn't. He presented Home Alive with a proposal to produce a compilation CD to promote local bands while raising money for self-defense classes. This proposal inspired some collective members to make another proposal to produce a CD on a major label. We were all on board for making a fundraising CD, but, of course, we had collective meeting after collective meeting debating whether to trust this guy we didn't know or go to a corporate label. We debated what community-based meant, and whose community, since some collective members were in community with major-label, record-industry bands, executives, and lawyers. The fundraising project brought up questions about the value of being a small, locally focused project versus garnering a wider audience. Was creative and political control more important than getting a bunch of money to be able to dream bigger, possibly make a bigger impact? If we went with a corporate label, bands on those labels couldn't simply donate a track. We'd have to become a nonprofit so they could donate their publishing rights, which is how money is made. A split happened similar to when we debated the NRA class, and it happened along similar lines. Were we a leftist, anarchist-oriented collective, or were we a progressive, liberal organization? Was putting out a CD on a major label selling out to corporate culture? Were we willing to become a nonprofit, change our collective structure, and report our activities to the state?

While we were trying to reach a consensus, the community in Portland our femme mentors were part of produced a CD called *Free to Fight* on an independent queercore label. The CD focused on hyperlocal community care and self-defense education. It featured all-woman bands and had a seventy-five-page zine full of art and community-based safety resources. It was explicitly feminist.

I wanted to make something like that. Our femme mentors were fierce about the political distinctions between the terms *lesbian* and *dyke*. In my imagination (and probably in reality), the process of making *Free to Fight* included conversations about the term *woman* and queer and trans inclusivity. Except for the brief interruption by Alexis, Home Alive didn't explicitly consider queer gender in our organizing. The concerns about all-women or women-only classes centered around straight members' fears of being exclusionary toward the cisgender men in their lives.

As I was realizing my attraction to trans and genderqueer people, other Home Alive members were also coming into their queer sexual and gender identities, including dealing with abusive same-sex partners. Straight collective members certainly had their experiences of trauma, fucked-up relationships, and abuse histories. The difference was that we queers were on unstable ground, questioning core aspects of who we were. In this context, we were the subculture while straight members had the advantage of being on more solid ground. They inherited an invisible hierarchy that was often reflected in the power dynamics behind the decision-making. We were all swimming in it, not always able to see it.

We went with a major label.

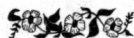

Eddie Vedder, Pearl Jam's singer, who some collective members were friends with, got his record label, Epic, to produce the Home Alive CD, which was called *Home Alive: The Art of Self Defense*. I didn't meet Eddie Vedder before, during, or after the CD project, but he once came to a jobsite where I was working as a painter for a company that sculpted concrete to look like granite. We made displays for zoos and aquariums and built water features and pools for the way-too-many new software millionaires. We were building the state's largest swimming pool for some rich asshole when I was told that Eddie Vedder and his wife would be coming by to decide if they wanted to hire the company to build their pool and that we shouldn't talk to them. I saw them climbing around the dusty site in very clean and very black outfits. I was in my tan Carhartts and forest-green pocket T-shirt and decided to follow instructions instead of introducing myself as a Home Alive founder.

Ironically, at the Epic Records offices, I was referred to as one of "Eddie's girls with the cause." Annoying as that was, it was impossible not to get sucked up into the ego-feeding bacchanal of making a major-label CD. Epic, a part of Sony, was located in New York. I arrived at LaGuardia Airport with the other collective members on a flight paid for by the label. I followed the collective members in bands who knew how to find the limo driver holding a "Home Alive" placard that the label sent. I drank free whiskey in a stretched Lincoln Town Car on the ride to the Madison Avenue offices of Sony Records. I got a special badge to wear around my neck that gave me access to the bank of elevators that sped up to the executive suites fifty stories above the sidewalk. I got to go through a cabinet that held thousands of CDs and take as many as I wanted, for free. I got to go to the executive cafeteria, where I could get anything to eat that I wanted, for free.

Another Home Alive collective member and I were in charge of designing the CD packaging. Assigned to an Epic graphic designer, we communicated our vision for the front and back covers and the sixteen-page resource booklet insert. We made sure that the less-known artists donating a track, like !TchKunG!, Tribe 8, Catfood, and Andrew Horwitz, were equally highlighted alongside Pearl Jam, Nirvana, Soundgarden, Joan Jett, and Ann and Nancy Wilson. We laid out the resource booklet with beautiful, intense, dark visual artworks donated by Seattle artists. The Home Alive logo I had made when we first started the collective, an urgently scrawled text made with a crayon pressed down so hard it crumbled as I drew the letters, looked amazing blown up on the designer's huge computer monitor. It was as thrilling to see my artwork there as it was to see it in sticker form on Joan Jett's guitar or on the refrigerator in a scene from the movie *Jerry McGuire*, which was shot in Seattle by Nancy Wilson's husband, Cameron Crowe. My anticapitalist politics didn't give my ego immunity from the thrill of being anointed relevant inside of the machine.

"Are we using the Michael Jackson jewel case?" an Epic executive asked while we all sat around a conference table way up above Madison Avenue in a room with floor-to-ceiling windows.

"Yes," I answered, not realizing I didn't matter.

She looked past me to the executive seated on my right and asked the question again.

I knew we were using the jewel case in question because it was one of many examples we had considered while designing the double CD. I'd had lengthy discussions with the graphic designer about the mechanics of the case and how it wasn't obvious that the CD cradle had to be pulled up to find the second CD. I learned that Epic believed the recent Michael Jackson album didn't sell as well as his others because of this jewel case.

In the evenings, when I went to meet friends in the dark, Ukrainian-owned bars on the Lower East Side, we discussed the news reports of Michael Jackson being accused of sexually abusing kids and the news that his sister, Latoya, was speaking out about childhood family abuse. I didn't doubt these stories, knowing too well what it was like not to be believed. Over bottom-shelf whiskey, I talked with my friends about the fact of Black men being falsely accused of rape in a white supremacist country, and the complications of the Jackson stories, that they were about male-on-male sexual violence and violence against Black women. Race, gender, and class couldn't be ignored as I tried to make sense of my role creating a glitzy public stage for Home Alive with a record company seemingly more concerned with design flaws in the package than accusations of the artist's predatory behavior.*

Home Alive and Epic hosted CD release parties in Seattle, San Francisco, and New York. Returning to New York for the celebration, I cruised through the airport with purpose, entitlement guiding me as I searched for the limo driver holding the "Home Alive" placard. For three days I was fed free alcohol and food. Glammed up in brick-red lipstick and black

---

* It's impossible not to mention David Meinert here, a project manager on the Home Alive CD who was exposed as a brutal serial rapist in 2017. Meinert preyed on women in Seattle's music, art, and political communities while building his own personal and political power. He obviously used Home Alive early on to seem credibly nonmisogynistic, even feminist. Accusations against him, as reported in the media, only go back to the early 2000s, but I have no doubt there were women raped by him in the 1990s. I'm going to safely assume they weren't believed by some of the same people who didn't believe me at the time. That doesn't make me clean in the situation. I'm filled with deep sorrow thinking about my own unintended complicity as a Home Alive collective member benefiting from Meinert's connections as a promoter and producer. I'm also filled with intense rage that Leigh Heron, the private investigator hired to find Mia's killer with the funds raised from myriad benefit shows our community put together, signed on to be a part of Meinert's "crisis management" team. Seeming to have no conscience or principles, Heron still promotes Mia's case on her website.

blocks of mascara smeared under my eyes, I felt like a Warhol superstar. I was part of interviews with national music media, I snorted cocaine in bathrooms with former MTV VJs, and I casually conversed with Jim Carroll, a Lower East Side poet I thought had died from an OD in the 1980s.

I stayed in New York an extra week to soak up art, along with more alcohol and drugs. A friend who had a spoken word piece on the CD was performing at an underground punk club. I called the Epic offices to see if I could pick up some Home Alive CDs for the show. I couldn't get a hold of anybody, so I took the F train to the Sony building. I waved to the security guard in the lobby, like always. She waved back but wouldn't let me access the elevators. I didn't have the special badge anymore. When the security guard called up for me, the admin person answering the phones said everyone was in a meeting. I hung out in the lobby for a while, waiting to catch someone I knew on their way out. Eventually, the guard said I had to leave. I sat on the sidewalk outside the main entrance watching people in suits rush along Madison Avenue. A couple of people dropped quarters into the empty coffee cup I hadn't yet thrown into the trash. It wasn't the first time people in suits interpreted me as someone who needed their pocket change. I leaned my head back, trying to see the top of the towering Sony building. I felt very small. Around four o'clock, when I knew the executives and their assistants left the office, I called up one more time from the nearby pay phone. The graphic designer I had worked with answered. She came down with a handful of CDs and wished me luck.

❧❀❦❀❧

The CD didn't sell well. I remember a collective meeting where someone said someone told them our demand to have control of the project was the problem, that we made it too difficult for the label to market the CD. I hope we created that big of a problem for a major corporation, but the accusation of us being demanding and difficult seems more like someone's misogynist feelings about the project. It's possible Epic never intended to market the CD, that the amount of money they spent on the Home Alive compilation was worth it to appease Eddie Vedder, who made them billions.

No matter whether *Home Alive: The Art of Self Defense* was always meant to be a tax write-off for Epic, the CD got traction with the help of independent PR consultants in Home Alive's extended networks. Girls and women and gay boys and non-binary kids from all over the world wrote us letters disclosing experiences of physical, sexual, and emotional violence, wanting to start a Home Alive chapter. We made a collective decision not to expand Home Alive through chapters. Since we grew out of a specific community in mourning, we suggested people start locally based collectives and create support networks for their individual and community safety needs.

Epic gifted Home Alive an amount of money much greater than the CD would have ever made. I don't remember if this was the label's way of ending their relationship with us or if the donation was negotiated by the lawyers helping us, an idea of Eddie Vedder's, or something the collective members doing the business end of the CD made happen. Any of those could have happened and would be interesting stories. However, the impact on Home Alive would be the same. The collective went from being a small, volunteer-run project with an annual operating budget of $7,000 to a nonprofit organization with a $250,000 bank balance. We rented a huge loft in an old textiles factory with enough space for an office and a classroom. We created a few part-time positions, expecting to be able to raise enough money to keep those funded. The stakes and possibilities became a whole lot bigger. It was a seismic shift we rolled with, like we rolled with most things: multiple long, drawn-out meetings full of fighting and frustrated tears. Or maybe that's just how I remember it.

To check my memory while writing this, I called Mich, who had also been a core Home Alive collective member.

"That's funny," Mich said, "I just came across a Home Alive newsletter that announced we hired staff in some boxes I was sorting through. It's the one printed in blue ink."

"That is funny," I said. "I just got boxes out of the basement of MJ's house and found my old Home Alive files. I guess I should look through them."

Memory is complicated. I trust it's hanging around deep in my physiology and psyche, swirling through my cells until ready to become thoughts. My art practice is sorting through old photos and drawings and piles of papers, then taking the fractured bits and fabricating them into legible shapes or words. I think of it as weaving a fabric representing the parts of my history stolen by violence.

Later that day, I talked to Zoë and told her about the Home Alive files. "Wow," she said. "I'm so curious to see what you have. It never occurred to me to save any of it." When I asked her why not, she said she had moved so many times in her childhood she hadn't developed a sense of nostalgia. I texted Mich: *Why do you think we both kept these files all these years?*

Mich replied: *I very explicitly kept them as institutional history, an archive. Now they're my personal internet, my data on how I became me, my evidence. I'm a part of this universe whether I know how to communicate it or not.*

I texted back: *I don't think I was as self-conscious about archiving. My files are a mess, not chronological. But I see how much Home Alive is the root of everything else I've done since. Like moving these boxes of old crap was instinctive, a future part of my healing process. It's definitely my story to tell as much as anyone else's.*

The unspoken part of this thread is that I published an article about Home Alive several years ago that unexpectedly reopened old wounds for other collective members. Some publicly stated that my story was wrong, that I should not "have the last word" on Home Alive history.

Mich responded: *I think you know Home Alive is your story.*

CHAPTER SIX

Outside the Collective

My time in New York made clear that those floor-to-ceiling windows overlooking Madison Avenue didn't provide safety from falling. The whirlwind of being treated like a rock star, then being treated like a bothersome insect, knocked me into a familiar abyss. Heroin, once my way out of these feelings, wasn't an option. Using the different tools I now had from the domestic violence shelter stay and Home Alive, I decided to create a Home Alive self-defense program for women in domestic violence shelters. "I'll work on that with you," Zoë said when I presented my idea at a collective meeting.

Flipping through the newsletter printed in blue ink I've pulled from my old files, I see that by the spring of 1997 we promoted "Curricula developed for and with domestic violence agencies." My Home Alive files remind me that we taught classes to women at day centers, where they spent time before seeking shelter at night, and to advocates working in confidential domestic violence shelters. I remember being disappointed that New Beginnings didn't want classes. They believed self-defense would contribute to arrests of abused women who fought back against their abusers. Shelter workers were aware that abusers commonly leave marks in hard-to-see spots and then call the cops to punish their partner, who may have smacked or scratched them in self-defense. Cops show up and use cop judgment and arrest the emotional person without any visible bruises. The cop didn't see anything happen, so it didn't happen. What they see is a scratch on the abuser's face and say: *Aha! All that yelling must mean you left that mark. You're the abuser.* I was bummed New Beginnings didn't see that Home Alive was expanding ideas of self-defense that could benefit other women like me who used their services.

My files contain letters of recommendation from other advocacy agencies that explain what we were doing beautifully:

As advocates working with these survivors, we feared encouraging women to engage in "self-defense" might directly result in the survivor's arrest. The facilitators from HOME ALIVE did an excellent job acknowledging that these were valid fears and helped direct the discussion to what could be or needed to be done for "self-defense" to be a safe term in the context of domestic/dating violence. This led to the group listing all the possible ways survivors are automatically engaging with self-defense. This list ranged from behaviors like breathing, grounding themselves, protecting key areas on the body to activities like journaling, drawing, or talking with someone safe. It also included natural psychological responses like disassociating and denial. We were able to identify positive associations with self-defense and domestic/dating violence. Most importantly, we saw ways of validating for women all of the ways they had automatically protected and taken care of themselves.

You know what I see in the newsletters? Mich texted. *That Mia's death set something in motion we had to chase.*

One 1994 interview in a queer punk zine confirms this idea:

Some people got together and decided to hold a benefit to fund a self-defense class, in an attempt to create a kind of forum for friends to get together and deal with a sense of loss and helplessness.

and

We broadened our definition of violence and self-defense towards something that's much larger than violence against women.

and

There is no leadership. We are the leaders.

The interviewer concluded that

Mia Zapata's friends are righteously pissed about the attitude held by some that she, and all those who dare eschew the mainstream, deserve what they get. (Sound familiar bashing survivors?) Home

Alive is based on the radical notion that "freaks" deserve to be safe too.

I find seedlings of healing and transformative justice in handwritten notes proposing collective structure, new self-defense classes, new organizations to partner with. There are media packets and flyers for events, and even the Home Alive logo sticker that circulated far and wide. I found a letter to some editor where I fiercely defended my world.

I appreciated [the article] on the death of Mia Zapata for the national publicity it gives to the case, which makes it harder for her murderer to hide. It's true that there is a sense of collective grieving in Seattle since it's a relatively small city and so many people have lost friends to overdoses, suicides, and murder. However there has also been a renewed sense of community in many ways rather than the feeling of hopelessness [the article] conveys. Many of us have made a conscious effort to keep an eye out for our friends and learn how to be safe in our homes as well as on the streets.

I find memories of the excitement and purpose I felt as part of the collective. Including a proposal for a video, *Killer Instincts*, Lydia Lunch and I tried to get funded. I had forgotten this but can now see me and Lydia sitting in cafés when she was performing in Seattle, dreaming up the never-made video.

There are some notes I wrote in preparation for a collective meeting when Home Alive wanted to partner with Q-Patrol, a queer vigilante group (modeled after Curtis Sliwa's Guardian Angels) whose leader was a known abuser. I was trying to show the connection between structural issues in the collective and the politics we were always fighting over:

—issues to resolve . . . contracts with people; how we choose who we work with; how to separate personal info from working policies; women on women violence.
—use this to continue the discussion about how we make collective decisions. I have strong concerns about the direction we seem to be moving in without discussion. Examples . . . Nonprofit status means restricting our resource info; focus on keeping our relationships with "big people" such as Joan Jett and Eddie Vedder etc. in good standing and letting our relationship with others such

as Rubber and Chagrin not be as significant (They both asked for months to do a benefit); All our volunteers right now are lawyers and accountants rather than the 100 people who've approached us over the last year; If we chose to work with Q-Patrol, that would be choosing an organization that doesn't value DIY ethics, that mimics the military and the cops in how they organize, that only acknowledges "law abiding" events and organizations.

I keep returning to the newsletters. Eight of them: 1996–1998. I don't have issues 1 through 3, or issue 10. The last one is issue 11. I don't know if more than eleven were made. Early issues have a call for a zine we were making where I was the contact person, something I don't remember but which makes perfect sense. These issues are full of movement building, artwork, testimony, poetry, anger and determination, and hope. Issue 5, the newsletter in blue ink, is titled "I Must Be Dreaming." The main article starts off with: "The changes around here are almost too good to be true, and we wanted to tell you about them."

Here we are at the seismic shift the Epic money created.

I remember really wanting one of the part-time paid positions. I remember clearly that I thought the Home Alive job would be a dream job because I had created it, because it was bringing together art and social change, because I wouldn't have a boss.

The newsletter informs me that I was the office manager at first, another thing I didn't remember until looking through these files. I remember being the community outreach coordinator, an early cousin of diversity, equity, and inclusion work. It looks like we hired two other collective members, one as the volunteer coordinator and one as the self-defense coordinator. The blue-ink newsletter reminds me that a fourth position went to a core collective member who had left but came back for the paid work. The fifth position, the development director, was hired from outside the collective. She had some nonprofit fundraising experience. Newsletters after this one say that the collective member who had left and come back to be paid had left again by mid-1997, when I had transitioned into community outreach coordinator. At the same time we added an operations coordinator, another person hired from outside the collective.

Staff positions forced a need to implement clearer operational structures. We created interlocking committees made up of core collective members and members of the board of directors and advisory committee. Issue 8 of the newsletter explains that the personnel committee, made up of two collective members and a board member, was to "oversee staff and the inner workings of the office including job descriptions, staff interactions, hiring, office procedures, and staff problem solving."

Yikes. In our own words, we created a system in which some people were workers and some people were overseers.

The invisible hierarchies became visible and entrenched. I remember my frustration at being held to account by people outside of the day-to-day operations, that our—at least intended—collaborative relationship had been subsumed by a worker/boss type of relationship. In a report I wrote in early 1998, I said:

> It was exciting in the beginning as we were being paid to do jobs we created. . . . There were moments of amazing triumph as tasks and projects became defined and solidified. But the overall feeling was of struggle as each person self-defined their role without direct supervision or a clear decision-making process, or without an overview of the needs of the organization financially and structurally . . . learning how to truly work collectively if the organization is going to remain a collective would be helpful. Or deciding not to be a collective . . . would make being an employee easier in terms of knowing how to get answers to be able to complete tasks.

The development director we hired from outside the collective, that we pinned our hopes of maintaining five part-time positions and a loft space on, was gone in less than a year. We fired her. I've had a memory of that story defined by discomfort and sadness, the beginning of my exit from the collective. In the mess of papers I have, I'm able to piece together some different stories about what happened:

- Home Alive was an organization that became an employer before it had the capacity and skills to be accountable for people's financial well-being.
- The development director took the job with an understanding of the title in the context of her former employment, not realizing Home Alive didn't have an infrastructure to support her work in the way she was used to being supported.

- The operations coordinator took a job she believed to be secure, that would have an infrastructure for raises and eventually offer health care, then found out that wasn't the case.
- A person with access to payroll records became concerned Home Alive was treating employees as 1099 contractors and could be in violation of labor laws.
- The personnel committee believed they were acting with appropriate authority in making decisions regarding employees' working conditions and for doing what they believed was best for the organization.
- Home Alive ran through the Epic donation money in about a year, seemingly another example of record companies wreaking havoc on young creative people not used to being on the inside of institutional power.
- Between the time of getting the donation and the development director being fired, four of the core collective members had left.

The article I wrote that opened old wounds for others was meant to be closure of my own wounds. I'm finding that closure in my archives.

What I remember is that I tried to be in solidarity with my coworkers who were upset about their working conditions. The archive reminds me I was also concerned, as a collective member, about the financial health of the organization and the development director's day-to-day skills for managing her job. I remember her being upset that she was going to be fired, that she feared the personnel committee members. I remember office conversations about Home Alive incorrectly handling being an employer and being open to litigation that would fall on the board of directors, most of whom were not core collective members. I thought it was a good idea to set up small conversations between different stakeholders with the goal of finding our way to the same page. I remember the personnel committee thought I was purposefully sabotaging their work. Reading a page of my own notes from this time, my word choices tell me that I was sure I was seeing an obvious inconsistency no one else was seeing and that I believed it was my job to make sure they did:

I'm trying to balance my own needs with that of H.A. This org is about providing others with info to make decisions about self-care, boundaries, and balance, and to feel empowered to exist in this world in the face of adversity. Yet all we do is knock each other down, particularly when we try to set boundaries and meet our own needs.

In my memory, I left as a direct result of how we handled the employment situation. My exit report tells me it was several months later, when almost all the original collective members had resigned, including the personnel committee members. I found my exit interview, a form clearly borrowed from another organization that wasn't edited to fit our needs. Answering the question "How did you feel about your pay and benefits?" I wrote:

The pay sucked for the amount of time I was putting in. What benefits? Home Alive should provide benefits for all staff over 20/ hrs a week and choose days off for holidays that reflect more than Christian and White American holidays.

For my answer to the question "Why are you leaving the job?" I wrote:

I left Home Alive as an Employee because I was very unhappy with the working environment and the lack of clarity in my position. When the financial crisis arose, I thought it made sense to lay me off. Since there was no active Personnel Committee, I made the decision to do so as a founding member who wanted to see the organization survive.

I didn't remember the absurdity of laying myself off from my dream job. That's amusing and depressing. Home Alive is obviously where I started to think of a job as my identity and where work and trauma became intertangled. I'm struck by the lack of attention given to the challenges of creating financial security on the unstable grounds of violence and trauma. We spent a lot of time blaming each other for why things fell apart. But of course, looking back, there aren't any individuals to blame, because we all had collective responsibility for the good and for the bad.

CHAPTER SEVEN

Cousins

There's another story in my Home Alive exit report. This one I never forgot. It's in my answer to the question "What was your favorite experience?"

> My favorite experience was speaking at the Woman of Color Breakfast at the Washington State Coalition Against Domestic Violence conference.

I was invited by my friend Toni to speak. When Toni and I were together, people often asked, "Are you sisters?" People who didn't know better also asked, "What are you?" We shared some—but also had very different—ethnicities. The thing we shared deeply was an exploration of our racial and ethnic histories our families didn't teach us about. My dark, swirly curls and black eyes, and regular encounters with others' assumptions that I wasn't white, formed another way I felt like an outsider in my family. When my dad once mentioned, in passing, that our family was Sephardi, I was intrigued. He's since both denied and confirmed that statement several times, intriguing me further. He's also said there are family histories suggesting our diasporic routes included the Iberian Peninsula and Holland before several centuries in Transylvania, which is where his father was born. Transylvania has a significant Roma population.

When I asked if any histories suggested we were also Romani, he scowled and replied: "We lived in houses." His outdated stereotype wasn't helpful.

My father has never provided helpful responses. Once, when I described my high school relationship as domestic violence, he said, "But you didn't live in the same house. Domestic violence is what happened in my family, not yours," using his impenetrable illogic that sets my system aflame. Another time he said, "You know about guns. I want to show you my new gun." His interpretation of what happened with Bryce, which I wrote about in painstakingly long letters to him, was that I had an interest in guns. I told him I didn't want to see his gun.

This was after the five years I chose to be estranged from my family.

"Your brother won't talk to me about guns," he said, knowing I liked to win whenever pitted against my brother. It tapped into my desire to be the better boy child instead of the difficult girl child. My dad was already taking the lockbox out of his desk drawer. "I've had it modified to be left-handed," he said. He rested his left pointer finger on the trigger and turned the barrel of the gun toward me.

"Don't do that," I said to him with a mitigating laugh. He responded to my request with his own nervous laughter.

I turned to leave the room, reeling heavily from his stubborn denial of my reality.

"Wait," he said. "I can't tell how much weight you have gained or lost since I last saw you. Lift your shirt."

My dad's need to have control over everything in his path is proof enough that assimilation into whiteness happens through acts of violence. Assimilation cut me (and him and my brother) off from being connected to my own history and culture.

During another absurd conversation, this time many years later and on the phone, my dad said, "You're not Jewish, I am." His generation of Jewish immigrants, characterized as successful in the US, was steeped in fear. Fear of European antisemitism and Nazis. He has told me, over and over, that he couldn't fall asleep as a kid because his parents fought loudly. More recently, he has said the fights were about the Nazi genocide, which was happening at the time and, I assume, directly impacting them. He's always said they fought in Hungarian, my father's first language that he stopped speaking long ago. He still has insomnia.

His father, my grandfather, died when I was a baby, and I met his mother, my grandmother, less than a handful of times. During a visit to her when I was a teenager, I remember her giggling conspiratorially with her second husband, sneaking sips of liquor from a flask not very well hidden in his inside jacket pocket. Sitting in a pink semicircular booth at a Miami Beach diner, she poured some of the cheap liquor into my diet soda with a wink. Later, back at her apartment, she spoke to my dad in Hungarian while he paced on the tiny balcony chain-smoking unfiltered cigarettes. She gave me bananas soaked in heavy cream. I ate it all despite my dairy allergy, enchanted by all the broken rules.

I have one picture of myself with my grandmother. It's from a visit to her in my late twenties. She lived in a senior facility outside of Washington, DC, near where my father had moved. She lived near my father because his older brother made him take responsibility for their mother's well-being after decades of near estrangement. Looking at the picture, I see my grandmother is withered and sunken, one hand holding tightly to the arm of the chair she barely balances on. The other hand rests on my shoulder; her well-manicured blush-colored nails stand out. So do my bitten-down black-polished nails. She has me in a full side embrace, our heads resting against each other's. I can see part of an old, sepia-toned photograph on her shelf. I remember feeling surprised that my relatives in the photos looked like the pictures in *Bury Me Standing*, a book about eastern European Roma. I cherish this photo of me and my grandmother. It's proof that our broken-apart family has had moments of an intertwined past, present, and future.

Within a year of that DC visit, I was in a tiny Hungarian town, transferring trains on my way to stay with a roommate's parents who taught English at a university in southern Hungary, near the war-torn Croatian border. Using the stipend Home Alive had decided to pay ourselves out of the Epic money, Zoë and I traveled to Prague together, renting an apartment for a month. I took a side trip to Hungary, where I had a two-hour wait at a station next to a newly built hotel and an old run-down bar. I went to the hotel for potato pancakes and to sample Unicum, a Hungarian-made liqueur that turned out to be a nasty, thick digestif that tasted like rotten Jägermeister. The person who served me had the same skin tone as I did, which was a revelation. It was the first time I saw what others saw when looking at me.

Empowered by the Unicum, I walked across the parking lot to the bar. The woman working there looked just like Lisa, my childhood friend who was also half Hungarian. An elderly man putting back shots ordered a Unicum for me. He asked the bartender to translate for us. She explained that, since 1989 and the fall of the Berlin Wall, they all learned English instead of Russian in grade school. She said the man was sure I was Hungarian and wanted to know where my family was from. When I answered, he slapped his knee and ordered me another shot. A few shots later, he walked me to my departing train, waving from the platform like a relative as I settled into my window seat.

"Why do you want to go to Hungary?" my father had asked before I left on this trip.

"To see where our family is from," I answered.

"Well, they're not there anymore," he replied.

We never talked much about my trip, but when I returned, he sent me a copy of a family tree on yellowing paper. I've looked at it several times over the last couple of decades. Now, as I'm writing, I pull it out from the folder in the drawer near my desk. I find my dad's name. Two of his marriages are recorded, but no branches for me or my brother. Still, I accept I am a descendant of these strangers. On the first page, there is a note stating this document was compiled in 1984 by someone named Enid. I find Enid on the tree. There she is, born in 1926, an older cousin of my father's. There's another set of notes on the first page. Notes I don't remember—or maybe that I've forgotten. One note states a fact I was taught: that my grandparents, Emmanual and Ilonka, were first cousins. I've looked at this document so many times trying to figure out who their parents were and how they are cousins. I never noticed it right there in a different note: *Alta was mother of Emmanual and aunt of Ilonka.*

Alta, my great grandmother. "The same man married two sisters," my dad says, as if that piece of information should be enough to answer all my questions. That same man is hard to find, even as I look at it now. But there he is, one man with two branches. One is Alta, the other is Sussa. Alta also has two branches, two last names, two sets of children. It's confusing. All the names, so many the same name, across three pages. Incomplete birth and death dates. My head hurts looking for answers that don't exist. It hurts more as I scan website after website about cousins and marriage. I find a statistic that says 10 percent of marriages in the world are between cousins. I find lots of anthropological studies about "cousin marriage." Finding out I'm an anthropological curiosity is, well, weird. Less weird is that I know other people whose grandparents are cousins. It's an immigrant thing.

Going back to the paper document, I notice several names have the notation "in Israel." Only 0.2 percent of the world population is Jewish, so it's probable I'm related to Zionists, to Israeli settlers. This disturbs me much more than my grandparents being first cousins. I never considered I could be related to people who have carried out the Zionist occupation and US-funded Israeli genocide against Palestinians. This probability gets heavier as I flip to page 2 and find again the names with the notation "d. Holocaust." These are my murdered cousins. I hold them in my aching heart, only knowing them abstractly. I ache for the horrors they must have experienced while realizing I feel a far greater distance from them than I feel to my Palestinian activist friends I call cousin, and who call me cousin. This fragile, yellowing paper bursts with my inheritance: my duty to heal. The crinkle of the pages reminds me to never stop demanding that Zionist violence cannot be committed in any of my cousins' names. There will be a Judaism without Zionism again. Palestine will be free again.

I turn to the final page, page 3, with new clarity. The planned decimation of a group of people that was never supposed to happen again is happening again as I write. The overwhelming horror of genocidal death is present outside of the history in my family tree. I understand what I'm looking at differently than when I looked at it before October 7, 2023, even though I always looked at it with anti-Zionist politics. At each demonstration, I have chanted, "Not in my name," knowing I had family killed in the Holocaust, I just didn't know who. I knew that 70 percent of Hungarian Jews were forced into Nazi concentration camps and one-quarter to one-half of Roma people in the same area were murdered by Nazis. I always knew it was more than statistically probable that more people on this yellowing paper were in the camps than those who have the "d. Holocaust." And here it is on page 3, where I find Alta, seeing her there for the first time. Wait. What's this? Next to my great-grandmother's name, and next to one of her children, my grandfather's sibling and my grandmother's cousin, is the "d. Holocaust." This is somehow new information, even though I've looked at this document before, even though it is plainly drawn out. My father has never said anything about our direct line being murdered by Nazis. Does he know? How did I not see this before? How have we never talked about it?

Trauma and Recovery by Judith Herman is the book that coined and defined the term *complex post-traumatic stress disorder*. The first time I bought the book, I found it in the self-help section of Red and Black Books, the feminist-socialist bookstore on Capitol Hill. I didn't like the spirituality of self-help, but this book seemed different. It was making connections between interpersonal violence and structural violence. I never finished reading the book, because my soldier-turned-anarchist roommate stole it, along with some of my other books, to pay for his part of the electricity bill. I don't remember when I got another copy of Herman's book, but there it is in the blue section of my bookshelves, which are arranged by color. I flip through the pages, finishing the book.

In chapter 3, titled "Disconnection," Herman writes, "Traumatic events call into question basic human relationships. They breach the attachments of family, friendship, love, and community. They shatter the construction of the self that is formed and sustained in relation to others." Then, in chapter 7, "A Healing Relationship," Herman explains, "Recovery can only take place within the context of relationships; it cannot occur in isolation. In [their] renewed connections with other people, the survivor re-creates the psychological faculties that were damaged or deformed by the traumatic experience. These faculties include the basic capacities for trust, autonomy, initiative, competence, identity, and intimacy."

When I went to Hungary, I knew I was carrying my grandmother, Ilonka, with me. I didn't know I was carrying Alta. I'm still surprised at how much of my father I'm always carrying.

CHAPTER EIGHT

Rock Stars

Dr. Beth E. Richie was the keynote speaker at the Washington State Coalition Against Domestic Violence conference where I spoke about Home Alive at the Women of Color Breakfast. I was mesmerized by the confidence she had in communicating her ideas. I listened to her discuss intersecting oppressions faced by Black women in violent relationships. My mind was on fire, sorting the differences of my experiences as a woman who isn't Black while hearing something familiar in the outsider status of the specific women's stories that were shared. The decision about getting a temporary protection order, for example. At first, I didn't consider getting one, because cops didn't equal safety in my community and I couldn't imagine being responsible for them unexpectedly knocking on the door to deliver the paperwork at a house full of weapons for a revolution and weed for tax-free income. The legal advocate at the shelter convinced me to file because she could help me arrange a legal alternative. Instead of cops, two of my comrades could deliver the court order to Bryce. Even with her being sensitive to the culture of my community, I was pulled between doing the right thing as defined by social services standards and doing what was right by my community. Finding people willing to serve Bryce stirred up chaos for others who felt similarly pulled between worlds, and, no matter how much I did to not involve the police, I was still perceived as betraying the community. Every move I made was considered a reflection of the community, just as every decision I was making to create personal safety also took my community into consideration. I didn't have the luxury of individuality.

I listened raptly to Dr. Richie speak about the ways misogyny, homophobia, and racism underpinned assumptions about who was and wasn't worthy of community and institutional protection.

I thought about how anxious I'd been when I had to go to the welfare office, how much social workers scared me. I thought about how I'd been questioned on why I, a woman in her late twenties with no children, needed public aid. My queer, improper femininity was a problem in the system. If I didn't correctly perform expectations I didn't understand, I might lose access to my rent money and food stamps. Dr. Richie's talk opened up new ways of thinking for me. I sat in that conference auditorium sniffling up snot while tears rolled down my face. I felt validated. And inspired. The conference program said Dr. Richie was a professor. I decided that's what I would become. I decided my new job-intertwined identity would be *Formerly homeless woman becomes college professor*.

A graduate degree in art seemed ridiculous, since I was already an artist, so I applied to the History of Consciousness program at the University of California, Santa Cruz, where Angela Davis taught. Following in her footsteps made sense. I set up a campus visit.

I flew down to Oakland and then rented a car for the drive to Santa Cruz, just over an hour. When I got to town, I drove up, up, up into the hills and then up a long, curving road into what I thought was the countryside. It turned out to lead to the campus entrance. A deer pranced by as I got directions from the security booth to the correct parking lot. Another deer was eating the piney foliage lining the parking area. Birds were chirping. I finished listening to the Fugees tape I was playing, took a deep breath, and got out of the car. Singing "Killing Me Softly" to myself, I walked toward the nearest building, hoping I was headed in the right direction.

I had an appointment with Ms. Walker, the History of Consciousness program manager. I walked up a flight of stairs and pulled open the door six minutes late, which I thought was early, since being at least fifteen minutes late was normal in my world. I walked down an empty gray hallway. There were flyers on a lone bulletin board I stopped to read. They promoted a conference revisiting Donna Haraway's essay "A Cyborg Manifesto." Haraway's office was next to the bulletin board. Karen Shirley had assigned "A Cyborg Manifesto" at Antioch in my contemporary art theory class. It's an early socialist critique of identity politics and gender essentialism. Next door was Teresa de Lauretis's office. I had a book of hers on semiotics and film theory that I didn't understand, but I knew she was a badass queer feminist. Then I walked by Angela Davis's office.

My palms were sweating. I stopped and stared at her nameplate, remembering a story she'd told the last time I heard her speak. She had said students would come to her office, see the "Most Wanted" poster with her face on it, and ask if it was real. I knew that shit was real, obviously a check in my favor to be able to study with her.

In Seattle, I couldn't spit without hitting a literal rock star, but after I heard Dr. Richie speak, intellectual activist professors became my rock stars. I had imagined History of Consciousness being more vibrant and pulsating than the Comet Tavern on a Saturday night. The silent, gray emptiness of the cold institutional hallway surprised me, but I suppressed my first response to academia and kept going.

Ms. Walker's office was at the far end of the hall, the only open door. A white woman in her fifties with short brown hair and glasses, she wore a lightweight plaid sweater loosely draped around her shoulders.

"What's your area of research?" she asked after inviting me to sit down.

"Um. Like. Feminism. Gender. Race. Art."

"Those are all interesting areas." Ms. Walker handed me a marigold piece of paper. It was a photocopied list of current PhD students. "You'll find plenty of people focused on related areas."

My research focuses on the queer Caribbean postcolonial subject through Marxist and Lacanian theory in order to reframe the location of the subaltern.

Areas of interest include Foucauldian theory, Psychoanalytic analysis, Revolution and the Subaltern, Utopian Communities, Hegemony, Frantz Fanon.

I wasn't sure which of these statements were related to my interests.

People had undergraduate degrees from Stanford, Wesleyan, and New York University. I was only familiar with NYU. When I was at Antioch, Sarah and I went to New York together for one of our co-ops. I worked at a health food store, where I stole our groceries to be able to afford the Lower East Side sublet we rented, and she worked at the NYU bookstore, where she stole the feminist theory books we thumbed through.

Ms. Walker told me the application deadlines and how GREs were weighed.

I nodded, thinking I'd have to find out if my ACT score could be accepted instead.

She told me eight to ten applicants are accepted into the program each year.

I nodded, thinking she meant eight to ten people apply.

"Is that your cat?" I pointed to a photo on the shelf behind her desk.

"Yes, that's Carmen," she said.

"My cat's name is Zar." I smiled in solidarity, thinking she made the decisions about who got into the program, and that this was a good sign.

Ms. Walker told me to come back at 1 p.m. James Clifford had office hours then.

"Is Angela Davis here?" I asked.

"She's not in town," Ms. Walker said.

I found a taqueria off campus. I pulled James Clifford's book *The Predicament of Culture: Twentieth-Century Ethnography, Literature, and Art* out of my backpack. I had read it in the same class where I'd read "A Cyborg Manifesto." It was so cool all these people taught in the same program. I'd brought a bunch of books, hoping to get them signed.

I returned to campus promptly at 1:15. This time, when I entered the sterile corridor, the first door on the right was slightly ajar. I saw the back of a thin, balding white man staring at a computer. I knocked, cautiously. Books were stacked and overflowing on every surface, including crowded on the shelves lining two walls of the office. Papers were piled haphazardly on the desk; a framed print of the image on the cover of *The Predicament of Culture* hung on the wall.

"Hello, hello. Forgive me. There is always too much email to keep up on. I'm Jim."

"Hi. Oh my god. It's really nice to meet you. Thank you for taking the time. I read your book in college and it changed my life."

"That's good to hear. Where did you go to college?"

"Antioch."

"The one in Ohio?"

"Yes. I graduated a long time ago." I wanted him to know that I had a lot of life experience, not just academic.

"What have you been doing since then?" Jim asked me. I told him about Home Alive.

I left his office and walked around campus before driving back to Oakland. I was acutely aware of my purple hair and tattoos, of my shiny, off-brand combat boots and new thrift-store dress. I couldn't put my finger on why, but I was uncomfortable.

When I got back to Seattle, I had an IBD flare-up so bad I couldn't drink
for a few weeks. I had to figure out how to get a prescription for the
expensive medications I needed, and I wasn't willing to go back to the
Harborview emergency room. Lisa, back in Chicago, was working in
medical billing and knew about drug companies' subsidy programs. She
sent me information on the manufacturer of my meds and then guided
me through the application process. Thanks to her, I got my maintenance
medication for free, along with a free colonoscopy at a university hospital
that confirmed I didn't have any cancerous cells.

Reading over the History of Consciousness application, I learned health
care was included with admission to Santa Cruz. Unfortunately, I also
needed a grade point average, which wasn't included in the thick package
of narrative evaluations making up my Antioch transcripts. I went and
signed up for a six-week summer course in the extension program at
the University of Washington called History and Martyrdom in Ancient
Rome. I chose it because of my love for Renaissance art. There wasn't
a lot of art in the class, but it covered events as brutal and bloody as a
Caravaggio painting. I received an A–. Transcript with a letter grade:
check.

Next, I needed three letters of recommendation. The grad student
teaching the class said he'd give me one. Check. My friend Leah, another
artist who I knew through Home Alive, connected me with her mother,
Cleo, who was working on her PhD. I volunteered as Cleo's research
assistant in exchange for a recommendation letter. Check. I still needed
one more. I wrote Karen Shirley. She said yes. Check. I was kicking ass.
An A– and recommendations from two grad students and my undergraduate art professor from ten years earlier.

I stopped going to the bar regularly and spent most of my time with
Sarah. She had recently moved to Seattle with her two-year-old daughter, Paulinka Mia, who was born five months after Mia was killed. Sarah,
Pauli, and I created a makeshift family. The days Sarah worked late, I
picked Pauli up from school. I'd bring her to my house to play with Zar

and make her macaroni and nondairy cheese with broccoli for dinner. When Sarah got home, Pauli and I would walk over to their house, two blocks away. We'd put Pauli to bed and then watch *Will & Grace*, since I didn't have a TV and wanted to see the new gay show. Sarah was the one now taking me to my health care appointments, taking copious notes on new protocols or driving me home while I was blissfully drugged up from another colonoscopy.

For the first time in my work life, I had a full-time job with health care benefits. My experience as a formerly homeless person helped me get hired as a case manager in the YWCA's Homeless Intervention Project, where I signed up unhoused people for employment training that led to work, even if the job was only for one day. Identifying more with my clients than with the other case managers, I made friends with some of them through a likely breach of policy. We had a kinship I didn't have anywhere else. One woman had taken a train all the way across the country to escape her abuser. We sat in my office drinking weak coffee from the break room and crafting a resume of work experience she didn't have. Eventually, she was hired as a (very slow) typist. She saved enough to move out of transitional housing into her own studio apartment. She crocheted a blanket for me as a thank you, a blanket I still have, which my cat Gracie loves to sleep on.

I would go out drinking with another client when she could find someone to take care of her four kids. Sometimes she brought her family over to my house to barbecue with Sarah and Pauli and my roommates. After she fell in love and moved in too quickly with a man who paid all her bills, she also quickly left him when she found out he was sexually abusing her thirteen-year-old daughter. I loved her for putting her kids before her man.

The HIP case manager job was part of Clinton welfare reform, what the US Chamber of Commerce called "a reassertion of America's work ethic." I could work as a case manager without a social work degree because the new legislation was rolling out fast and needed staffing. During my first team meeting, the program director explained, "We're shifting focus from human development to economic development. It will be turbulent for some time." And it was. Each week, a longtime case manager quit. New case managers arrived, carrying boxes into another empty office. A few months later, they carried their boxes out. I had to send too many Black women to job-readiness trainings with titles like "Appropriate and Inappropriate Work Clothing" that were taught by white instructors. I refused to send clients to an EPA hazmat training for a two-day job cleaning up toxic waste when we needed to inflate our numbers for the next round of federal funding.

I lasted six months.

The next hurdle in applying to grad school was taking the GRE. I signed up for a prep course at the U-Dub Women's Center, a place where I'd taught Home Alive classes. On the first day of the course, a hippie-age white man with a long gray beard, wearing shorts and a tie-dye T-shirt, stood at the front of the stadium-seating classroom. *How annoying he's a man*, I thought, sipping the soy chai latte I'd bought walking over from the bus stop.

He started the class saying, "You don't need to know math, you just need to know how to take this test." *He's not so bad*, I thought, taking another sip of chai.

I studied diligently after working at my new job as a case manager with Jewish Family Service. (My supervisor was much more chill than the one at the YWCA, but this is where I learned other Jews considered me "unaffiliated" since I hadn't had a bat mitzvah.) Zar Bar lay across my pile of scratch paper, pencils, erasers, and plastic sharpeners while I sat at the dining room table my roommates and I had found on the curb in a fancier neighborhood. My roommate Marc put on upbeat Chilean music and set out a recycling can for the papers full of numbers and symbols I'd crumple in frustration.

It was the first year the GRE was being offered online, but I didn't have a computer so I took the test in person at Seattle University. It was only offered on Saturdays at 8 a.m.

This is what I remember:

If _____

_____

_____

_____

And

$(xx)(xxy) > (xy) + (xy)$

Exhausted from waking up earlier than usual, I struggled through the four hours of testing, there until the end. Algebraic formulas stayed out of memory's reach under the fluorescent lights and institutional gray walls. The analytical section went smoothly but would be weighted the least in my applications. Fortunately, the reading-comprehension section had a question about Marcel Duchamp's *The Large Glass*, a painting I'd learned about at Antioch.

When it was over, I walked outside the dank building into an unusually sunny Seattle day. I unlocked my bike and rode over to the Comet, craving familiar darkness. I sidled onto a barstool and ordered a pint of hard cider. This was a grunge music scene haven at night. During the day, when Marcus was tending the bar, there were mostly other Black men drinking beer and watching sports.

"I just took the GRE," I said to Marcus.

"What's that?" he asked with his heavy Bronx accent.

"A test to get into graduate school."

"You're going to grad school?"

"We'll see."

"Well, hell yeah, shots all around for the professor!" he said as he served the three of us in the bar at noon on a sunny Saturday.

History

I didn't get into the History of Consciousness program.

PART TWO

INSTITUTIONALIZED

[LOS ANGELES

AND SANTA FE]

Claremont

I got into a cultural studies program in Denver, a master's degree designed for working adults that I can't find any traces of on the internet. I liked that Denver was in the mountains but thought I'd be uncomfortable among all the athletic white people who skied. I also got into the cultural studies program at Claremont Graduate University, on the far eastern edge of Los Angeles County. Los Angeles had a bad reputation in Seattle; many of the wealthy people changing the city had moved from there. On the other hand, the night of the 1992 uprisings—after the cops caught on camera beating Rodney King were acquitted—was one of the best times Bryce and I had together.

One of our anarchist friends came over to tell us something big was erupting and we should find the TV. I dug around in the storage closet and found the old black-and-white a former roommate had left behind. We plugged it in and turned on the news. Our soldier-turned-anarchist roommate joined us. The four of us were captivated. Black residents were taking the streets of their underserved neighborhoods. Not knowing Los Angeles, we couldn't decipher the complex racial relationships unfolding with their Korean immigrant neighbors; what we saw was a thrilling Black-led takedown of white supremacy.

Bryce looked out the window and reported that no one was in the streets. We thought it was suspiciously quiet for our predominantly Black, politically active neighborhood. The four of us piled into Bryce's car and drove around looking for protests. The Central District was quiet. Bryce turned toward downtown, and as we crested the hill on Union at 15th, a red glow emerged in the sky, evidence of upheaval.

At 7th and Pine, we parked the car and joined a pulsating crowd pushing toward Olive and 5th Avenue. A brick was tossed through a liquor store window. Someone reached through the broken glass and

handed out bottles of alcohol. I got a fifth of top-shelf whiskey and immediately drank from it, passing it to my friends. The window of the Betsey
Johnson store was smashed open. A butch with a green mohawk jumped
in and started handing out clothing off the mannequins. I got a floppy
straw hat with spots of blood on the wide brim. I felt glamorous in my
designer couture, sipping fancy whiskey in the middle of the street.

"Jessica! Jessica! Look!" Bryce was jumping up and down on the roof
of a police car.

From the other direction, I heard someone else yell my name. "Jess!
Jessica! Help me lift this!" It was June, a woman I knew from a neighborhood antiracist coalition I was a part of. Dressed in a suit and heels, June
was struggling with a huge concrete planter in front of Bank of America.

"Dude! That's too heavy!" I ran over to her.

"Fuck this place." June kicked at the bank windows. I joined her.

"How's your son doing?" I asked.

"Healing. So is the other boy. Meet me at the hospital tomorrow at
three o'clock. I'm holding another press conference."

June's son had been shot in front of Garfield High School. She
refused to press charges against the kid who'd fired the gun. June held
press conferences from the steps of the hospital every few days to counter
the media narrative insisting the boys were rival gang members. June was
a Black mother on an abolitionist crusade to educate the city and ensure
another young Black man didn't go to prison.

"Jessica! Goddamnit, get over here. Stop socializing." My
soldier-turned-anarchist roommate glared at me from a few feet away.
"Stay with the affinity group!"

June gave me a hug and ran to catch up with some people from the
neighborhood coalition. I turned toward them but changed my mind
and walked back over to my friends. I didn't want to risk ending up on
my own when the police inevitably attacked us. I looked longingly at
June and my Black neighbors when my white and Indigenous anarchist
friends ran off to throw bricks at a jeweler's and yell about South African
blood diamonds. But I also made it home safe that night.

The following week we got ahold of the Watts gang truce through
an LA zine-maker. The document called on the city of Los Angeles to
meet the Crips and Bloods dollar for dollar to restore broken streetlights,
develop parks in empty lots, and create jobs programs. The agreement
was never reached, because the city refused to negotiate with the gangs.

A lot of current and former gang members, along with former Black Panthers, implemented their part of the plan anyway. In the year after the 1992 uprising, gang homicides in Watts were reduced by 44 percent. I chose LA over Denver, hoping I'd find the community activists who'd crafted the gang truce.

CHAPTER ELEVEN

Cultural Studies

Sarah and Pauli helped me pack Zar and our stuff into a U-Haul. We secured my 1982 Toyota pickup onto a trailer and drove from Seattle to the casita I had rented on Lincoln Avenue in Pomona, California. Sarah and Pauli stayed for three days to help me settle in. We found a couch and dishes and a brand-new scratching post for Zar at a thrift store down the street. We planted succulents in clay pots on my four-foot-by-four-foot cement porch. Before they left, we drove into LA and explored Hollywood Boulevard. A tattoo artist let Pauli sit in their chair and kindly put a rub-on Samoan band around her upper arm. We saw semi-famous actors we couldn't name and got kicked out of the main entrance of the Hollywood Wax Museum for loitering too long without paying an entrance fee. Then Zar and I were on our own.

The first night, I was shaken awake by what sounded like a bat cracking against the side of the house. Zar hunkered down, his golden eyes morphing into wide black pupils. I checked the doors and windows. The sound lasted for another full minute. I called 911 while the house shook. "It's an earthquake," the dispatcher told me.

The next night, a searchlight from a police helicopter lit up my bedroom every thirty seconds while a garbled, amplified *Stop running!* bounced through my window and off my walls. I hadn't role-played this scenario in any of my self-defense training. I didn't know whether to prepare to protect myself from someone crashing through my front door or hide in the bathtub to avoid police bullets that might spray through my windows. I grabbed Zar and sat inside my closet until the helicopter noise drifted away.

One of my first days driving home from campus, a searchlight from a police helicopter trained down so brightly on a man running down the street, I could clearly see he was Latino. I didn't know what I was supposed to do, or could do, as a witness in an actual Orwellian scenario. I drove to the end of the median dividing the street and did a U-turn. I saw the man slip through a hole in a chain-link fence and disappear into the bushes of an overgrown lot. I drove home to do my reading for my seminar, a section of *Discipline and Punish* by Michel Foucault.

I loved my pickup truck. It was my first vehicle since I was eighteen, when I bought a VW Bug and drove it until the engine blew and I couldn't afford to fix it. Nearly fifteen years later, when I had the job painting concrete rocks, I needed a truck. I had finally felt like I could afford to keep a vehicle running, especially since one of my roommates taught me how to change the oil and brake lights. I bought my 1982 pine-green pickup for $1,000. Sarah sewed leopard-print seat covers and matching curtains for the camper. The vise-grip pliers I replaced the window handle with added a tough, punk femme touch. On my first day of class, I drove to campus and parked in the graduate student lot. A BMW pulled out of a spot next to where I'd parked. A Mercedes station wagon was in the spot on the other side. The only other pickup trucks I saw were driven by the maintenance crew taking care of the perfectly manicured campus.

I walked over to the building where my first class was being held. There were a bunch of well-dressed smokers walking in extremely anxious circles around the outdoor courtyard. As I got closer, I saw they weren't smoking; they were talking on cell phones. They were MBA students; the building housed the Drucker School of Management. The fancy cars and people in suits threw me off. The few graduate school students I knew in Seattle didn't have money and/or were older women changing their paths after surviving the early part of their lives. I wasn't prepared to be around so much wealth.

My second class, held that evening in a different building, was a required ethnographic research seminar. I was excited about this one, thinking it would have a similar approach as James Clifford's *The Predicament of Culture*. My understanding of ethnography was that it was a decolonial practice intervening on racist metanarratives created by anthropological research. I thought it was interconnected with rematriation and returning stolen artifacts in museum collections to Indigenous tribes. I was wrong. The sociology professor who taught the class, a very nice white woman who researched divorce, led us through a research method called "participant observation." The semester-long assignment was to pick a site, participate in the culture, and draw conclusions from a position of having stakes in that culture. It was a counter to academic positioning that put the researcher on the outside, a supposedly impartial observer. *Okay. That's not terrible*, I thought.

During the evening class sessions, my cohort and I shared notes and helped each other determine a direction for the final papers we'd be presenting conference-style. I wasn't prepared for so many of my colleagues to be significantly younger than me. I was only thirty-three. But a lot of them were just out of college. And the other person in her thirties, who was married to a man and had kids, one of them graduating from high school, considered herself middle-aged.

One night, a classmate flipped through his reporter's notebook, raised his hand, and told us he had chosen to observe a strip club. I thought he was joking. He read: "I followed her to the back room. I realized I could have sex with her if I wanted. The power felt palpable. She pointed to a chair for me to sit in and began grinding her ass in my face without touching me. The club serves liquor. If it was a dry club, she could have touched my crotch with her writhing ass."

He said he understood that his research may be controversial but that men go to strip clubs every day so he wanted to know what happened there.

I'd visited a lot of friends on their shifts as dancers at strip clubs. I thought he was an idiot to think paying someone for a dance meant he could have sex with them. Wasn't he confessing to using academic research to get away with rape? I looked around the room for some sisterly solidarity but didn't observe any obvious allies.

I raised my hand and asked Mr. Potential Rapist, "Have you ever read Annie Sprinkle or Carol Queen, or anything by sex workers writing about their own experiences?"

He said no. He said he wasn't interested in the workers; he was interested in writing about strip clubs for men like him. Men who didn't go to strip clubs.

I asked, "But aren't you a man going to a strip club?"

He said, "It's different, because it's for research."

Maybe, I thought. But it still seemed like a lot of bullshit. I looked around the room again, searching for signs of annoyance with this man for wasting our time with his naive misogyny. I observed blank faces.

Before the end of our first year, he had an essay accepted for publication in an anthology put out by a leftist academic press known for cutting-edge scholarship.

❦

The small tuition stipend and ten-dollars-an-hour work-study job I had wasn't covering tuition, rent, and everything else. The person in the financial aid office showed me projected payment plans and encouraged me to take out more loans. The projected numbers were significantly greater than my income before graduate school. But they were imaginary numbers as far as I was concerned. The financial aid worker assured me that I'd earn a high enough income to easily pay back the loans. I didn't believe her, but one of my classmates who was older than me, a single mom with kids, advised me to take out as much as I could, that loan companies let you make small payments forever, there's no harm. This is one of the reasons many of us now in our fifties and sixties still have student debt. Back then it was true that we could easily set up affordable payment arrangements and that student loans weren't attached to credit scores. I took out the max allowed, because that was the only way I could cover all my expenses.

Part of my expenses included the health care I'd thought the school provided. Turned out Santa Cruz, a public university, provided health care to graduate students. Claremont, a private university, did not. Part of my mandatory fees paid for limited emergency coverage, and I also had access to the student health center, but its scope of services was Band-Aids and the morning-after pill. I applied for the California low-income health care program but was rejected because of my "preexisting conditions." They included depression along with the IBD, so I went off the depression meds I had recently been prescribed and applied again, hoping that having only one preexisting condition might make a difference. It didn't matter, because the funding for the program was cut for the following year. I called Lisa, who found an IBD research study in LA that I qualified for. For those two years, I had the best health care I've had to this day.

❦

Nir, the chair of the cultural studies department, taught a class called Genocide and Mass Murder. I took the class thinking it might include Judith Herman's *Trauma and Recovery* and be a way to learn more frameworks for making connections between interpersonal and structural violence. That book wasn't on the reading list; however, Nir was Israeli, fluent in Arabic, and distraught over the Rwandan genocide because he believed never again meant never again.

The classroom was a small, white windowless box with two conference tables pushed together. Each session, I took a spiral notebook and two pencils out of my backpack while the seven other students plugged in laptops. For fifteen weeks, using the United Nations' 1948 Genocide Convention that first defined genocide under international law, the goal of the course was to determine whether historical violence, such as the Armenian or Native American genocides, fell under the legal definition of genocide. *What the fuck*, I thought. But yes, apparently through the lens of the UN treaty, these events could be debatable history. Inside of institutions, genocide could become a question of legal definition, not a fact based on the impact human beings experienced. It was alarming to learn that the horrific wars intended to erase groups of people could be academic fodder and ranked as greater or lesser crimes.

Indigenous scholars, who wrote books with reams of footnotes, were considered controversial academics. Nir argued that US colonization of Native Americans had to be parsed out and not understood as a singular genocidal event, that—according to the UN treaty—there couldn't be five hundred years of genocide. One of my young classmates, appropriately appalled, spent the semester shaping an academically sound counterargument. But at the end of the semester, when she presented her research, she had concluded that the laws created by colonizers held more weight than Indigenous academic, oral, and cultural histories and that, yes, there were too many different incidents with different reasoning against different tribes for there to have been five hundred years of genocide. I was immersed in a new type of danger. I thought about starting a self-defense class to minimize the impacts of institutional gaslighting and trauma. I still think about that.

I observed that the other students called Nir "Dr. Abrahamson." At Antioch, everyone used first names. We called the dean of students "Steve," the president "Al." Karen was Karen. Faculty, administrators, staff, and students all used first names with each other. I tried to adapt at Claremont but eventually gave up.

I had a piece in an art show in Pomona, and Nir was the only one from my program who came to the opening. The gallery was in the

Pomona arts district, an area around 4th Street that was a short drive from my casita and unironically segregated from the rest of town by an iron gate with the words "Artist Colony" welded into the arch. It's where I did my ethnography project, and the show was one of the ways I was a participant. The colony was an economic revitalization project led by politicians and real estate developers. I attended the monthly meetings between developers and local artists at a collectively run gallery that had been in the neighborhood for fifteen years.

The show was about dolls. Back in Seattle, when I lived with Katie, Shakti, and Zar, I had made a large charcoal drawing about the night Bryce shot the gun called *Barbie's Dreamhouse*. A disproportionately large, dark-haired, and naked Barbie fled from a house that had been cut open. The crumbling insides were exposed while a small figure with dreadlocks stood on the stoop pointing a rifle at her. Nir didn't say much about the drawing, but he hung out and had a plastic cup of cheap wine with me, chatting jovially as I introduced him to people. The next semester, I was awarded one of the few paid teaching assistant positions in the department. Nir assigned me to a queer, Jewish media studies professor at Pitzer College who had produced the first feature film ever directed by a Black queer woman, and who became my mentor. That assignment made all the difference in the direction I eventually headed.

CHAPTER TWELVE

Anarchists in LA

Activists from all over the world were in Seattle. The World Trade Organization was having its biennial Ministerial Conference at the convention center, and massive antiglobalization demonstrations had erupted. I'd wake up in my casita, make a cup of Earl Grey, feed Zar, and put on *Democracy Now!* to listen to interviews and roundtables discussing NAFTA, the Clinton administration–backed international trade agreement, and the militarization of the US-Mexico border. Consumer goods could flow freely across the border while migrants seeking economic opportunities were arrested, deported, and murdered by the US government. Indigenous and non-Indigenous family farmers spoke about their struggles against Monsanto, which was forcing them from their ancestral lands and razing rainforests to produce genetically modified crops of fake foods and poisonous pharmaceuticals. Abolition activists were exposing the prison-industrial complex and the disproportionate incarceration of Black and Brown people. Discussions about billionaire-funded laws destroying workers' rights to unionize made connections to the rise of modern-day slavery in the Global South. Feminists of all genders and races were drawing connections between trans and cis women trafficked, raped, and murdered in Mexican factory towns and along pipelines destroying US Indigenous and Canadian First Nations communities.

The "Battle in Seattle," as it was dubbed, occurred a few months after I moved to Los Angeles. I was preoccupied with the fifty thousand activists, artists, and intellectuals from across the globe fighting the financialization of everything on the same streets where I had protested the Gulf War, taken over abandoned buildings for low-income housing, co-organized an anarchist-led march against neo-Nazis, and wheat-pasted and stenciled art against anti-queer health care policies and misogynist antiabortion laws. These were the streets I had walked through with Mia. The ones forever changed after she was killed, and where Home Alive reclaimed some sense of safety. Twelve hundred miles away, I felt like part of the crowds.

I obsessed over the news, learning new narratives about familiar territory. I yelled at the radio and TV in my new academic language. I was mostly in solidarity with Pacifica Radio analysis, but NPR annoyed the shit out of me. I had thought I was an NPR fan until I heard too many of their reporters repeating the same antiactivist narratives. Their boomer story went like this: People had a right to exercise their free speech, but these activists are doing it wrong; they're tackling too many things at once instead of having a single message delivered through a 1960s-type charismatic leader. I'd lecture my radio, going over 1980s and '90s activist movements and strategies. Antiapartheid student encampments in solidarity with South Africa. ACT UP. Third-wave feminism. Horizontal organizing. Intersectionality. I took their boomer nostalgia personally, annoyed with its long shadow over activist culture as the news cut to a Monsanto ad disguised as a sponsorship message.

That was November. In August, the antiglobalization movement was convening in Los Angeles for the 2000 Democratic National Convention. Mich was living in LA, other Seattle friends came down, and we all met up in the streets outside the Staples Center. When the cops decided the "Free-Speech Zone" had been breached during a Rage Against the Machine show, we dodged rubber bullets to the beat Ozomatli played as the band members jumped off the stage and led us away from the fray. It was an intense and fun day. I captured parts of it on the video camera I carried with me, and I brought my footage to the Independent Media Center. They were a DIY, grassroots, anticorporate media hub made possible by the new portable and affordable digital technology. The IMC sites had become a critical part of the convenings.

The new technology provided a path from the 1992 LA uprisings to the IMC and the anticorporate globalization movement. The LAPD officers who were caught on camera beating Rodney King were caught because George Holliday, a guy with one of the new portable cameras, heard a commotion outside his apartment. Holliday went onto his balcony and recorded what became one of the first widely seen cop watch videos. Holliday wasn't an activist. He called the LAPD to see if they wanted the video. Infamously, they did not. Holliday then called a local news station, which aired the video. It was a culture-shifting moment.

There was a video, uncontestable proof of the continuing, systemic anti-Black racism governing the country. Of course, though the video resulted in charges against the cops, the jury acquitted them of using excessive force, and days of uprising occurred. Portable media did not end racist policing in the US (then or in 2020, when cameras caught the police murder of George Floyd, a Black man, and sparked another national uprising). What the new technology changed was the ability for most anyone to use a camera and become part of the narrative. Media could be made from the bottom up, on a low or no budget, by individuals, citizen journalists, and artists. More than one story at a time could be told, challenging white supremacist, misogynist, anti-trans and -queer, colonizing narratives. It's an undeniable cultural shift with a tool that can be used in struggles for equity.

The normalization of a militarized police force repressing citizen revolts is another path from the 1992 LA uprisings to the WTO protests. The Seattle police used similar tactics in 1999 as the LAPD used in 1992. I had a VHS tape when I was researching the topic that highlighted the LAPD training the SPD post-1992, a video I couldn't find while writing this. What's important is that cops riding through the streets on tanks, hanging off on all sides in soldier-like formations, and indiscriminately spraying chemical agents into crowds were new tactics in the US in the '90s.

Ready for the moment and embracing the chaos were anarchists. Showing up in "black bloc," dressed in all black from head to toe, including wearing black ski masks, anarchists emerged, visually, as a unified formation. They threw tear gas canisters back at the police and built barricades out of dumpsters that sometimes got lit on fire. Unafraid of meeting violence with violence, autonomous reporters and corporate media equally beamed a spotlight onto my former community. An arcane political ideology that hadn't held public sway in nearly a century and that was only of interest to a small, marginalized corner of the left and some punk musicians, anarchists were suddenly a cause of cultural anxiety.

As the LA convergence at the DNC approached, the local Fox TV station, which actually used the call letters KCOP, juicily ran a three-part story called "The Anarchists in LA." I set my VCR to record each night. In my leopard-print beanbag chair with Zar Bar in my lap, viewing through a cultural studies lens, I was enraptured. A shaky, handheld camera followed the well-coiffed, middle-aged reporter as he walked up an unpaved, overgrown path to a house seemingly deep in the woods near Eugene, Oregon. According to mainstream news, Eugene was anarchist central. According to KCOP, anarchists were a unified group of violent outsiders with a mission to destroy the violence-free world in which KCOP's Los Angeles viewers lived. The reporter was greeted by a tattooed, messy-haired person in a black ski mask. The reporter was quite interested in the wood-burning stove—aesthetically, not politically. Then the report cut to a shot of assumed anarchists wearing black ski masks and burning flags in the middle of a small-town street lined with evergreens and other foliage of the Northwest. Then the report cut to— whoa, wait ... footage from the 1992 uprising in LA. Black people were smashing windows and grabbing things out of a store on a tree-barren street, running down wide city streets carrying boxes of diapers. KCOP edited these disparate images together, implying its viewers should see the Eugene anarchists in black ski masks the same way the station implied its viewers should see their Black neighbors: as outsiders.

KCOP took three days and nearly twenty minutes of airtime to craft a narrative that placed racist anti-Black tropes onto mostly young white leftists in black masks, presuming Black LA residents and anarchist demonstrators were equally outside threats to the Fox station's viewers' way of life. I had found my thesis project.

❊❊❊

A Chicanx-run anarchist café in MacArthur Park called Café Luna Sol was my favorite place to do my research. Away from the annoyingly bucolic suburbs, I'd eat deliciously glutenous homemade vegan empanadas at a table in the back room of the café surrounded by my books, photocopies of articles, and spiral-bound notebooks. One day, I left one of my key references, Todd May's *The Political Philosophy of Poststructuralist Anarchism*, to go to the bathroom and noticed a flyer for an upcoming event at the café on racism in the anarchist movement. I made a note of the date and returned to my reading.

The day of the event, the tables had been folded up, making room for the overflow of people. Tan metal folding chairs were set up in a large circle. Punks of different races and ethnicities were wearing similarly torn black jeans, faded black T-shirts, and black bandannas around their necks. There was a group of New Black Panthers in black tactical fatigues and dark sunglasses. A few people dressed in button-down shirts, looking more like accountants, handed out communist newspapers. Some Anti-Racist Action anarchists set their newspapers on the chairs while the green anarchists fought with the anarcho-socialists over whose additional agenda items should go first.

The meeting organizer whistled loudly, calling people to take a seat and begin introductions. It only took five people introducing their affiliations for Maoists and Trotskyists to break out into a heated debate. Eventually, the older Black man with deep ebony skin sitting two chairs over from me, wearing an orange-trimmed dashiki and large wire-framed glasses, stood up and interrupted the chaos. "I'm Ghaisi. I have a newsletter, the *Pelican Bay News*. I'm looking for some of those Seattle anarchists to help me." I leaned over and whispered to him that I was from Seattle. Twenty minutes later, when a few more people used their introduction to argue that racism wasn't a strategic topic for the left, Ghaisi nodded toward the door. I nodded in agreement.

Outside, Ghaisi told me that he was born and raised in South Central and that his newsletter was mailed monthly to men in Pelican Bay, the prison where he'd spent most of his adult life. Out of prison and sober for a decade, he organized with people who wrote the 1992 gang truce. I told him how significant that document was in my decision to move to LA. We planned to meet at his office the following week.

That day, I pulled up in front of the single-story stucco building on Normandie Avenue and parked my green truck near the security gate. Ghaisi opened the metal door and gave me a hug. Inside, he introduced me to his office mate, Michael Zinzun. Mike was in his fifties with a thick gut and hip-length graying dreadlocks, most of which were tucked neatly into a knitted hairnet. He smiled mistrustfully at me, and I could see where he'd lost his eye to a brutal police beating. I knew of Mike because he ran the Coalition Against Police Abuse. I had read how instrumental he'd been in the gang truce negotiations. A stunningly masculine person named Moniqua walked into the room and handed Mike a stack of flyers. Moniqua looked at me in a way I have no language to describe, but I viscerally remember feeling acute awareness that whatever we may have had in common on paper, I could never fundamentally understand Moniqua's experience of race, class, and violence.

Ghaisi and I spent a lot of time together. We worked on his newsletter. We hung out in coffee shops in both of our neighborhoods. We met with people who participated in the 1992 uprisings. We went to Watts to visit community gardens created in areas the city still hadn't repaired since the 1965 uprisings. We went to political lectures at museums and community centers. We went to art events that Mike and I both had artwork in. Mich often joined us. She had finished grad school and had lived in Palestine/Israel, organizing against the Zionist occupation. More masculine presenting than she used to be and fully committed to anti-Zionism as a Jewish person, Mich generally wore a keffiyeh wrapped around her neck. Ghaisi usually wore his University of the Hood baseball cap, and I'd often complement my vintage dresses with a purple faux-fur jacket. My old and new lives were vibrantly interconnected.

Zar spent a lot of time outside our casita in Pomona, absorbing the Southern California sunshine. His beautiful long, black silky fur was falling out in patches around irritated areas on his once-fuzzy butt. He had been bitten by a racoon a few years earlier and didn't respond as expected to the treatment. It turned out he had an autoimmune disease and the racoon bite had exasperated it. I was always worried about him. I talked about my fear of Zar dying with Maura, a Home Alive friend who had moved to LA after breaking up with her infamously shitty, and closeted, movie star girlfriend. We spent the day on a hike in Griffith Park and then eating noodles in Thai Town. I fell asleep on her couch, too tired to drive the forty miles back to Pomona. When I got home the next day, I found Zar trying to scoot to greet me at the front door, his back legs disturbingly immobile and spread out.

I dropped my keys and ran to him. His breath was shallow. He couldn't lift himself up. He turned his head toward me and blinked his amber eyes. I scooped him up in a towel and sat on the bed holding him. He stretched his head, indicating he wanted to be on the floor. I laid him on the bedroom carpet. He tried to crawl toward the bathroom. I picked him up and put him on the tile floor. He pointed his chin toward the tub. I placed him gently on the cool porcelain, where he lay still, panting. I petted him and sobbed. He let out a howl, a howl I now know is a death howl. He tried scooting his dying body around the tub to get comfortable. I sobbed, mad at myself for pushing him off me two days earlier when he wanted to sit on my lap because his bald patches had been oozing grossly. Guilt knotted my intestines.

Zar howled again.

I felt each and every one of my skin cells turn papery thin. I felt my arms and legs throb with the beat of the thick ball of grief blocking my lungs from taking air in deeply. My sinuses felt like shattered glass.

Zar sucked in a few soft, uneven breaths.

I picked him up again and put him on my lap. He didn't struggle. He gave a weak howl. Ten minutes later, his breath slowed to a stop. I felt his body stiffen.

❦

"Oh, damn. I loved that cat," an actively alcoholic ex I called said. "Go get another cat right away. Just go." The only thing I trusted about this ex was their expertise in avoiding feeling pain. I went to a no-kill shelter and adopted Bella, a beautiful calico. At her free checkup, the vet said Bella had advanced feline leukemia. Per their policy, the shelter took her back to care for her and gave me a voucher for another cat. I wasn't ready for more heartbreak. Instead, I volunteered at the shelter to get my cat fix. Within a few weeks, an eight-month-old kitten with deep Caribbean-blue eyes entranced me. I picked her up to see if she would lean on my left shoulder, a gesture of Zar's I missed. She pulled her head back, looked at me with her gorgeous eyes, shifted her body, and leaned in to rub her nose against my right check. I named my little trade-in Sadie Viva. Sadie for a former client at the YWCA, to remind me of my life before graduate school, and Viva for Mia, as in Viva Zapata.

❦

I felt my body thicken as I became a driver instead of a bike rider. My new lifestyle led me to a new addictive behavior: the twenty-four-hour drive-through. I'd stop on my route home from campus, stuffing myself full of fried, breaded food that made me feel sick but kept me from seeking out drugs. The delicious, disgusting, greasy food-like chunks were how I avoided slipping further into the depths of the grief I hadn't escaped when I left Seattle. New layers of fat thickening my body protected my brain from the messages my gut tried to send to my heart.

I interpreted the numbness as safety until a searing pain prevented me from straightening my spine into a standing position. I maneuvered my fully bent-over body to the phone to call 911. The EMTs who showed up were nice enough, but all they could do was offer me a ride to a hospital. It cost $150, so I declined. The sobering reality of no options eventually loosened my spine enough to get in the truck and go to the drive-through for some more fried chunks.

The positive side of becoming a driver was that I didn't need to live within biking distance of campus, not that I ever rode my bike to campus. The summer before my second year at Claremont, Sadie and I escaped the suburbs. We moved to an apartment in LA near the corner of Santa Monica and Western, on a one-block street aptly named Institute Place. We became friends with our upstairs neighbors, Luis and James, who always had alcohol and cocaine. We'd keep both of our apartments' doors open for Sadie to have upstairs and downstairs accommodations. The boys decided to adopt a kitten, a gray tiger-striped one named Cristal, for Gina Gershon's character in *Showgirls*. Sadie and Cristal would gallop through the hallways together, entertaining the neighbors, a duo of best fur friends.

LA had become the most affordable big city on the West Coast following the dot-com explosion. Marc, my Seattle roommate who'd played Chilean music while I studied for the GRE, had moved to Pasadena for a job. A gentle, uncomplicated guy who loved to drink beer and ride his bike, Marc helped me learn how to use a Thomas Guide, the pre-GPS map needed to make sense of LA's knotted freeways. Marc picked destinations—the Long Beach aquarium, taco stands in East LA, dinner with Mich and her parents in Manhattan Beach—and I'd flip through the hundreds of spiral-bound pages to find a street and then its map coordinates, trying to follow a system made out of paper that made even less sense than the one made out of concrete and steel.

I spent a lot time with Maura. We went to see dyke bands at queer bars and flirt with butches. We became friends with Jennifer and Leon, gorgeously tattooed, born-and-raised LA queers who met when they lived in the same court-ordered sober house. Leon was a chivalrous, old-school butch on his way to becoming a trans man. Jennifer was stunning, the most beautiful woman in the room whether she was in a low-cut high-femme outfit or a cheesy velour tracksuit. She never lorded her beauty over anyone and was hilarious when she easily put men and butches in their place while they tripped over themselves trying to flirt with her.

Leon insisted on helping me find good spots to scout when I was working as a production assistant in the casting department on a film being made by my media studies mentor's partner, the director who had been targeted by Jesse Helms. My job was to hand out a flyer for a casting call. It said we were seeking "African American butch or tough women, 18–25." The stereotyped language made me cringe. Leon told me to get over it. "Stereotypes is how everyone thinks," he said. "When I was in prison there were whites, Blacks, and Mexicans." I didn't agree with him and never stopped being uncomfortable as a white-passing person representing a Hollywood film as I walked into beauty shops and Chinese restaurants and through swap meets lining the streets still wrecked from the 1992 uprising. No one else seemed as concerned as I was. People always took the flyer and, after reading it, asked for one for their friend. I checked back weekly at Michelle's XXX and the Akbar, and the bartenders would give me free drinks and send people who fit the look over to me. "I told you," Leon said.

At school, I was writing papers so badly that the writing center didn't know how to help. I had won awards for my writing back in high school and had tested out of grammar requirements my senior year, but I couldn't wrap my brain around the language of theory. I continued to exacerbate my IBD with fried, gluten-full, dairy-licious food to avoid the creeping feeling of failure. I managed to miss the deadline to turn in my paperwork to graduate. Actually, what I missed was the fact that I even had to do this step. Now, in order to graduate I had to pay $2,000 to stay enrolled over the summer. I already had taken out the maximum amount of student loans, so I charged the tuition fee to my credit card, which was weighed down with a partial tuition payment from the previous semester. I figured I'd be employed soon enough and I'd get the card paid down. Despite this paperwork mishap, things were looking positive. One of my mediocre essays was published in an academic journal, and I had received a grant from the Institute of Anarchist Studies to finish my thesis project, a video—not a paper—called *Paint It Black*. My rent was covered, and I was on track to meet my September 1, 2001, deadline.

CHAPTER THIRTEEN

I'm Queer, My Partner Is Trans

Paint It Black screened in art galleries and film festivals that summer, including up in Seattle, where I visited Zoë and other friends. I had a job interview scheduled for September 13, two weeks after my degree would be official. It was for a grant-funded position at the California African American Museum.

Early on September 11, Luis banged on my door to make sure I turned on my TV. James brought a pot of coffee, and the three of us sat on my couch holding the kitties while we watched news of the planes flying into the World Trade Center and images of people jumping out of the fiery towers before they collapsed. We took turns using my cordless phone to check on our people in New York. I had messages from several activist lists to the effect of, "The chickens have finally come home to roost. Delete this message!"

The morning of September 13, I put on my interview outfit: a pair of black pants, a deep plum short-sleeved top, and a lightweight oversized men's blazer, a graduation present from James that he'd stolen from the costume shop where he worked. I called the California African American Museum to confirm the address. The person who answered the phone asked me to hold. Ms. Johnson, who I was supposed to meet with, clicked onto the line. "Jessica, I am so sorry to tell you this. I'm right now coming out of a meeting where we were told all grant funding is being diverted to Homeland Security. The position is gone."

A week later, I put my interview outfit on again and drove to Century City in my green truck for an interview with a small, privately funded nonprofit that archived recovered art collections that had been looted by the Nazis. The executive director said, "You have the perfect eclectic skills for this position, but I'm sorry to tell you the National Endowment for the Arts has rescinded our grant. That money is being redirected to

Homeland Security. Can you believe it?" I nodded, thinking I'd have to go back to making pizza. The executive director continued talking. "What we'd like to do is offer you the opportunity to write a grant, and if you are successful, the job is yours. Of course, the research and writing would not be paid." I couldn't believe it.

Harder to believe, they weren't the only small nonprofit arts organization to make that absurd offer. It was wild how many interviews resulted in an offer to write a grant for their organization for free, with no guarantee of paid work. In the first wave of the 9/11 economy, arts and cultural spaces were decimated, stocks fell, tourism and travel industries collapsed, and my newly minted graduate degree became a liability before the piece of paper arrived in the mail. I signed up for a temp agency along with everyone else in the country who was flailing under the government's latest disaster capitalism investment.

❦

Daily, I called the temp agency and was told there still weren't any job requests. Then, one day, they called me. There was a half day of work in Sherman Oaks. It was a flat fifty-dollar payment. I wiped the vegan cookie crumbs off my rumpled leggings. I didn't bother changing, just put my interview blazer on over my black T-shirt and clipped my hair into a messy topknot. The address I drove to looked like an empty office building. I pushed open the front door and took the elevator up to the fourth floor. A young woman with long blonde hair greeted me. She was a little too pretty, a little too hip to be a suburban office worker. But as I had learned, LA stereotypes were different. The sparse reception area was noticeably quiet. There weren't computers or any personal items at her desk, just a phone. It rang. Then she asked me to follow her down a strangely empty hallway. Like when I walked down the History of Consciousness hallway, it felt similarly off.

The receptionist knocked on a door that was opened by a man with a lot of tattoos and rockabilly sideburns, dressed in the same color Carhartt pants I used to wear on the construction site. He wasn't an office worker. "Have a seat," he said. "Mr. Kennedy will be ready in a minute." This reception desk also only had a phone. No nameplate or pictures of pets. The phone rang and the rockabilly guy pointed to the door across from where I was sitting. He didn't get up to introduce me to Mr. Kennedy, just told me to go in. I didn't know what to expect but almost laughed out loud when I opened the door and saw a skinny guy with too much hair product in an ill-fitting suit sitting behind the large thrift-store-quality executive desk. Mr. Kennedy got up, walked over to me, and held out his hand. He could've been younger than me. I wondered if he was a porn producer or a wealthy idiot playing boss in an inherited business.

Holding up a copy of my resume, he said, "So, you went to Claremont. My dad taught out there."

I smiled.

"It looks like you would be great for the job. Can you start today?" he said.

"What's the job?" I asked.

"I need you to do some faxing, some filing, some basic stuff like that. You get paid your hourly rate through the temp agency. Can you start right now?"

"Um, okay? How long do you need someone? Is it full-time?" I asked.

"We can work out whatever schedule you need."

I tilted my head and squinted at him.

"Really. Come on, sit over here." He walked back to his chair and motioned for me to follow. I walked over and sat down. He stood behind me and pointed to a piece of paper on the desk. "This is a list of people you need to fire. I have to go to a meeting." He ran out the door before I fully registered what he had said. I looked at the list. The first person was being fired for laziness and a bad attitude. *I hope this dude isn't Black*, I thought as a Black man walked in the room. He was wearing gray cargo pants and a gray work shirt with a name patch that read "Darryl."

"Where's Mr. Kennedy?" Darryl asked.

I stood up and held out my hand. "I don't know. I'm Jessica."

"Why am I here?" Darryl asked.

"Um, I don't know. He just hired me and ran out of the office."

"Am I being fired?"

"I guess so."

"Why?" His voice rose.

"I don't know. It says here . . ." I paused. "It says here it's because you aren't, um, doing a good job."

"What the hell?" Darryl yelled.

"I don't know," I said. "It says some shit that seems fucked up to me."

Strangely, Darryl just turned and walked out of the office. Almost immediately, a Latina woman about my age walked in. My list said to tell her she was late all the time.

"Oh my god," she said. "Am I being fired too?"

"I guess so," I said.

"I have three kids. I'm a single mom." Strangely, she too just walked out of the office. Something was off.

A white woman in a wheelchair came in.

"Oh, hell no!" I said. "What the fuck is going on?"

A bunch of people with headsets rushed through the door, including the people just fired and Mr. Kennedy, who held out his hand, laughing. He wasn't in a suit anymore.

"I'm Jamie Kennedy. This is my show. You were great." He was an actor I'd never heard of.

Darryl also held out his hand to me, laughing. "Man, you had us feeling like shit." It was Craig Robinson, who eventually played Darryl on *The Office*.

Someone with a clipboard said, "Just sign here and you'll get your fifty dollars."

"You're kidding," I said. "You went to a temp agency to take advantage of people needing work?" I was so pissed. I told them I needed to step outside for a minute. The rockabilly guy and the person with the clipboard walked me back down the deceptive hallway to the elevators. When we walked through the first reception area, they made sure to stay between me and a man in a business suit waiting for what he thought was a job interview.

"Just come back up when you're ready," the rockabilly guy said, pushing the elevator button for me.

Outside, I called Maura, who was used to navigating the film industry thanks to her shitty ex. Maura gave me advice on how to negotiate for more money. I paced around the parking lot a little longer. The man from the waiting room came outside. He had a big smile on his face.

"That was fun," he said. "Did you have a good time?"

"I thought it was kinda fucked up."

"Man, I love LA. What a great way to make fifty bucks." He walked over to the bus stop in front of the building.

I went back upstairs. Eventually, I signed an agreement not to sue the show and they paid me $200. Rockabilly guy walked me to the elevator again. He put his hand up for a high five and said, "You got more than my day rate."

❧❦✿❦❧

Sadie and I moved out of the Institute Place into a house on Winona Street in the part of East Hollywood where Thai Town and Little Armenia came together. We lived with three other queer artists, two other cats, and one dog. In honor of Winona Ryder's highly publicized pill addiction and shoplifting arrest, we dubbed our home the Winona House.

One of my roommates made a new friend named Juaquin at a trans support group. Juaquin had crystal-clear warm brown eyes that also gave off a slightly evil glint I couldn't resist. The three of us went to queer art and film events together, and one night Juaquin said, "I like you. Like that." It was cute, until two months in when he asked me to marry him.

Remembering an old domestic violence advocacy checklist about signs of a potential abuser that included immediate proposals, I answered, "This is going to end with you hitting me, isn't it?"

"I would never hit you," he said. I wondered, but I paid attention to the fun sex and tucked away the red flag.

While we were waiting for our fried foodstuffs at a twenty-four-hour drive-through after an intensely sexy romp, he casually mentioned a physical fight with his most recent ex. *People change*, I told myself. *I've changed.* I grabbed the french fries and ate a handful.

For our six-month anniversary, I drove the fifty-four miles from the Winona House to Juaquin's house in Corona. It was a rental property his parents owned. He'd moved in earlier that year after his break-up and, I later learned, his attempted suicide. Juaquin lived with five drooly, extremely large dogs and three very annoyed cats. He had been away at a ten-day-long new age workshop in Ojai, another red flag I tucked away.

"You're late," Juaquin said when I walked in the door. The juju he'd just appropriated had already worn off.

"I can't control traffic," I answered. His eyes went dangerously flat. I clenched internally but kissed him, trying to keep the moment calm. "Look what I made you!" I pulled out the collaged book I had made, capturing all the good parts of the last six months. His eyes softened.

"I ran a bath for you," he said. "Look. I sprinkled petals in the water. They're from the rosebush I got at my grandmother's house last year.

When I went to Argentina with my mom. You know." I didn't really, but Juaquin had warmed up the tub and I sank in, determined to relax.

Later that night, while we played with his dogs in the backyard, Juaquin said, "You're going to leave me."

"Why?" I asked.

"You obviously want to leave me," he said with a flat voice. "Don't leave me," he said, and grabbed my wrist. I broke free easily, exactly as I had learned, exactly as I had taught. His eyes widened in surprise. Then he laughed.

"Okay, tough guy," he said, grabbing both of my wrists. I flicked free.

"Nope." Juaquin laughed and pulled me down to the ground, sitting on top of me. "I'm not letting you leave me." I bent my right knee and used my foot to twist my hips. Juaquin flew off me.

"Goddamnit! You and that self-defense," he said, no longer laughing.

Body memories of childhood and half memories of fights with D'Cazzoni accusing me of wanting to leave him instead of admitting he had slept with someone else fluttered through my psyche.

"Please stop. I just want to hold you," Juaquin said. "I love you."

"I love you too," I said, remembering that lying is an act of self-defense.

For the next few hours, Juaquin yelled and cried, dared me to leave, and then blocked exits. Eventually, he wore himself out. I felt the energy shift. I suggested we go to bed.

"You won't leave, right?" he asked.

"Right," I lied.

I crawled into bed, pretending to sleep while churning over the best route out of the house without making his dogs bark. When I heard Juaquin snoring, I got up and collected my things, making sure I could feel my truck keys in my bag.

"What are you doing?" Juaquin asked.

"The bathroom," I answered, dropping my bag.

"Why are you bending over your bag?" Juaquin asked.

"I tripped on it."

Juaquin got up and pushed me into the bathroom. "Okay. Pee."

I can always pee.

An hour later, I slipped out of bed again. This time I made it out the front door and to my truck before Juaquin appeared in the doorway.

I turned over the engine. He ran in front of the car.

"Don't go," he said.

"I have to," I said.

He looked at me, no love in either of our eyes. He stepped out of my way.

I drove home. I petted Sadie while I watched the clock tick. I had two hours before I had to go to work at the part-time museum job I'd finally gotten.

After work, I called the Gay and Lesbian Center's violence prevention program.

"I'm bi and my partner is trans. He held me hostage in his house. I had to escape. I'm looking for a support group."

"You know this is the Gay and Lesbian Center, right?" the queeny, male-sounding voice on the other end of the line responded.

"I'm queer. My partner is trans," I said, trying a different identity.

"Did you get our number from the resource list for court-ordered programs?" the person asked.

I repeated that I was queer.

"I don't think we can help you," the person replied.

I looked up City of Los Angeles domestic violence programs. I made an appointment with one that had the word "feminism" in its description. I got an appointment for a few days later. In the waiting area, filling out intake paperwork, I felt like the world's biggest loser. A young dyke took me back to her office and asked me about my past relationships. I answered honestly. She looked at me softly and said, "I'm sorry you've been through so much. Nobody deserves that."

I'd never heard those words before.

Ghaisi looked terrible. He'd lost a ton of weight but had a hugely distended belly.

On the recommendation of a neighborhood healer, he was taking colloidal silver. He bought me a bottle because she told him it'd also help my IBD. When he said he was pissing blood, I insisted he see a doctor. It was liver cancer, a result of contracting Hep C in Pelican Bay that of course was never treated. Ghaisi said he wouldn't go back to "Killer King," the notorious King/Drew hospital where he'd gotten his diagnosis.

"Shit, Jessica. I could go there with a splinter and end up dead. I need one of them Jewish doctors at Cedars." Cedars-Sinai was an expensive private system where Hollywood stars went. A few days later, he called, asking me to go with him to an appointment at Cedars.

"How'd you get that?" I asked.

"I went to the emergency room. They can't turn you away for not having insurance," Ghaisi said. "My shit is so bad they gave me another appointment."

He needed chemo. They said it might extend his life by years. I drove him to his weekly treatments. Then he got a bill. "C'mon, Jessica. I'll show you. We go get this written off by their indigent fund." He got that first bill written off. Then he got a second and third bill, and a letter demanding payment.

"Jessica, that sister in Patient Care isn't listening to me on the phone. We need to go meet with her. You give her some of that white logic." I told Ghaisi I didn't want to be used in his gender battle with a Black woman. He said that I'd see what he meant.

The Patient Care director wore a crisp beige suit and had extra-long manicured purple nails. The two of them seethed through the dense class dynamics. He was a formerly incarcerated Black man dying from years of untreated symptoms in a racist health care system, a former addict who'd survived as a chronic scammer for most of his life. She obviously had her own story, and it didn't have space to show empathy toward Ghaisi. She shot palpable disdain his way as he shot back overly forceful demands to wipe out all of the tens of thousands of dollars he was being charged. He played every card he had, while she looked on, bored. He got indignant. She kicked us out. He told me to be whiter next time.

The chemo wasn't working. I was with Ghaisi when the doctor said he had less than six months to live. In frustration, Ghaisi left the doctor's office and headed for the Patient Care department. He was determined to win something that day. We traded off arguing the pointlessness of billing a dying man, the inevitability of these bills going to collections. The Patient Care director tapped her now aqua nails on her desk, not saying anything. After a few hours, or maybe it was only a few minutes, she opened a file drawer and sent us away with paperwork to have the rest of his bills charged off.

At the four-month mark of his six-month sentence, Ghaisi was still going strong. He'd stopped chemo altogether and was taking a special concoction the neighborhood healer had made for him. We kept going to activist and art events and editing the *Pelican Bay News*. Then his mom got sick and was rushed to King/Drew. He was visiting her every day, calling me to see if there was anything to do in the evening. "There's a panel at LACE on the theater arts program at Chino Correctional," I told him one night. He said he'd pick me up in an hour. Two hours later, I was annoyed that he hadn't shown up and that I hadn't heard from him. I had my period and was hormonally impatient over his inconsideration. Another hour later, he pulled up in front of my house and honked his horn. The shock of his horn rattled me further. I broke down crying outside the open passenger window of his car. "Get in the car now, Jessica," Ghaisi said, using a tone I hadn't heard from him before. We drove in silence to the convalescence center where his mom had been moved. On the way back to my house, he said my public tears could have got him shot. I apologized. I was genuinely sorry. He remained cold. It was the first time our trust in each other didn't cut through all our differences.

He stopped calling. I gave him space, worried about time.

I called him on his birthday.

His brother answered his phone. "Ghaisi's dead. The memorial was last Saturday."

I still want a do-over.

The temp agency finally had a real job for me: I was working part-time in the admissions office of a small private college specializing in psychology graduate degrees. I also had a part-time job in the education department of the Museum of Television & Radio, a job I'd gotten through a friend. Neither gave me health care.

Processing admissions applications felt dangerously close to being a secretary, even though that job had a genuinely easy-to-work-for supervisor. I really liked what I was doing at the museum. I got to create and facilitate classes using the museum's media collection. So instead of staying in an easy situation, including a better commute, I asked my high-strung supervisor at the museum for more hours. She gave me exactly a half hour too few to qualify for health care. I quit the admissions job. Lisa found an IBD research study I qualified for at Cedars.

At the museum, I added the George Holliday video to the civil rights lesson, bringing the discussion about using media to influence social change more up-to-date. The classes were designed to meet K–12 curriculum standards, but I found I most enjoyed teaching the community college classes that came in for field trips. We'd meet in the airy museum lobby, and I'd guide them through the heavy wooden doors into the windowless auditorium. The students were mostly of color and had been very young in 1992. They got excited seeing footage of the events they'd heard about. They shared what their family members had told them, making connections between their own history and the history of resistance to racial oppression.

These interactions reminded me of my goal to make my story *Formerly homeless woman becomes college professor*. I knew more about what that meant now. I'd recently been at a talk at an anarchist bookstore in Echo Park where a history professor said being a tenured professor meant an obligation to speak out about the Bush administration's war crimes in Afghanistan and Iraq. This professor said having tenure was as secure as being a Supreme Court judge. That sounded good to me. I applied to PhD programs.

❦❦❦❦

Yeah, I didn't get into any of those programs.

❦❦❦❦

My video thesis was the problem, or at least a problem. PhD programs weren't impressed with my ability to translate written words into visual images. My skills in making theory aesthetic and accessible wasn't the proof of my intellectual aptitude these traditional academic programs were looking for. I was distraught over the rejections. I called Mich. She said, "You spent your whole life kicking over institutions. Why do you expect the doors to be thrown open when you knock?"

Oh, right.

I tried again, this time applying to two MFA studio art programs in the LA area. I triple-checked the health care policies, scholarships, and teaching assistantships. I also made sure both programs had queer, racially diverse, feminist faculty.

I ran into a professor I hoped to study with at a group show opening where I had a piece. It was at the One Institute, a queer archive. Professors were a part of the queer and trans community in LA, as if it was normal to have graduate degrees.

"I applied to your department," I told her.

"Your work is really great. I hope you find a good fit," she said, putting a consoling hand on my shoulder. I checked the University of California, San Diego, off my list.

When I didn't get either a thick acceptance packet or a skinny envelope with a rejection letter from the University of California, Irvine, I decided I was so far down that pile of applicants I should just give up. Then I got a call.

"Did you get in anywhere?" the professor on the other end asked. She was one of the people I noted in my application who I wanted to study with.

"I don't think so," I answered cautiously, not sure if it was the correct answer.

"Okay. We have you on the waitlist. You're not dead in the water yet." She hung up.

A week later, the acceptance package arrived. I called to say yes, I would attend the program.

CHAPTER FOURTEEN

I Like Dildos, I Like Art

Irvine's MFA program was mostly crit classes, a form of torture where one displays their artwork for classmates and professors to pick apart. You get so beat up emotionally that it feels physical. For the record, it can be done differently. My cohort of nine people, with an average age of around forty, were committed to mutually assured destruction from the get-go. The main instigator was a forty-something boomer dude with a long gray ponytail (yes, he was white). We got deeply embattled over a replica of an orange on the invitation to our first group show. Ponytail dude presented an image of a hand reaching out to grab an orange that looked too much like a hand grabbing a breast. He insisted it was about feeling squeezed in by the Orange County suburban culture of Irvine. The former Japanese television news anchor disagreed with his inter-pretation, pointing out that images of oranges were a pervasive part of Orange County branding, from her kid's soccer team uniforms to shop-ping malls. She said the image could be read as commercial advertising.

Ponytail dude said, "You're wrong."

His animosity broke the last straw I was clinging to in an effort not to engage, having swallowed my voice in surprise at his blatant misogyny. I pointed out the heterosexist read of the design. Ponytail dude snorted dismissively and gave a knowing nod to the forty-something gay white guy, a teenage actor on those 1980s after-school specials. Gay white guy chimed in: "It can certainly be read that way, but I see it as a lesbian image. Don't you, Jessica?"

"Yes, Jessica," ponytail dude said. "I thought you would like it. Your art is so lesbian."

Well, fuck me, I thought. My blurry, intentionally pixelated blown-up video stills of masculine-identified genderqueer friends wearing pissers, packers, and hard silicone dicks had been completely misunderstood. I sat back, swallowing my voice again, along with my bruised queer ego. I was in a het danger zone aided by misogynist gay men where my queer femmeness was getting cannibalized by nasty, fleshy dicks-for-brains.

"You're worse than the Taliban, censoring artistic freedom through your fear of sexuality," ponytail dude said. The fifty-something African prince, like from Black royalty, with a British accent chimed in: "Girls. It's just an orange." Then shrugging his shoulders, he raised both his hands and made a squeezing gesture.

I looked at my feminist musician classmate. She had her arms crossed protectively over her chest. So did my studio-assistant-to-a-famous-feminist-artist classmate. She mouthed, *What the ... ?* to me. I was going to open my arms and shrug in response, but they were also protectively covering my chest. The meeting came to an end without any resolution. Ponytail dude said he'd send a follow-up email for the next meeting time.

He did. And signed off with *CU Next Tuesday.*

❧✿❧

Tuesday night, in our required crit class, ponytail dude was screening his current video. "It explores privacy and surveillance," he said.

He turned out the lights and clicked on the projector. Fading out of black onto the screen was a slow camera pan across a row of young girls' asses peeking out from under their matching cheerleader skirts. Cut to a montage of teenage girls in red-and-white uniforms from behind, adjusting their bra straps and underwear. Cut to a shot from the bottom of an empty staircase. The frame filled with even younger girls in the same red-and-white uniforms gathering at the top of the stairs. The camera was still focused upward as the girls walked down the stairs in formation. Flashes of their matching white underwear came into focus with each step.

The video went on like this forever. Or maybe three minutes. The class silently watched; the professor didn't interrupt. The video ended with ponytail dude photobombing the frame, flipping his long gray hair to reveal his grinning face behind cheerleaders bent over and stretching. My heart was pounding when the lights came on. My voice stuck in my throat once again, swallowed in speechless surprise.

The twenty-two-year-old suburban kid freshly out of a fancy undergrad art school (yes, he was also white) spoke first: "This is a twenty-first-century commentary on the panopticon. It brings up the impossibility of individuality, of complicity, of being unable to escape from the mediated gaze that fetishizes young girls." I wanted to smack him and his naive, masculinist use of theory.

"Yes," gay white guy said. "We fetishize youth. The camera forces us to desire things we don't want."

Go to fucking therapy, I thought, slouching further down in my seat.

"Well, I think this is just brilliant," added the Black African prince. "You are the observer and then the observed. One must consider what it means to be a bomb. Can we read this as a commentary on blowing up social conventions? But in jest, of course. You must tell us your intent."

I closed my eyes and clicked the heels of my combat boots together. I opened my eyes. Nope. I wasn't at home. Ponytail dude was talking.

"As you know, I live on campus," he said. "I was walking around with the camera this weekend when I came across this cheerleading meet. Just as I got the tripod set up to tape it, one of the coaches said I couldn't. I couldn't believe it. This is a public university. It's public space. More than that, they are in my backyard."

"Well, that's interesting about public space," the African prince said.

"Exactly!" ponytail dude continued. "Not only that, but there was also a gender discrepancy happening. I used to coach boys' baseball and parents always had video cameras. Would they have told me to put my camera away if those were boys? No. When I was a high school teacher, I had to keep my classroom door open when I met with a female student. Not if I was meeting with a male one. That's sexism. I wasn't going to stand for it, so I held my camera down against my leg and caught it all from that one angle."

"You can't be serious," I said. Accidently out loud.

"Jessica?" our professor said. It was the first time he'd said anything since class had started.

I was ungrounded but aware enough to know I had to be really careful or whatever I said would be thrown back at me.

"Dude," I said. "How are you any different from the men on Hollywood Boulevard taking video of women for porn sites, nonconsensually?"

"Yes. Jessica, that's exactly it," ponytail dude said. My face must have said what I was thinking, because he also said, "The 'it' I'm engaging, the question I am answering, is about the fetishization of women's bodies and sexual desire. I thought you, of everyone, would understand."

I couldn't help myself. I started listing titles of books on feminist film theory. I listed feminist artists who had done work since the 1970s on the male gaze or on queer desire. I listed off pop culture films where teenage girls kill their abusers. I spewed anything that came into my head until ponytail dude said, "I don't need Feminism 101 from you, Jessica."

"Okay, you two. C'mon," gay guy said.

"You're right," ponytail dude said to gay guy. "I see what you mean. I have another version with a soundtrack, but I thought that one was what might be too much. I don't know, should I show it?"

The professor said yes.

The lights went back down. The pan across the cheerleaders' asses appeared with the opening chords of "Thank Heaven for Little Girls."

I got up and left class, remembering that leaving is an act of self-defense.

❁❁❁

"I need to go West Hollywood, tonight," I said to Mich, calling her on the cell phone I'd finally given in and bought once I started driving out to Irvine. I felt safer having it when I slept overnight in my campus studio. I usually went to the more racially diverse, less trans-discriminatory bars on the East Side, but I needed some old-school, "no boys allowed" dyke culture after a couple months of institutional art. Mich was up for it.

It took me two hours to drive the forty-five miles from campus to Mich's apartment on Mariposa Avenue in Koreatown. Then it took us thirty minutes to drive the seven miles to the Normandie Room, one of the two dyke bars on Santa Monica Boulevard. We walked in and were beckoned over to a table by the person making a documentary on Mia and the Gits. She introduced us to her friend Mag, the only other masculine-presenting person in the bar besides Mich. Mag was leaning up against the wall between our table and the jukebox, wearing a lime-green zip-up hoodie and a tie and sipping a clear cocktail through a straw. I ordered a drink and went to flirt with Mag. We talked about art, though Mag never mentioned being the artist who made the bright cheerful art on the walls. We talked about bars we liked to drink in and, under the pretense of getting together again as a group, exchanged numbers. Mag wrote down Mag's name as "Von." All signs were pointing to the complicated gender I loved. I called Mag/Von a coy few days later. Mag/Von didn't call back. Well, okay, fuck Mag/Von.

Back in Irvine, I had a one-on-one crit with one of my older dyke, feminist advisors about my pieces on genderqueer identities. She said the video stills of my popsicle-blue dick drying underneath my favorite blue bras hanging on the towel bar inside the gold-and-pink-tiled shower stall that hadn't been updated since the 1980s worked better than the video stills of my trans-masc friends, which looked to her like they were stuck in 1970s lesbian-feminist porn. She said I needed to make more images of more people in order to convey the shift in gender I was portraying.

"I've taken video of everyone I've slept with," I said.

"You must know other people with dildos. Ask them," she advised.

Some crits were on point.

I emailed Mag/Von, instead of calling. *I like dildos. I like art*, Mag/Von replied, signing off the email with "Von." We met up at a bar near my house where trans women and their admirers hung out. Von pulled a handful of poetry magnets from her pocket that he had stolen from the rich lesbian film producer's party Von had come from. I was charmed by this rebellious, class-warrior artist. We made word poems and talked about art and gender. Von had been in a scooter accident right after we met. Von still had a bruise from a faceplant on the cement. That's why Von hadn't called me back. From then on, we went to see queer art, performances, and bands together when I wasn't in Irvine. We went to Jennifer and Leon's holiday party and ended the evening with some other friends going on a midnight shopping spree at a twenty-four-hour women-owned sex shop. We kissed for the first time in the back seat of one of my other dildo models' Jeep. That date became our anniversary.

❦❦❦❦❦

"Jess. Are you sitting down?" Danielle said over the phone. "They found him." I knew exactly who she meant. Nine years, six months, and three days since Dan had called to tell me Mia had been murdered, she was calling to tell me a suspect had been arrested. I did a search and found multiple articles online showing a familiar picture of Mia next to a stranger's mug shot. Their faces locked together side-by-side in a media narrative seared into my memory, filling in blank space in my nightmares. I wish I didn't know that's the last face Mia saw.

I traveled up to Seattle for the trial. I sat in the observers' section of the courtroom alongside friends from Antioch and the Comet, alongside Mia's family. A huge stony-eyed man with an emotionless stare sat at the defense table embodying the collective pain, anger, and imaginings of the very worst that had hung over everything I had done for the last decade.

The medical examiner who had performed the autopsy on Mia's body had the foresight to create a sample from the smallest trace of DNA years before it was common practice. Cold-case investigators regularly submitted the sample to the national DNA database established by the FBI a year after Mia's murder and expanded in the wake of 9/11 by the US war criminals who drafted the Patriot Act. My friend's brutal murder, along with my grief, were bound up with white supremacist technological warfare that terrified me. These technologies are why Mia's killer was found. It's almost too much to take in.

For a decade, I thought this asshole held the key to the unaccounted-for eighty minutes between when Mia left her friend's house and when her body was found. If this mystery was solved, I reasoned, violence against women would be solved. I wanted answers and resolve where there wasn't any. What there was was a sign outside a courtroom with *Zapata v. [Fuckface's surname]*. The white plastic letters letting me know I was in the right place had once spelled out my and Bryce's last names in front of a different courtroom, when we had the protection order hearing that turned out to be punishment for both of us, resolve for neither. It turned out that Mia's killer had come to the US on the Mariel boatlift, as one of the formerly incarcerated Cubans taken from jails and psychiatric hospitals—including queers imprisoned for being queer—and sent against their will to the US, a Cold War fuck-you on all sides. Time and history folded together over and over into more and more violence. Impossible grief over impossible loss stacked heavier with more impossible layers.

In Seattle, I went to where Mia's body had been found, a place I had visited many times since her death. The street had changed from a dead-end road at the edge of an empty lot to a connector road for a block with newly built homes. Kids' toys were strewn across front yards, suggesting a safety that has never been real. Gentrification had paved over more than one community's grief. I lay down in the spot and set the camera on my chest, the rhythm of my breathing like a metronome. My breath quickened and slowed with the sounds of tires on pavement as cars swerved around me. When I couldn't take it anymore, I got up and pointed my camera toward my feet, walking from the Central District to Capitol Hill, capturing footage of past and present while tracing a path from death to life.

I had to be back in Los Angeles before the jury convened. I was home alone when a friend in the courtroom texted: *The Jury's coming back with a verdict.* I jumped up from my desk and ran back and forth across the living room, through the dining room, and down the hallway to the three bedrooms. I didn't stop running around my house until my phone pinged again.

Guilty!

I felt immediate relief. It was unexpected. An unjust system can't produce justice. Yet the iceberg of fear made up of the unknown started to melt. I didn't need to sort thoughts of Mia's rape and murder with thoughts of prison abolition, the Cold War, imperialism, and the racist injustice system. I needed to grieve. I lit candles on my altar and simply ached for my friend.

⁂

I had a crit with Catherine, another of my older dyke, feminist advisors. I was showing her the piece I'd edited from the Seattle footage. I reserved a classroom, set up the DVD player and monitor, and tested the playback. Everything was working. I went to my teaching assistant assignment in the classroom across the hall. When I returned an hour later, a cord had been taken from the setup. I had three minutes to fix the situation. I ran to the A/V cage, but it was closed. I ran to my studio, grabbed a pile of cords, and arrived back at the classroom as Catherine floated through the doorway in her full regality, carrying an intimidating air of success. She looked at the mess of cords and dark monitors and, without saying a word, walked across the room and folded herself into a yoga headstand against the wall. I felt very small and sweaty.

Ponytail dude opened the door. "I saw you trying to get into the cage, do you need help?"

"Yes," I said. I hated him more than ever.

He helped me sort through my cords and find that none were what I needed. We walked over to a locker where he stashed A/V equipment and found the right one. He told me he'd had a crit with Catherine earlier. On his cheerleader video. He was disappointed that all she had to say was, *Okay, keep going.* I was disappointed to hear that too. We went back to the crit classroom and got the DVD player and monitor attached again. I thanked him. He grinned like an idiot. I let him have the win.

Catherine watched my video from her upside-down pose. When it ended, she said, "The lipstick smeared across the face is too cliché." She unwound her long body out of the headstand and said, "I can't possibly give you any more feedback based on what I saw." Then she floated out of the room.

❦❦❦

Feedback on my art that I still carry student debt over:

"Isn't that the most basic thing you can do with charcoal on a piece of paper?"

"No. I don't know what you're doing, but no. Do something else."

"All I see is a reference to *The Vagina Monologues*."

"Oh, are you still making autobiographical art?"

"Why are these pieces so small?"

"The piece seems done. There's nothing to say."

❦❦❦

I was the only one in my cohort earning an MFA for the explicit goal of teaching. My classmates planned to be the next LA art stars. "Those who can't do, teach" was said without irony more than once, including by teachers.

"That guy is an idiot," more than one person said about our professor who wrote a book on the significance of community colleges in higher education.

"You know how the art world is. They like to 'discover' people," a successful Arab feminist artist, and alum from my program, said while we chatted at an opening.

Los Angeles had overtaken New York as the capital of the global art market. The average price of a piece of contemporary art went from $7,500 to $30,000 during the 2000s. It was a billion-dollar market that higher education wanted a piece of. MFA programs proliferated, profiting off the artists who had moved to LA to find fame.

I got really good at name-dropping and feeling entitled to being at dinner parties with lots of forks in the place settings. I got drunk on smooth wines that cost as much as my household's monthly electric bill. When my dildo project was censored by a Catholic institution at an exhibit on queer identity in San Diego, I contacted the National Coalition Against Censorship. My name and art are in the same archive as Robert Mapplethorpe, David Wojnarowicz, and Karen Finley. I got to know

Cheryl Dunye and Tim Miller and other artists I used to read about, who were censored by Jesse Helms during his homophobic rampage against the National Endowment for the Arts. A queer art historian well known for books on queer art censorship included my work in his lectures. I felt historical. Important. I almost forgot I wasn't going to graduate school to become a famous LA artist.

CHAPTER FIFTEEN

The Year of Magical Teaching

During my last year of the three years at Irvine, I was hired as an adjunct professor at California State University, Fullerton. I got the job through a femme friend who recommended me to her department chair. I had a brief in-person interview while sitting outside the campus cafeteria at a concrete lunch table, and the department chair hired me on the spot, saying, "Oh hell, let's just do this. I need to get somebody in here and I'm sure you'll be great." I had two sections of an American studies class called Introduction to American Popular Culture, which I changed on my syllabus to Introduction to US Popular Culture, not knowing it was a standardized name for a general education requirement. A gen-ed class meant there were students from communications, nursing, kinesiology, religious studies, and a whole bunch of other majors outside of humanities.

Hurricane Katrina struck New Orleans a few weeks into the semester. I was able to use the Kanye moment, when he said on national TV that George Bush hated Black people. I had students collect dog blankets and gift cards for survivors who had been bused to LA, an exercise to learn the material relevancy of popular culture. I brought in my zine collection to inspire students to make their own, and then we held a zine fair. It was an interdisciplinary course, and I had fun facilitating students through theory and praxis. My student evaluations were overwhelmingly positive. My chair's evaluation, less so. He informed me that teaching wasn't a popularity contest and I shouldn't use so much visual media, that I should add in more text-based reading assignments. Oh yeah, and change "US" back to "American" on my syllabus. Still, I was hired to teach two more sections the following semester.

I had done it. I was *Formerly homeless woman becomes college professor*.

I sent an email thanking my mentor at Claremont. She replied that there was a one-year position available in Pitzer media studies, covering someone going on sabbatical next year, and asked if I wanted to apply. I did. During the phone interview, my mentor asked what classes I wanted to teach. It was the first and last time I was asked that question. I got the job, one of only a few people who had one lined up before graduation.

According to the National Center for Education Statistics, I was one of 13,500 people in 2006 who graduated with a master's degree in visual or performing arts (its government name). I started my career as a professor making $49,500, the most I'd ever earned up to that time, and the most I'd ever make as a professor. I had health insurance as part of the job, and the insurance also covered domestic partners. I'd even accidentally negotiated a travel reimbursement for my commute. The dean finalizing my hire offered moving expenses, and I said that I didn't need to move but joked I could use gas expenses. Pitzer, one of the Claremont Colleges, also reimbursed me for travel costs and fees for conferences once I started the job. I was able to build my CV by presenting on panels and network for tenure-track positions. I was even reimbursed for travel to job interviews when they were at one of those conferences. This was all impossible without institutional support, but now I could participate when professional colleagues invited me to show my artwork and publish my writing. At forty years old, I finally could imagine a future that seemed possible. Life felt good.

❦❦❦❦❦

During the year of magical teaching, I didn't mind working in a borrowed office. I stepped over the boxes filled with books left on the floor in front of the wall-to-wall bookcases by the professor on sabbatical, imagining the day I'd be filling bookcases in my own office. I was content enough with the two cleared-off shelves where I set some of my favorite queer studies, cultural studies, gender studies, and critical race studies books. I also set copies of the videos and textbooks I'd chosen for my courses on the shelves, along with some of the academic journals I was published in. I propped up DVD cases of my own videos, highlighting the cover art I'd designed. I added a toy model of DNA and a mini ceramic chicken in honor of Mia, plus a picture of me and Von in Belize, a trip paid for with part of a stipend I'd received for my thesis show.

Figuring out my professor couture was fun. I traded in carrying a bike bag for pulling a lime green rolling briefcase I found used online. I hired my two femme friends with a business supporting queer and trans folks in finding their professional style to help me find my "aging punk femme" look. It included upscale vintage dresses accessorized with animal-print silk scarfs and either knee-high red zip-up boots or purple lug-soled cowboy boots. On Fridays, Von and I met friends at Kung Pao Kitty on Hollywood Boulevard for soju-and-dumpling happy hour. On Saturdays, we bought mountains of cocaine with Von's old bandmates and hung out in West Hollywood. On Sundays, we nursed our headaches at Hamburger Mary's brunches, drinking two-for-one stevia-sweetened "Gym Queen Mojitos." Life felt good.

❧❦❧❦❧

My salary wasn't allowing me to make a dent in in my $85,000 worth of student loans. By the end of the fall semester, tripping over somebody else's crap in an office that wasn't mine became annoying. As the spring semester wound down and I could count the days until the year of magical teaching would come to an end, along with my salary and benefits, those books were full-on anxiety-provoking. PTSD and survival economics could stretch a year into forever. Now that I had degrees meant to manifest a career and tens of thousands of dollars of debt, time moved faster.

I scored an Intro to Video summer class at Pitzer that would get me through to the next school year and the three media studies classes I was hired to teach at Scripps, another one of the Claremont Colleges. It was another yearlong position, as an adjunct visiting professor instead of a visiting assistant professor. I didn't understand the different academic titles, though I did understand that as an adjunct professor instead of an assistant professor, even though I was teaching some of the same courses, my pay was nearly half: $28,000 for the school year instead of $49,500. Also as an adjunct, I wouldn't know whether my job was a go until enrollment numbers were confirmed. At the Claremont Colleges, that was a week before the semester started.

While I was teaching the summer class, Von and I moved to an apartment in West Hollywood. The rent was surprisingly less expensive than what we were paying in East Hollywood at the Winona House. Our new building was full of older gay men, elderly Russian women, and young born-again-Christian soap opera actors. The gay men watched out for us. One neighbor hired me as a home health care aide for his aging mother through the state funds he received. Another farmed out a photo-editing gig for a talent agency to me, where I clipped images of actors off of gossip sites. And an Antioch friend working at a gay porn production studio in the Bay Area hired me as a remote video editor. My porn name was Aileen D'oeuvre, in honor of Aileen Wuornos.

I thought I was handling things. I thought the part-time teaching supplemented by multiple gigs while applying for tenure-track jobs was working. The eating out, drinking fruity cocktails, and doing lots of cocaine felt just fine. Except I started having trouble catching my breath while walking up the single flight of stairs to my apartment. My knees hurt. I couldn't feel my guts. My mind and body were silently angry and inflamed. I went shopping for new jeans and found out I was four sizes bigger than when I'd started the year of magical teaching. Life didn't feel so good.

My Scripps classes were confirmed. I carpooled out to Claremont with two tenure-track colleagues, doing my best not to trip over the emotional wedge I felt between us as my career was spiraling downward alongside their upward paths. One day, hefting myself into the cab of my pristinely composed, Hong Kong–born, queeny colleague's shiny new truck, I made a comment about being bigger. "I noticed," he said, side-eyeing my lack of grace. The baggy clothing I was buying at Ross and Target to replace the vintage professor outfits weren't hiding my extra roundness as well as I'd hoped. The red boots that didn't fully zip up over my calves anymore lay on my closet floor next to the deep-olive-green, just-below-the-knees, form-fitting skirt. So did the tailored black skirt suit with the pink satin lining I got at a consignment shop and would wear with a striped vintage polyester button-down shirt when I had conference presentations. It didn't matter. My adjunct position didn't include travel funds.

In high school, I'd read my mom's copy of Susie Orbach's *Fat Is a Feminist Issue*. I supported femme visibility movements that celebrated fat bodies. But the scars from being ostracized as a fat kid and being picked last in gym class, my father's controlling interest in the size of my body, and being a woman in a misogynist culture all easily trampled any feminist consciousness. I had an interview for a tenure-track job at a small college in New Jersey, but instead of being excited I went into a panic about what to wear. My femme stylist friends rescued me. They found a bright-green polyester vintage dress with large, round white buttons and an oversized white collar. They told me I was sexy at every size. So did Von. I tried to believe them while I tied a purple silk scarf around my neck and stepped into the matching purple creepers I'd found at a thrift store on Melrose.

My excitement over the interview was also tamped down by the fact that being flown out for a job actually meant having to have the middle-class resources to buy a plane ticket and pay for a hotel room and car rental, which the college would later reimburse me for. I filled out one of the many unsolicited, predatory credit card offers promising zero percent on purchases for fourteen months. I bought a special blue plastic envelope to hold all the required paper receipts I had to attach to the reimbursement processing form.

My first meeting in New Jersey was with the dean of faculty. When I told him that my partner was from Vineland, a nearby town, the dean gave me his analysis of class disparity in the area and told me about the programs supporting first-generation college students. Von's family fit the description, though I was just trying to assure him that moving from California wouldn't be a problem. Then he told me about his research on Romani Holocaust survivors, which was fascinating. He confirmed the historical routes my Transylvanian family might have taken. It all seemed like a good sign.

My next meeting was with the department chair, who didn't show up. Neither did two of the four hiring committee members. The two faculty members who did show up didn't know how to get into the locked smart classroom that had the necessary technology for the teaching demonstration I'd been asked to prepare. I was supposed to have presented to a classroom full of faculty and students, but no one was on campus. That all seemed like an ominous sign. I gave a truncated version of my lecture to the two committee members while we crowded around my computer inside a small, empty room usually reserved for student club meetings. Afterward, they bought me lunch in the school cafeteria. It was obvious they had already decided who to hire. My interview was an expensive, time-consuming charade.

Driving back to my hotel in the rental car, I saw a bar advertising two-dollar well drinks. I stopped to drink several rum and Diet Cokes, wondering if any of Von's family was in the bar. When I got to the hotel, I wanted more. The only thing open was an Italian restaurant that delivered. Italian food hurts my guts more than any other type of food, with all the gluten, dairy, tomatoes, green peppers, onions, and garlic. So I ordered a calzone, a meatball sandwich, mozzarella sticks, and eggplant parmesan, enough to destroy any feelings other than pain. Not wanting the delivery person to judge my binge, I pretended someone else was in the room when the food arrived. Then I closed and double-locked the door and crawled onto the bed to spread everything out in front of me. I charged a movie to my new credit card and ate my way through *Juno*, waiting for the abortion scene that disappointingly never happened. When I was so full that I could no longer chew, when I felt the tomato sauce moving behind my sternum and tasted the burning sensation of onions, garlic, and green peppers as I swallowed, when my head was so foggy I couldn't think, when it hurt too much to take a deep breath, I stopped eating and broke down, sobbing. Life felt like shit.

❀❀❀❀❀

The tenure-track hiring cycle was over for the school year. I joined a diet program that feigned health care legitimacy by setting up in a corporate drugstore adjacent to the pharmacy. I paid for it with the credit card the diet program offered to people without insurance. Workers in lab coats drew my blood, weighed me, and gave me vitamin B shots that would supposedly boost my metabolism.

Twice a week, I woke up, peed and pooed, didn't eat anything, and walked the mile to the drugstore for my weigh-in. I'd pee again in the public bathroom next to the pharmacy. Later, when Jennifer relapsed again, she said it was where she would shoot up after filling her Vicodin prescriptions. One time, while I was sitting on the hard plastic chair that served as a waiting area, Mindy Kaling from *The Office* walked up and signed in. She sat down next to me. It seemed an awkward place to fawn over her work, but I did let her go ahead of me to show my appreciation. She said, "Oh, aren't you sweet" in a singsong voice.

I was uncomfortable working out at my neighborhood YMCA, because in Hollywood it was still a Hollywood gym. Von bought me some workout DVDs, trying to be supportive while also hoping I'd stop whining. There turned out to be a Jillian Michaels box set in the mix. She wasn't yet known for being a racist idiot; not much was known about her at all. I put on one of the DVDs and my queerdar pinged. I wasn't the only one curious about her. A quick search came up with tons of lesbian gossip sites tracking her, reporting sightings of her at the Abbey and other West Hollywood queer bars, debating whether the woman with her was her girlfriend. I worked out to the DVD insistently, pushing the rewind button at my favorite sections. There was the place in the kickboxing workout where Jillian's hand lingers just a bit long on the shoulder of a woman with short bleached-blonde hair. They exchange sly smiles as Jillian slowly slides her hand away. The woman gives Jillian a sassy comeback, and Jillian chases after her while they both giggle. In a different workout, Jillian wears sweats that say *GIRLS TENNIS*, flagging which team she plays for. Jillian only calls out the names of women in the background, never men, and in one telling moment, a man excited about meeting his reps goal throws his arms around Jillian and lifts her off the ground. She pulls away from him, practically punching him. She doesn't look at him again for the rest of the workout. After a few months of obsessing over these queer codes, my arms were more toned and I could easily carry groceries up the flight of stairs to my apartment.

❦❦❦

While getting in my steps, I noticed for-rent signs in the windows of almost every apartment building in my neighborhood. Houses with for-sale signs had couches, books, clothing, and kids' toys strewn across lawns as if the former owners had rushed out in the middle of the night. It was 2008. The government had bailed out the corporate investment banks that had preyed on people's manufactured dream of owning a home, and it was all playing out like a nightmare. This application round, arts and media studies positions were even scarcer. I mailed out my thick application packets. They cost forty to sixty dollars each. That didn't include the costs of copying and printing my seven-page CV, two-page cover letter, one-page teaching philosophy, nine-page sample syllabi, five-page published writing sample, and the DVD reel of my creative work. I charged the costs for my hoped-for academic employment to the same credit card I'd used to pay for my calamitous interview in New Jersey. In return, I received slim envelopes with terse rejection letters. In 2008, the letters included explanations about budget cuts and departments being defunded, signed off with an ominous *Good luck.*

More credit card offers came in the mail, with credit limits anywhere from $8,000 to $25,000. I applied for every single one, storing them in a drawer for emergencies. Inevitably, rent or groceries became a monthly emergency. So did my maintenance medications. And the new alternator for the car. And the worm medicine for Sadie. And the emergency surgery for Puppy, Von's cat.

Sometimes I added Von's name to the applications, a wry nod to our coupledom being recognized by the banks but not the state—not that we cared about state-sanctioned marriage. We wanted to learn how to love each other outside of capitalism. The problem was that we could have debt in each other's name but only be on each other's health care at the whim of a benevolent employer. Sharing a credit card felt like we were scamming something, a het capitalist rite of passage for queer anticapitalists. We split all our living expenses but kept separate bank accounts. So the credit cards wedded together our bus passes and gas, our bar tabs and tattoos, our student loan payments that were on different deferment timelines. To (mostly) avoid overdrafts and late fees, I transferred balances about to go into a high interest rate to a new zero percent offer, keeping payments at a minimum.

I noticed a surprisingly high minimum payment on one card and rooted through a pile of statements shoved in my desk drawer. There was a $20,000 balance on a card I didn't use. I dug deeper and found charges to my personal checking account that I knew nothing about. I showed Von, worried there had been identity theft. He said no, those were his charges. A chair he and his siblings bought for his dad as a Christmas gift. Von had charged it to the card and then didn't ask the others to pay him back. Drinks with Crosby, his ex, at the Frolic Room. Dental work he didn't like to talk about. It turned out the credit card with his name on it was just a second card attached to my account. We were wedded together in my bank account. All my fears married all my worst behaviors. It wasn't pretty. I assumed Von was purposefully fucking with me.

The feeling of a giant thumb pressing down and preventing me from getting ahead of the exponential debt that grew no matter how hard I hustled overshadowed all my ruminating. More education hadn't changed my circumstances, it had only created more pathways into more impoverishment. Von racking up more debt in my name felt intolerable, another thing I had no control over, another thing dragging me into the depths of disarray. Von didn't understand why this was a line that couldn't be uncrossed. I didn't understand why he didn't feel what I did. We fought and fought and fought until I kicked him out.

Several friends intervened. They helped him understand his responsibility to our shared life and helped me understand he hadn't acted with intentional malice. I finally agreed to meet and talk. It was the first time we had discussed the impacts of our different class backgrounds on our relationship. We kept meeting and talking, digging into the emotional differences we had toward money.

We both have mixed-class realities, though I started out with middle-class security while he started out in generational poverty. His family banded tightly together through deaths, unemployment, and homelessness while my property-owning people fractured further with each trauma. Von and I both worked all through high school, but I got to spend my paychecks on things I wanted while his paychecks helped support his family's basic needs. He learned to spend what he had when he had it because there may never be more, and also because there was a church community that would provide in an emergency. I learned I was supposed to save for the future, and that success meant financial stability through individual achievement. For Von, a job was just a job, and he felt free to quit on the spot and find another if he was fed up. For me, a job became my primary identity, something that reflected on me rather than the employer.

Despite these differences, both of our families valued reading, art, and education. Those threads, along with our shared scrappy survival skills, created something different together from how we were each raised. Neither one of us had been taught how to budget or financially plan. We both were used to closing our eyes and crossing our fingers between paychecks. "We're Americans," Von said, dryly, unpatriotically, during one of our meetups.

He admitted he had fucked up, that he shouldn't have paid for drunken escapades with Crosby or cover the recliner he couldn't afford. I accepted he hadn't done anything on purpose and that I had responsibility in the clusterfuck of our finances. He didn't want to lose me. I was pretty sure I didn't want to lose him. (I mean, I didn't suddenly trust in love or anything.)

I remembered some of the charges on the card were for our trips to Morro Bay and Las Vegas, much-needed breaks only made possible by the credit card. Von's dental work was an expensive emergency due to having rotten teeth from childhood poverty. He had been in constant pain and didn't have dental insurance to cover the treatment that would give him relief. Then there was Puppy's emergency surgery, where Sadie heroically donated blood, their adorable little paws joined together with intravenous tubes. That cost a lot. There was no way to avoid debt in the midst of a global financial meltdown that was forcing us into debt.

When he moved back in, we both worked seven days a week. On a rare evening at home together, we watched the documentary *Maxed Out: Hard Times, Easy Credit and the Era of Predatory Lenders*, by a filmmaker named James Scurlock. The film explained predatory lending through interviews with people who had lost everything, including loved ones, due to this disastrous practice. It highlighted experts criticizing the rise of credit scores as a measure of individual value and convincingly argued root causes of the ever-expanding wealth gap. It was made before the Great Recession, the Fight for $15 labor movement campaign to raise the minimum wage, and the Occupy Wall Street movement. As credit scores and the wealth gap were not yet basic concepts, they were challenging to understand. I was taken with a Harvard University law professor named Elizabeth Warren. She was unknown at the time and hadn't yet gotten bastardized by electoral politics. Warren effectively simplified the economic consequences of the middle class disappearing through a billionaire coup. It was materially different than my anarchist fantasies of disappearing the middle class.

Maxed Out helped me realize that not being able to pay off credit card debt was by design. Filing for bankruptcy was a logical next step, not a personal failing.

We made an appointment with the bankruptcy lawyer in the same building where Von worked as the office manager for a queer film festival. He'd noticed her office on his way to the gendered bathrooms the building management refused to change. He found out that bankruptcy cost $1,000 and that we could pay in installments. I gathered all the necessary documents proving my debt-to-income ratio met the conditions for a Chapter 7 charge-off, then met the lawyer at the US bankruptcy court in downtown LA. I cut across a plaza of shuttered high-end stores and entered the courtroom waiting area, which was packed to capacity. In February 2009, the wait to go before the judge was more than an hour, though it took less than five minutes for a formal ruling to get rid of my $35,000 credit card balance. I celebrated by buying a pair of black tights for 90 percent off at a store that was going out of business across from the courthouse building.

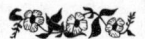

Because of the recession, over the next few months, Von's dispatch job at the limo company was cut and his queer film festival job was under threat of being cut. My photo-clipping and gay-porn-editing gigs disappeared. I was offered only one adjunct class at Scripps for the following school year, which paid $7,000 and would be another drastic cut to my teaching income.

Not having to pay down credit cards, we put all of Von's paychecks from his second job into savings and dreamed up plans to escape LA. We decided to move to New Mexico for a year after I finished teaching my Pitzer summer class. I had visited a Home Alive friend in Santa Fe when Von and I almost broke up. I fell for the quiet beauty of the big open spaces and rough craggy landscapes lit up by lightning storms and shooting stars. I met a bunch of queer folks in Santa Fe, including younger Antioch graduates, and I met a tattoo artist perfect for my next tattoo. The small town seemed like a good place to make decisions about our future, compared to the dying embers of LA.

On the chalkboard-painted closet doors in our living room, we wrote:

SAVINGS: March = $2000
April = $2000
May = $2000
June = $2000
July = $2000
August 16 = Grades Due
August 20, 2009 = $10,000. LEAVE LA.

In May, I gave notice to Scripps that I wasn't going to teach the one class they had offered for fall. The next day, I was flooded with calls and emails from recent MFA graduates asking me to recommend them for the class. I don't know how they knew I was giving it up, but the intense competition for shit-paying adjunct positions made it depressingly clear there was no job market for a teaching career. My MFA degree felt more and more like I had fallen for a Ponzi scheme. I was ready to move someplace new and figure out what else I could do for income. But first, I had to finish two more weeks of the 2009 spring semester, turn in my grades, and teach my last summer class. My summer class was my contribution to our moving costs.

The problem was that I hadn't received the email with my teaching contract. That email always included deadlines for ordering books, the classroom assignment, the student roster, and other important administrative details. I called the Pitzer registrar's office. They told me the course wasn't on the books, that they didn't have me scheduled to teach. Crap. No one had called to let me know there wasn't enough enrollment for the class to be a go. I bent over to pick up a shirt I had flung on the closet floor, and my back went out. I couldn't unbend or walk. I lay in bed for a week. I was depressed and in pain, plus my face was swollen from an allergic reaction to the muscle relaxers I'd been prescribed. I was absorbed in grief and self-pity over the unceremonious end to my teaching career. I was a shit partner for Von, who was actively grieving over his father's death six months earlier. We fought a lot.

❦

When I could sit up again, I filled out an unemployment application. I would get at least a couple thousand dollars, which would help with the move.

Then I got a call from the Pitzer summer program coordinator.

"Where are you?" he asked.

"What do you mean?"

"We had five students waiting for you in the classroom today," he said.

"The registrar said the class was canceled."

"Well, it's not. Can you teach it?" the coordinator stated more than asked. "It's seventy-five hundred dollars you must need."

Indeed. I updated the syllabus and, two days later, traded in sweatpants for one of my femme professor outfits that almost fit again. While I was on campus, I stopped by to see the coordinator and we figured out that communications about the summer class had been sent to my pitzer.edu email account, which had been closed when my position as a visiting professor had ended. Since then, I'd had a scripps.edu email address. Pitzer and Scripps were both part of the Claremont Colleges, and the classes I taught were part of the same intercollege media studies degree, but the HR departments were different. Additionally, the summer program used yet another HR department. There were a whole lot of HR administrators, yet no one to track where or when I taught, despite being a professor in the consortium for three years. It was insulting. But at least I was getting my summer class and pay. My academic career could end on a high note, teaching my favorite course, one I had designed: Censorship in the US.

CHAPTER SIXTEEN

Professor Staff

Our small moving van was overstuffed. We blew a tire less than an hour into the fifteen-hour drive to New Mexico. We found the closest rental van lot, catching them just before they were closing. They called in a larger replacement truck for us and, assuring us it would arrive, went home for the day. We waited for two hours in an open concrete lot under hot blazing sun. We lost several plants, including the jade tree Lydia Lunch had given me and the monstera from our neighbor's mother. We fought over whose fault it would be if the cats died. Then the larger truck arrived and we once again, but without the help of friends, packed all of our boxed-up belongings into a moving truck. We got back onto the eastbound Interstate 10 freeway with Puppy relentlessly and irrhythmically scratching at her carrier while Sadie cried and foamed at the mouth.

On the final evening of our three-day journey, we rounded Interstate 40 at Albuquerque and headed up Interstate 25, the last leg of the drive. Eight miles from our exit onto Saint Francis Drive, a lightning bolt flashed huge and bright over the Sangre de Cristo Mountains. It looked like it had been drawn with a silver metallic Sharpie through a sky as cobalt blue as Sadie Viva's eyes. Von and I grabbed hands and squealed at the undeniable Santa Fe magic.

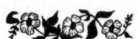

We unpacked our boxes into our friend's refurbished garage, which we'd be staying in for the month. We set up a corner for the clothing we'd need and another corner for the litter box. The cats explored anxiously while I explored employment options at the grocery stores where I bought expensive anti-inflammatory foods. Cash registers and credit card transactions had become computerized since I'd last worked retail. I made up experience but never pushed send. It turned out I had more invested in my graduate degrees than I'd realized and wasn't ready to let go of my dad's American Dream.

My Home Alive friend brought me over to the community college to meet some people she knew. On a tour through campus with a person who worked in enrollment, we ran into the chair of the media arts department. I was introduced as an artist and media studies professor. The department chair asked me what I taught. I told her all the relevant classes, except for Photoshop. I never wanted to teach Photoshop again. Catherine, my yoga headstand mentor, had said Photoshop would be my bread and butter. I thought I could avoid that fate, somehow still thinking I had control over academic hiring processes.

"Do you teach Photoshop?" the community college department chair asked.

"Sure," I answered, doing my best to keep a team-player look on my face.

She asked if I could do a quick teaching demonstration. I began by explaining how to log in to the computer with a school ID. I explained how to navigate to the desktop icon as well as the start menu to open the program. Before I actually opened the program, she offered me two intro sections that started the following week. My ability to patiently explain how to log in to a computer, not my art or design skills, got me hired.

Photoshop was one of the most popular classes at Santa Fe Community College. Media arts and photography majors were required to take it. Most art majors took it. High school students seeking college-level credit took the class along with retirees sorting through family photos and local artists building portfolios. A day before the semester started, I was offered a third intro section. There were so many sections added each semester that the course catalog simply listed "Professor Staff" as the instructor.

Being hired as an adjunct professor was unlike any other hiring process I'd ever gone through. When the department chair offers work, which is the first step, it isn't a guarantee of work. Even with a written promise of hire, called a teaching contract, nothing is formalized with HR until the window for registration closes and an ever-changing magic number of enough students have paid tuition. This is the contingent part of being contingent faculty. The job can be taken away at any moment, until several different administrative departments meet deadlines based on tuition and enrollment instead of curriculum and pedagogy.

The investment into an academic degree and obtaining the education necessary to then educate others in the same system is devalued by the system itself. Whatever one thinks about academia, it's important to see the irony where an institution with a mandate to move people into the workforce is also the institution that has created one of the larger contingent workforces. When I was teaching, it was at about one million; in 2023, it was one and a half million. And of course the same thing has happened in most once-secure sectors. The problem with higher education is not only a basic question of elitism and privilege, the problem is also that higher education has become a quintessentially neoliberal arena where a very few are profiting off the debt of a vast majority while also shifting the ideological landscape to the far right (a statement even truer as this book goes to publication than when I first wrote that sentence several years ago).

I went to the community college HR office after I'd agreed to teach the first two Photoshop classes to find out how much I was going to be paid. In the meantime, I'd been in a period of wage theft. With no signed contract or knowledge of the conditions of employment, I still had to prepare a syllabus. This meant becoming familiar with the textbook chosen by the department; reading, researching, and designing exercises and lectures; and also coming up with various ways of testing students' knowledge gained for them to pass the class and also to help generate necessary institutional data. The system gaslights faculty into accepting that income is secondary to the "privilege" of being a professor.

The HR department staff had left for the day. The next day, I called to make an appointment. They told me they wouldn't have contracts ready until the first day of classes, so they didn't know my specific income. I assumed I'd be paid somewhere between the $3,900 per class at Cal State Fullerton and the $7,500 at Pitzer. The somewhere between was a big, life-impacting range.

My first teaching day was a Friday, and HR was closed by the time I wrapped up my back-to-back classes. On Monday of the following week, I went to HR in between my classes, but they were closed for lunch. On Wednesday, I arrived two hours before my classes started and was able to finally get ahold of my contracts and find out my pay.

The salary listed was $1,950 for each semester-long class.

"Nineteen-fifty?" I asked, thinking there was a typo.

"Yes," the HR person said.

"For sixteen weeks of work?" I asked.

"Yes," the HR person said.

"I've been teaching for four years," I said.

"Here?"

"No."

"We only count the years you've taught here."

I hadn't imagined an even more insulting possibility than all the cuts to my salary I had already taken. It was hard to hold my body up as I signed the three teaching contracts.

When we moved to New Mexico, I didn't know the state vied with Mississippi as the worst place in the country for K–12 education. When I accepted the teaching job instead of looking for a retail service job, I didn't know higher education was an afterthought in the state budget, that unemployment was extremely high regardless of great, or not-so-great, recessions, while adult literacy was extremely low. As a part-time worker, I could apply for unemployment. The New Mexican EDD case manager told me to apply in California instead, where I was technically still a resident, that the weekly benefits would be higher. I followed their advice, and while I was a professor at a community college in New Mexico, my salary was subsidized by the state of California. Higher education was a house of cards ready to topple, but I somehow still felt personally responsible for my failed academic career. I wanted to leave—but also, maybe, just maybe, things would get better.

⁂

Teaching three Photoshop classes sucked. I had tech-savvy high school students frustrated with how slowly we had to move for the tech-illiterate seventy-year-olds. I had artists working on sculptures who wanted to do one very specific thing with the program that I didn't know how to do. I had middle-aged men explaining my own lesson plans to me and twenty-something men absolutely sure I was incapable of teaching them anything they didn't know. When I used twenty minutes of a three-hour lab class on a media-studies-type lesson about copyright law, showing a video about a controversy over the well-known Barack Obama "Hope" poster between Shepard Fairey, the artist, and the AP photographer who'd taken the original photo, not one student wanted to engage in discussion.

A call for applications to teach a class called "Volunteer in the Community" in another department showed up in my school email. I applied. And was hired. I happily dropped one of my Photoshop sections for the new class. Volunteer in the Community had been taught by the director of the Service Learning department, which had lost state funding and was being shut down. The director had negotiated a teaching position, the administrative staff person had been hired into a different department, and the student worker had had to find another job. The Volunteer in the Community class, which was more case management than teaching, was the only remaining element of the once fully staffed program. Students took one, two, or three credits, which determined how many volunteer hours in a nonprofit organization they had to do. I helped place them, oriented them to processes for reporting hours, assigned two short papers, and facilitated one wrap-up class session. They could sign up for the class anytime between the start of the semester and the week after midterms. Students took this class if they were short on credits to continue receiving the state lottery scholarship funds every New Mexican high school graduate was granted. They took the class to meet minimum required credits to take out student loans. Because of the state's high unemployment rates, both pools of money were commonplace post–high school income options. A new influx of volunteer sign-ups would happen after midterm grades, when students found out they were failing a class. Community college administrators relied on this class for enrollment head counts, part of the state funding formula.

"They were only going to pay an adjunct one credit for that course," Susan, the admin staff who worked in the adjunct faculty office, told me. Sitting at her desk behind a *THE GODDESS is in* nameplate, Susan said, "I told him it wasn't right to pay someone only one credit to do all the work needed for that class. I told him that paying somebody only six hundred dollars was criminal. Everyone in the department meeting just stared at me. I wasn't supposed to open my big mouth. I was just supposed to be taking notes like a good girl." Susan was significantly older than the dean, a second-wave feminist and class warrior who took me under her wing like a surrogate parent. She gave me one of the few locking cabinets in the adjunct office so I didn't inadvertently violate student privacy laws by taking the files home, as the dean who hired me had suggested I do. Susan made sure one of the five computer stations that served three hundred contingent faculty members was open for me to use to create the necessary tracking documents for volunteer sites and student volunteer hours. And she kept me informed of gossip and administrative bullshit while I worked in the office.

Because of Susan, I was paid $1,950 for three credits, instead of $600 for just one. However, the Volunteer in the Community class was actually six credits, and I should have been paid $2,700 (the math doesn't add up because higher ed logic doesn't add up, but that's the breakdown of how credits were paid). Six was the total number of credits printed in the course catalog, because it's the total when a one-credit class, a two-credit class, and a three-credit class are added up. But there was no oversight committee, no market-based reasoning, and no union to keep the college from balancing its budget on my back. Contingent faculty working conditions were only just starting to become a regular topic in higher education. The ratio of tenured or tenure-track to contingent faculty had completely flipped from 70:30 in the 1980s (the Reagan-Bush era) to 30:70 in the 2010s (the Obama era), a neoliberal goal achieved in the fallout from the Great Recession. My academic generation started degrees with some of the older assumptions about job security and then had academic jobs turn into a gamble before we emotionally caught up.

"Academia has never offered guarantees," a tenured faculty member would almost always post in the comments under articles on adjunct faculty working conditions, chastising precarious workers for not knowing any better. Tenured faculty who, by their own admission, hadn't been on a job search in decades would tell us, in anonymous comments on blogs, that we weren't hired because we weren't qualified. In an economy with a 10 percent unemployment rate, those of us with graduate degrees fared statistically better than those who didn't or couldn't continue education beyond high school, and still, when people with health care and job security said, "If you're so unhappy, why don't you just leave?" I felt ashamed and responsible for everything happening to me. It reminded me of when I was sixteen years old and sobbing in the driveway of Luke's house after another brutal fight. His mother, a social worker, pulled her car in coming home from work and, as an aside on her way into the house, said to me, "Why don't you just leave him?" I absorbed the message coming at me from all directions all through time: It was my fault.

The next semester, there was a new person preparing the adjunct contracts in the HR office. In addition to my two Photoshop contracts, I was handed three others that accurately reflected the six credits for the Volunteer in the Community class. I signed them quickly and walked over to the adjunct office to ask Susan what she thought I should do. "Take the money and run," she said.

Later in the semester, while meeting with the dean about the humanities classes I was going to take over from another adjunct who had found a full-time, nonacademic job, he said, "I saw your contracts were processed for all six credits." I held my breath. "We'll just let it go," he said. I sighed with relief and didn't ask any questions.

⁂

Von didn't want to be *she'd* anymore. In LA, living close to his family, Von accepted being referred to as "she," even though he preferred "he." Or just "Von." His actual preference was no pronouns. When we moved to New Mexico, he decided to use only masculine pronouns. He was less sure about what he wanted to do for work.

We met an older femme named Starling at a party who liked surrounding herself with younger butches and trans guys. Starling was opening a restaurant. She hired Von as a dishwasher, and he quickly worked his way up to lead cook.

Starling and her baby-butch partner, Mack, were drug-addled drama dykes and terrible bosses. They accused the one Black employee of stealing from them. They paid everyone under the table, firing people randomly with no recourse or ability to collect unemployment. They gave free meals to employees' friends and partners, then periodically freaked out about money and demanded employees pay for meals in full. At the height of Santa Fe tourist season, when they could have made enough to offset the slow winters, Starling and Mack took an eight-week European vacation. They had Von and two other employees run the restaurant for a temporary one-dollar-an-hour raise—from eleven dollars an hour to twelve dollars an hour. The night before they left, Mack got so high she took a chainsaw to the six-foot-tall wrought-iron fence surrounding the patio area, cutting it down to a three-foot disaster with dangerously jagged edges. That left Von and his coworkers to deal with the early stages of a lawsuit while Starling and Mack were swimming off the Isle of Lesbos.

This embittered Von to restaurant work, but not culinary work. He enrolled in the culinary arts program at the community college. His queer professors helped him get a job in campus food services, where he became a full-time staff member. He was still only making eleven dollars an hour, but he had all the things the college didn't give adjunct faculty: health care, sick days, paid holidays, retirement, and invitations to staff parties.

Von also had a locker for his coat. He had a place to store his books for the free classes he took, another one of the benefits of his job. Not so great was that he had to punch a time clock and wear a uniform. He walked down the hall anonymously in his chef whites with an Ozomotli T-shirt hidden underneath. When I walked down the hall, I was greeted by students who called me "Professor." I wore a more casual femme punk look, usually a black T-shirt with a gray button-down sweater over a brightly colored miniskirt and black tights. Still in knee-high boots. I was responsible for starting and ending my class on time. If I was a few minutes late, as long as students didn't complain, no boss chastised me. And yet, I had to carry around my coat, books, folders, handouts, lunch, water bottle, and gym bag while rushing from the parking lot to the adjunct office, to my classroom, to my next classroom, to my car, to my next job. I always felt like a visitor on campus.

I would go on unemployment over the December breaks when the college closed, while Von continued receiving paychecks. In the summer, starting in May, I'd go on unemployment again, until classes started at the end of August. The cafeteria closed for July, so Von would go on unemployment then. His weekly EDD check was fifty dollars more than mine. According to government calculations, I made less than eleven dollars an hour.

❧✦✤✦❧

"Professors on food stamps" was becoming a thing. There was a 2012 *Chronicle of Higher Education* online article titled "The Ph.D. Now Comes with Food Stamps." A single white mom struggling as an adjunct professor was featured and said, "I am not a welfare queen. The media gives us this image that people who are on public assistance are dropouts, on drugs or alcohol, and are irresponsible. I'm not irresponsible, I'm highly educated."

Raising the specter of the racist, misogynist "welfare queen" stereotype, an issue introduced by Ronald Reagan during his 1976 presidential campaign, was telling. Too many adjunct stories played on white middle-class anxieties that many highly educated people hadn't learned were racist. Too many adjunct professors were shocked that the system was failing them for the first time, when they had done "everything right." I understood the shock of failure, but the system had been failing a lot of us for a long time.

Stacey Patton, the journalist who wrote "The Ph.D. Now Comes with Food Stamps," covered higher education and race issues, a rare combination that's still too rare. Patton, who is Black and was an adjunct at the time but is now a tenured professor, also interviewed a Black adjunct professor named Kisha, who said, "I had to work against my color, my flesh, and my name alone. I went to school to get all these degrees to prove to the rest of the world that I'm not lazy and I'm not on welfare. But there I was and I asked myself, 'What's the point? I'm here anyway.'" Kisha's sentiment was closer to my food stamp story, which was exactly what the white single mom was trying to distance herself from.

On typical rainy November day in Seattle in 1992, my food stamp booklet fell out of my coat pocket into a muddy puddle as I reached into my friend's VW van to grab a bag of rice and block of tofu from the bounty he had collected at food banks that day. When I got back to the Bunker, I separated the paper food stamps from one another and left them to dry at the base of a radiator. Once they were dry, I collected the crinkled but crispy one-dollar and five-dollar stamps, folded them in half, and stuck them between the cardboard covers of the empty booklet on my bedroom floor. Then I read the letter I'd received in the mail from my father, an out-of-the-blue not-guilty plea about how he'd never sexually abused me. This sent me spinning.

I didn't think my father had sexually abused me, so why was he writing this letter now? It was confusing. I wanted heroin but was recovering from the catastrophic relapse.

I was going to have to quell my craving with junk food, but it was late and dark out and raining too hard to ride my bike to the store. I heard Bryce's car pull into the driveway. I pulled on my hoodie and ran out to ask for a ride.

"For what?" he asked.

"Potato chips," I said.

"Everything okay?"

He knew potato chips were my substitute for heroin. We drove to the neighborhood grocery store where Bryce's friend from high school worked. I went in to get my party-size bag of barbecue chips while Bryce waited in the car. At the register, I handed over a food stamp from my no-longer-damp collection.

"Let me see your cover," the store manager said.

"You take my food stamps all the time," I said.

"Let me see your cover!" he demanded.

The panic that led me to the chips intensified. I handed over my booklet.

"Your numbers don't match."

"What the fuck are you talking about?" I said. I was genuinely confused. I had enough money to buy what I wanted.

"How do I know you didn't buy these on the street?" he asked.

There was a line of people behind me. I was embarrassed. I felt like I had been caught using, which made me dig in harder.

He pointed out that the serial number on the stamps didn't match the serial number on the booklet. I pointed out that he knew me and I shopped there with food stamps regularly.

"Pay cash or move on."

I didn't move. I felt like I was under a heat lamp. I couldn't put words together.

"Pay cash or move on," he said again.

I wanted to be lying in my bed, eating until the only pain I felt was in my guts from too many chips. I wanted to hit somebody, or myself. I spit at the dude blocking me from my relief, set the chips down, then turned to walk out of the store.

I walked into a wall of security guards that may only have been one person. I was in a thick, dark hole. Someone grabbed my arm and pulled. I stomped on the foot in front of me, pushing the body away from me. More large men in uniforms surrounded me, grabbed at me. I punched and kicked and fought for my life. My black leggings with holes along the seams of the thighs were slipping down my hips. I tried to pull them up and someone shoved me to the ground. I was yelling and twisting. Faces too close leaned over me, held me down. Handcuffed me.

I was pulled up to my feet and dragged over to a plastic chair near the front door.

"Fuuuuuuuuck you!" I yelled over and over and over.

I was pulled off the chair by the handcuffs, my arms twisted behind my back. In the beer aisle, out of sight of the customers in line, I was knocked to the ground and dragged across the floor by a man I didn't know. I kicked at anything I could. He dragged me between the swinging doors of the employee-only area, pulled me up from the ground, pointed to a chair, and told me to shut up and wait.

Wait for what, for what, for what echoed in my head. I don't know if I asked out loud. I looked around. I saw pictures of women in bikinis on the walls. One was naked, straddling a billy club. I wasn't confused about why I was there anymore. I sat down and waited. I refused to let them scare me.

Bryce's friend from high school walked through the swinging doors, bent in close to my face, and tsked at me while wagging his finger. Some amount of unknown time passed. Then some cops walked through the swinging doors. I was being arrested for shoplifting.

For what? Nothing was real.

The cops perp-walked me through the store and outside to the police car, where they bent my head and put me into the back seat. Bryce was there, hands cuffed. He wouldn't look at me.

"Why are you here?" I asked.

"Fucking hell, Jessica. I looked up and saw you fighting off a bunch of dudes. I ran in and jumped on one of them."

I felt flattered that Bryce tried to protect me.

While we waited for the cops to finish collecting stories from witnesses, Bryce said he had weed in his wallet a friend had given him to give to me. He said it'd be my fault if he went to jail. I apologized. I said all I wanted was to buy potato chips.

"Maybe you should go back to heroin," Bryce said.

We both laughed.

We were held at the Capitol Hill precinct, the only ones there late on a Sunday night. The cop on duty let us wait in the same holding tank. She said we'd probably be let go on our own recognizance. A while later, we weren't let go; we were put in another cop car and brought to the King County Adult Detention Center on James Street. It was crowded. We were separated into our respective binary gender holding tanks.

I sat on the floor and watched the clock on the wall slowly tick forward. At 2 a.m., I still hadn't been called to go to whatever was the next step. It helped knowing Bryce was just down the hall. At 3 a.m., two University of Washington students were placed in the tank. They were giggling, which made other women ask them their story. They were tripping on LSD. One student's boyfriend was the main LSD dealer on campus and had been set up by undercover cops. They were with him at the time of the arrest. They said they weren't worried about being in jail, he'd take care of it. They were more worried about their Korean parents finding out they hadn't been going to class. They got nicknamed "the fry babies."

At 6 a.m., me and the fry babies were brought to a window where a guard handed us orange pants and shirts with *King County Department of Corrections* emblazoned on the back.

"Why are we getting orange ones?" one of the fry babies asked.

"Because we can shoot you if you try to escape," the guard answered.

The girls giggled.

I didn't. I did say, "I was supposed to be released on personal recognizance."

"Shift change. No one here to process the paperwork," the guard said.

We went up to the cells in time to be served breakfast. I gave my bread away, since I didn't eat gluten. It turned out to be a good tactic to be left alone.

The cells were concrete rooms crowded with bunk beds. No bars. Large solid-metal doors with a small reinforced window. Like a public school classroom. After breakfast, all of the doors swung open and the hall was filled with hundreds of women rushing to line up for the showers. I saw the fry babies. They weren't giggling anymore. I saw a Black woman from my cell high-five another Black woman and yell, "Shit, cousin, I haven't seen you in months!" They hugged, jumping up and down and screaming until a guard separated them.

A guard noticed I was limping and asked if I wanted to go to the infirmary. The woman in line behind me told me to say yes, that it's better there. For twenty-four hours, I was in a much quieter place with a single-stall bathroom to use. There was even a tiny sliver of a window with a view of downtown. When I was sent back into general population with a crutch, a bandaged foot, and only one shoe, I felt vulnerable. I gave my bread and most of my other food away to keep my cellmates on my good side.

There was nothing to do but sleep. Except I couldn't. I had no idea when or how I was getting out. I realized I needed to make a call, but I wasn't sure who to. Bryce was also in jail. My friends lived in squats without phones. Obviously, I didn't have family members to call. Then I thought of a friend who lived in a collective household and had a roommate who worked for legal aid. I hobbled out to the hallway phones the next time the cell door automatically opened.

"Everything okay, DV girl?" the guard asked. Being nicknamed "DV girl" in jail before I understood my own domestic violence story is a profound experience I'm still processing. I accepted the title and asked how to make a call.

My friend knew I was in jail. "Why didn't you call sooner?" he asked.

"I didn't think of it. A lot was going on. How did you know I was in jail?"

"Bryce told us."

"Did he call you?"

"No, he's been out since yesterday morning. His mom bailed him out."

My stomach dropped. Bryce had left me in jail and was hiding out at his parents' house. When I called him there, he said he didn't bail me out because he was mad at me for putting him in a situation where he had to take a shit in a holding tank in front of other men. I hung up on him and went back to my cell.

My name was called over the loudspeaker the next day to go to my hearing before the judge. While I was waiting, a woman who took a liking to me braided my hair into cornrows, telling me it helped my chaotic frizzy hair look more put together. The public defender I met with for less than five minutes was concerned about the cornrows, but there wasn't time to take them out. She told me to plead guilty. I told her my friend in legal aid had advised me to plead not guilty. She said I could do what I wanted. I asked the woman who braided my hair which way to plead.

"Always plead not guilty, baby," she said. I did and was released with a court date for six months later. The legal aid roommate found interns to take my case. They thought my situation was clear discrimination, a poor woman who tried to use food stamps but instead got beaten by security guards. We made a deal with the prosecutor. If I pled guilty, I would get time served plus twenty hours of community service and the charge would be off my record in three years.

Waiting in the courtroom for my case to be heard, the judge tossed out the case before mine, a white punk boy with bright blue hair who had skateboarded on a public sidewalk. My lawyers said that was a good sign.

When it was my turn, I stood up and answered, "Guilty." The judge looked at me, looked at her paperwork, looked at me again, and said, "Spitting isn't okay." She gave me time served, but she also gave me a hundred hours of community service. Even the prosecutors were surprised. I don't know if I was surprised. I know I got the message, which was familiar. I was being punished for being female and doing femininity wrong. Two decades later, I didn't want to be a professor on food stamps, for different reasons than my colleagues.

CHAPTER SEVENTEEN

Adjunct Representative

Von had worked at Walmart in high school in a small agricultural town in Arizona that welcomed the employment and convenience the gnarly corporation offered. This is what I thought of every time I read an adjunct blog calling us the Walmart workers of higher education. The Walmart comparison was meant to highlight corporate interests creating working conditions in higher education similar to those in retail. And yet, economic similarities didn't always mean class similarities. Having graduate degrees is both materially and culturally different under capitalism.

Von attended fourteen different schools as a kid. His family moved a lot because his father, who loved technology and was always tinkering with a new gadget, had gotten a community college degree in a long-defunct computer system crushed early on by the monstrous tech giants. When I was teaching in Santa Fe, solar panels were the hot new certification program. Solar panel installation certificates were lauded as the new public-private partnership that held the key to economic development. Prison corrections officers, medical billing, CNAs, website design, video-game technology, MRI technologists, and on and on. Majors that train students to do a very specific thing. When that specific thing is no longer the thing, students are left to figure everything out without formal critical thinking skills helpful for economic change and cultural adaptation. It doesn't mean those students aren't critical thinkers, it means it's one more way those who are systemically excluded since before elementary school remain on an exclusionary track through college, collateral damage in the war on everything.

The Walmart messaging also made me think of Crosby. When they were together, she and Von started a band called Shitting Glitter that, long after Von left her and the band, Crosby still fronted. She was a seductive performer, a girl in drag-queen gear who sang about the pain of being female in a beautiful trained voice. When Von and I were first dating, Crosby would wear his old Walmart name tag onstage, which bugged me, annoyed that she was publicly making a claim to Von. One drunken night, I jealously pointed to the name tag and said, "That should be mine now." She looked down, hesitated, then handed it over to me. I clipped the name tag to the lampshade on my desk, tapping on it as I edited gay porn or graded papers.

❦

It was hard to listen to the Gits. I could do it when I needed to feel more deeply than my defenses allowed. I could let the music I knew so well pull me back in time to a past that didn't fit anymore. The album released after Mia's death had a cover of Sam Cooke's "A Change Is Gonna Come." I never heard the band play it live, never heard Mia sing it when she was alive. I listened to that song differently. It's gorgeously haunting, full of hope, and pain, and tragic histories. It evokes a longing for so much more. I still chat about that longing with Mia.

❦

If any change was going to happen, I had to talk to other adjuncts at the community college. Susan, in charge of scheduling the faculty development program the week before fall classes started, helped me make sure adjuncts had our own discussion session. She introduced me to the chair of the faculty senate, the campus governing body where faculty weigh in on institutional business (without institutional decision-making power). The senate chair appointed the senate adjunct representative to work with me. We had a representative? Things were becoming more bureaucratic than I was comfortable with. Fortunately, the adjunct representative was a stoner. He taught astronomy and had gotten involved with the senate when he realized he was never getting a raise the way things were. Twelve of the three hundred adjuncts showed up to the meeting, mostly because we were given a sixty-dollar stipend for attending the development day. No one said much, but everyone filled out the job-satisfaction-type survey we had prepared and put their non-campus email addresses down for the activist list we were starting.

We sent out a few emails with information on adjunct organizing around the country and proposed another gathering for next semester. Twenty people showed up this time. There was a lot of anger and passion about the personal and professional crises each person was facing. Some people insisted we had to storm the president's office the next day. Others thought we should appeal to the faculty senate to make demands on our behalf. A group of fiery, unapologetic older white feminists in their seventies talked about their decades-long battles for equality in academia. The entire group displayed a strong sense of solidarity combined with a total lack of patience for figuring out concrete demands and action steps. I couldn't decide if the meeting was a success or failure.

Over the next few weeks, the adjunct office shifted. Our community of disenfranchised employees were engaging with each other regularly. My older feminist friends invited me into their circle, reporting on the daily insults they experienced and swearing up a storm against administrators. Other faculty chatted about classes or the weather for a few minutes while making copies before running off to class. The adjunct rep and I met regularly in the break room behind the office to draft email blasts about campus policies that affected adjuncts. Susan clandestinely created an email list of all three hundred adjuncts for us, a surprisingly hard task since the college didn't keep accurate data on who was teaching each semester. We also drafted separate messages to the thirty people whose non-campus emails we now had, starting a discussion about potential actions.

The first action was attending the faculty senate meetings together as a group. That led to the faculty senate chair asking me to run for the second adjunct rep position, which hadn't been filled for a couple of years. It was also the first time I ran for an elected anything. I was secretly thrilled, which was more embarrassing than winning an uncontested position.

As an adjunct representative, I had to attend the monthly senate meetings, sit on a small committee meeting during the rest of the month, and collaborate with my co-rep to bring adjunct faculty viewpoints to senate business and votes. Both of us were paid $150 for the semester, an amount stipulated in the senate bylaws. Between the faculty development stipend and the faculty senate stipend, I made $210 for sixteen weeks of college committee work. Before taxes.

❦

Monty was the new faculty senate chair. His priority was getting raises for faculty. I was on board. My co-rep couldn't be at the meeting where

Monty went over his proposed new pay scale, projected onto a screen that was so old it needed to be pulled down with a rope. I sat alone in the back of the room taking notes. I didn't see adjuncts listed on Monty's chart, so I raised my hand and asked if the chart only included full-time faculty.

"Yes," Monty said.

He pointed to the next person with their hand up.

"Wait," I said. "Do you have another one proposing new adjunct salaries?"

"No. But you can create one," Monty said. "Please let the next person ask their question."

"Wait, I'm trying to understand. Doesn't the senate represent all faculty?" I was genuinely confused.

Monty seemed impatient with my question, but he replied that full-time faculty members were paid so far below the national average that it needed immediate attention. He was referring to the sixty-eight out of three hundred and sixty-eight faculty members who weren't adjuncts.

Okay, but we're all paid far below the national average. Shouldn't we work on raises for everyone?

I didn't make that simple, obvious statement because the feeling in the room was institutional. The focus was on supporting the already most enfranchised group through math that didn't add up. My thoughts formed into a clumsy reply, pointing out that adjunct faculty salaries were a topic in the recent issue of *The Chronicle of Higher Education*.

"That's not what we are discussing here," Monty said with a chastising tone, reminding me I was still speaking out of turn.

Then he threw me a bone: "Look. Once we get our raise, we'll help you." He physically turned away from me, ending the interaction.

I looked around the room for allies. The only other adjunct was the wife of the vice president of academic affairs. She was looking at her phone.

❧❀❦

Monty's gaslighting pissed off my co-rep so much that he quit. My new co-rep, Carmen, had been teaching Spanish at the college for ten years. When she first started, she was a new mom and didn't have time to deal with the job exploitation. Now she was fed up. She and I met in the adjunct office regularly, planning our next move in the faculty senate. We also talked about the colorism and racism Carmen, who was Mexican, experienced in our progressive little Spanish colonial town. We talked about the transphobia and homophobia Von and I dealt with regularly on campus. We shared each other's annoyance at being infantilized as women and adjuncts. She was a relief.

Carmen had a master's degree in business administration and understood the admin-speak in ways I didn't. She was able to let Monty's stupid comments roll off her back in ways I couldn't. I found it impossible not to challenge him. Carmen would remind me that putting Monty in his place wasn't our battle. I let go enough to focus on presenting our concerns to the senate. She did mathematical magic with the adjunct salary chart, finding the shockingly inaccurate errors in the equations.

Doing a job a VP should have done, Carmen spent weeks on abstract problems until she created uniform steps. I said we needed to include a salary increase before we presented it to the senate. Carmen said she was ahead of me, that she had included a 2 percent across-the-board raise that wouldn't be noticeable because it was clean math. I said it wouldn't be noticeable for any of us either. I argued for a 5 or 10 percent raise. Carmen explained the math and why, for now, we had to keep to 2 percent. "Trust me," Carmen said. I didn't have a choice. I didn't understand the math.

Monty acted as if he couldn't understand Carmen's English, so she asked me to lead the senate presentation. It didn't matter. He stopped us halfway through, telling us we were taking up too much time. We decided to go directly to the administration. Carmen set up a meeting with the vice presidents of finance and human resources. "Trust me," I said to Carmen. "I'm going to organize other adjuncts to join us." I got eighteen other adjuncts to show up to the meeting. The vice presidents kept saying how surprised they were by a group of adjuncts together. It surprised them more than the salary chart having been so poorly calculated by their departments. We walked away from the meeting with an agreement for the 2 percent raise. After taxes, this would be less than ten dollars on most people's monthly paychecks. I thought it was an insultingly low raise that barely seemed like a win, but there hadn't been raises for faculty of any rank in five years. Carmen and I had proven raises were possible despite what the administration said. We had gained the trust of our adjunct colleagues, who were ecstatic.

Monty, on the other hand, was cartoonishly pissed. He said we went rogue. He said we went over his head. He said we should have asked his permission to negotiate a new salary for adjunct faculty, which we found hilarious in general, and also because that's exactly what he had told me to do. Monty tried to get revenge by attempting to sow division between me and Carmen. He invited her to speak at board of trustees meetings without me. At faculty senate meetings, he would only call on me, saying we both didn't need to speak to adjunct issues. He went so far as putting his back to me at a public function when I said hello and then pulling Carmen into a conversation. He thought he was conquering a threat to his tiny little power. It didn't work.

Adjunct faculty were seeking us out. Someone who taught with ASL interpretation came to us when the new department chair hired a friend instead of the adjunct faculty's longtime trusted interpreter. Another person needed space to store their belongings during the several hours between their 8 a.m. and 2 p.m. classes because lugging everything around was creating back problems. Several people were mad about having to meet with students in the cafeteria instead of a private office. We couldn't always, or even often, resolve the issues, but we were able to listen and empathize. We built relationships. I got people's contact information for our email list and regularly sent out articles about national adjunct organizing campaigns. Carmen made a spreadsheet of the concerns to bring up at faculty senate meetings.

❧❦❧

"Not today," Monty said. "Today we need to decide whether or not we support a ban on single-use plastic bottles."

"Sorry, guys. Next meeting," Monty said at the next meeting. "It's imperative we decide which board of trustees candidate to recommend."

"Hey guys, stop interrupting," Monty said. "You can make a motion at the next meeting."

I hated Robert's Rules of Order. My introduction to this parliamentary standard for majority-rule decision-making was when I briefly served on the Central District neighborhood council in Seattle. I wasn't elected; I was just loud. A friend who owned a house had asked people to attend an organizing meeting to intervene on the implementation of Weed and Seed, a racist federal program targeting Black and Brown youth. White homeowners taking over the area thought it was a great idea for some blocks of the Central District to become federal, instead of city, jurisdictions. Weed and Seed would make possession of an insignificant amount of weed a federal crime. A Black or Brown kid dealing in the streets would go to prison for decades, while the white homeowners—and a lot of us punks, artists, queers, and anarchists of different races who rented in the neighborhood—could get high on our front porches without consequence.

At the organizing meeting, I'd spouted off about my white neighbors who were inadvertent soldiers in the drug wars, bringing racist policies into the neighborhood and then, when they had kids, moving out to the suburbs for the "good" (white) schools. An older gay leftist in a Che T-shirt clapped and said I should represent the group at the neighborhood council. Nobody objected, so I became a bridge between leftist activists and the yuppie precursors to NIMBYs.

I was already active in a Black-led, multiracial coalition, the one where I'd met June, who I ran into during the protests against the LAPD beating of Rodney King. The coalition was led by a neighborhood minister and met at the socialist bookstore on Union Street. They were open meetings meant to build community and relationships. Homemade baked goods lined the table where we signed in. The meetings were held in the evenings and started with singing the Black national anthem, "Lift Every Voice and Sing." Volunteers interpreted for Spanish speakers. There was childcare, and kids ran around while we broke into working groups. Handheld fans helped cool down the crowded room that didn't have air conditioning. People raised their hands to get on stack to speak, but it was a norm to interrupt other speakers with shouts of agreement or anger.

The neighborhood council meetings were different. They were almost entirely made up of white people. They met in a classroom of an empty middle school early on Saturday mornings. The ten people chosen to attend sat around a long conference table under fluorescent lights. A hard copy of *Robert's Rules of Order* sat in front of the elected officers; they referred to it regularly. Once in a while, someone was chastised for speaking out of turn and told to raise their hand and get on stack. When called on, they spoke in quiet, even tones about high property taxes and poor school quality and the large tax breaks they would get through Weed and Seed. They all agreed that the money provided for after-school programs would be great for other people's children.

The neighborhood council asked me to invite members from the community coalition to present at a Saturday meeting. Two young Black women, both of whom had gone to the middle school where the council met, volunteered. On the day of the meeting, I met them at 9:30 a.m. in front of the building, the time I'd been instructed to arrive with them. We walked up the two flights of stairs to the air-conditioned conference room, all of us giggling uncomfortably as I turned the handle on the closed door.

The council president nodded at me and pointed to a seat at the table, indicating I should sit where I had at the other meetings I'd attended. I motioned for our guests to join me. The council president shook his head and pointed to chairs on the side of the room. I was confused. They weren't. They rolled their eyes at each other and wouldn't look at me. I wish I'd had the guts to object, but instead I sank into the brain fog disrupting my thinking process.

When I looked at the agenda on the table, the coalition speakers were listed last, at 11 a.m. I picked up my notebook and moved to a chair beside the two women. They asked me something to the effect of *What the fuck?* All I could do was shrug. Around 10:15, I asked if we could move the agenda item up. Nope, the council president replied, the agenda had already been voted on.

"Fuck this," one of the women said loudly.

They both stood up and left the room. I paused for a beat, but then followed. The three of us ran down the stairs shouting phrases peppered with a lot of *fuck*s.

That night, drinking vodka and orange juice with my roommate, Jane, I told her about the meeting. "I have the perfect song for this moment," she said. She went to her record stack, and the twangy opening chords of Helen Reddy's "I Am Woman, Hear Me Roar" filled the living room. We leapt around, channeling the dulled-down boomer feminist anger into an ironic interpretive dance while singing along to the chorus. Then we drafted a manifesto called "Roberta's Suggestions for Disorder."

I wish I had Roberta to place right here for you to read. I tried. I sent Jane an email: *I have this fleeting thought you mentioned you had a copy of our Roberta manifesto. Is that a memory or a hope?*

Jane wrote back that Roberta might be in a box in her studio where she kept art we had made together in the '90s. Also, she wrote: *I'd been thinking about you. Thinking about how the friends you have when you are super young and not-yet-formed have such a profound effect on how you live your entire life and how you think about things, even if you don't stay in touch. You and I were at least partially formed when we met, but I've also been thinking about those years and that circle of people and what parts of it I've retained and what I've left behind.*

I replied: *Yes! Roberta represents an absolutely formative time in life. The bond with you was made through trusting each other's shared anger, creativity, and coping mechanisms. The Roberta night was on the bridge between second- and third-wave feminism, anticapitalism outside of any political doctrine, and the world we wanted. It was punk performance that didn't care about having an audience. It was a pre–social media moment that only lives on in both of our memories. We have a visceral understanding that younger generations who have never lived without the internet can't experience.*

To which she replied: *Full disclosure: Mine was not an entirely original thought. I read it somewhere, can't remember where. Probably a review of a book I'll never read, I don't know. I love that, generationally, we don't exist. There's a lot to be said for figuring things out and growing up being mostly ignored. Roberta is not in the box I thought she was. I recall these:*

Ignore all rules.

Ignore all suggestions.

Listen to country music really loud.

You're not crazy, you're just thinking.

Jane said the suggestions were in no particular order, but I have to say, two and three make perfect sense together.

Also, it was Jane's household I stayed with when I left the shelter.

The former-adjunct-rep astronomy professor was coming to faculty senate meetings again. He suggested we propose a motion stating: *Adjunct faculty business must be on each agenda.* It passed. At the next meeting, *Adjunct Faculty Business* was last on the agenda. Same with the following meeting. Then we stopped getting to the last few items on the agenda.

We proposed another motion: *Adjunct business must be in the first three items of the meeting agenda.* It passed.

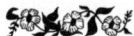

At the next meeting, Monty said adjunct business had to be a specific topic, it couldn't just be a general item.

"The topic is 'adjunct business,'" I said.

"That's not a topic," Monty replied.

"We'll share what we have when we get to our agenda item."

"I don't remember agreeing to that," Monty said.

Spring semester ended without reaching a resolution to Monty's made-up problem.

I went back on unemployment and antidepressants over summer break.

In the fall, there was a new college president. A Cuban woman in her sixties, she had a background in Hispanic-Serving Institutions at the federal level. I wanted to be hopeful.

"Adjunct business has to wait," Monty said to me as we walked into the lecture hall for a special faculty senate meeting with the new president. I ignored him and immediately got on stack to ask how she planned to address adjunct faculty concerns.

"This isn't the top of our agenda," the president answered.

"Adjunct faculty are struggling," I replied, ignoring Robert's rules on direct replies.

"Look," the president said, "no one is going to make a living as an adjunct. In the beginning of my career, when I was an adjunct, I had to rely on my husband." Then the president wryly laughed and said, "I suggest you marry well."

"Some of us can't legally get married," I said.

The room broke into applause. I was mortified.

I didn't (and don't) consider equality under existing laws a pathway to queer, or any other collective, liberation. I did (and do) consider marriage an antiwoman, antifeminist institution. The props I received served as a mirror reflecting back to myself how far I had compromised under constant economic struggle. The fight for fair pay and tenable working conditions was already so far inside the machinations of capitalism, so much about and retaining a manufactured concept of class, that I had much too easily, much too publicly, slipped into a caricature of revolt. Trying to get my ass into a seat at the table, I ended up sitting halfway down in the wrong seat.

Marriage was all over the New Mexican news. Due to no language about gender in the state marriage statute, several county clerks had issued marriage licenses to lesbian and gay couples. The licenses had been upheld in recent rulings. Marriage equality activists were celebrating. I appreciated the monkey wrench to the system from an unexpected place; it's a key principle I taught my students. Every semester I had them read the essay "Calling All Restroom Revolutionaries!" from Mattilda Bernstein Sycamore's anthology *That's Revolting: Queer Strategies for Resisting Assimilation*. The essay was about a group called People in Search of Safe and Accessible Restrooms (PISSAR), who had created a checklist I turned into a group assignment. I'd send mixed-gender groups of students to campus bathrooms to identify if a bathroom was accommodating to people who have periods, people who have penises, people with mobility disabilities, and/or people who needed to change a baby's diaper, among others. The objective was to understand that space isn't gendered, that bathrooms become gendered through enforced cultural norms. The first time I did this assignment at the community college, an administrator called campus security because she'd seen who she presumed to be a man (he was) go into the wrong bathroom (that was the point). The guards barged into my classroom while the students and I were debriefing the assignment. I was ordered to immediately follow the guards out of the room to answer questions. With only five minutes left until the end of class, I wanted to formally dismiss the students rather than let the chaos of being policed for challenging bathroom gender norms completely disrupt the assignment. Without thinking about consequences, I told security to wait. They guarded the door while the students exited and then herded me into an empty stairwell. Pretty quickly, the guards understood the assignment. Nothing came of the questioning, but I was extremely rattled. And I was rattled again now, in this faculty senate meeting. I hated that I was winning points from my colleagues for being a good gay.

Well, from most of them.

Monty leaned over from behind me and whispered, "She's an older generation. She didn't mean what you think."

"I know what she meant, Monty."

"Don't overreact, Jessica."

I hated my job so much.

"We have only one topic to discuss today," Monty said at the start of the next faculty senate meeting. "Everything else will have to wait, including adjunct business."

Carmen and I had prepared a presentation on how the proposed new budget was going to impact adjunct faculty. We found a discrepancy between the president's stated policy about extra course assignments—that we couldn't have them—and the historical practice of overloading assignments as a regularly relied-on part of adjunct faculty income. We'd brought the issue up before. Monty said to bring "proof." Our presentation was a strong combination of Carmen's data-making skills and my narrative-making skills, but it was never seen. Monty took us off the pre-planned agenda, changing the meeting to a full-time-faculty-only discussion of unionizing with the American Association of University Professors. He said they had tried to unionize in the past but adjunct faculty had voted it down. I asked for more of an explanation. He said not to worry about it, to trust him.

Later that day, I ran into Monty in an empty hallway I was cutting across between classes. He walked up to me and, pulling up his usually hunched-over back, made his full height clear. Looking down at me, Monty said, "You understand without a full-timers' union there will not be an adjunct union, right?"

"I understand we need to work together." I backed up a step, putting some distance between us.

"Jessica, you understand what I'm saying. Correct?" Monty leaned in, closing the gap between us again. "You need to let me lead. Once we form our union, we'll help you." He squinted his eyes. He looked like Mr. Burns from *The Simpsons* more than ever.

I felt an instinct to drop my book bag and cock my fists.

"Okay, Monty," I said, remembering that lying is an act of self-defense.

He backed up. I ducked around him, pushing back tears of frustration while taking in deep breaths. I walked slowly, trying to bring my focus to my lesson plan for my Gender and Culture class.

That night, I sent an email to the national adjunct listserv I was on asking who the AAUP rep was for my region. It was Joe Berry, an elder of the adjunct organizing movement who wrote a book called *Reclaiming the Ivory Tower* that was regularly referenced on adjunct-activist social media. Joe's email address was easy to find, so I sent him a message.

Dear Joe,
The full-time faculty at my college are discussing unionizing without the adjunct faculty. What should I do?
Jessica

Dear Jessica,
Here's my number. Call me.
Solidarity,
Joe

I didn't know what to expect when I called. I had mixed feelings about the labor movement. On the one hand, the Haymarket martyrs, Emma Goldman, and the history of radical Jewish activists from the turn of the 1900s had influenced my politics. On the other hand, in the 1990s the labor movement seemed extremely masculine, conservative, white, and straight. It had tried to crush leftist environmental activism on the Olympic Peninsula in Washington state. Pickup trucks with *Union Proud* bumper stickers also had American flag stickers and Jesus fish. The trucks were often parked next to cop cars at businesses displaying signs that said *No Shirts, No Shoes, No Environmentalists* and *We Shoot Spotted Owls*.

Joe and I spoke on the phone for a therapeutically long time. He was interested in all the gory details about the faculty senate fight.

"Jessica, here's what you need to do," Joe said. "Double the number of adjuncts coming to the meeting. If you can grow from two to four, that shows them you have numbers. Numbers are power. Then you do it again and again. But for now, start small."

Then Joe gave me the number of the AAUP New Mexico organizer. "Call Jason," he said. "That's who Monty must be talking to."

I called Jason the next day.

"You have to include adjunct faculty," I said.

"Our policy is to include adjunct faculty in all new chapters," Jason said. Then he let me speak for a therapeutically long time, asking smart questions and empathizing with my anger. It was the first time I had spoken to someone who wasn't an adjunct but cared about the intimate horrors of my job.

Maybe, just maybe, the labor movement was how to make change at work. It certainly wasn't going to happen by playing nice with administrators.

✿❦❀❦✿

"Hi. I'm Miranda." A woman with chin-length cherry-red dyed hair and nearly translucent skin introduced herself to me in the adjunct office. "Susan said you're the one sending the emails to adjuncts. Thank you."

Miranda wore a green polka-dot minidress with black leggings and black chunky-heeled Mary Janes. My colleagues in New Mexico usually dressed in the colors of the parched desert. I was intrigued.

"I'm glad you're reading them," I said.

"Did you see SEIU is organizing adjunct unions? I've always wanted to be in a union. I'm stone poor, a single mom on food stamps, and teaching seven classes between here and Northern this semester."

"That's rough."

"Yeah. And I just left an abusive relationship. I had to stay in a shelter." I told Miranda I'd been in a shelter also. When violence defines your life, you go deep fast. We chatted for a few more minutes, and then she rushed out of the office to her class. I rushed out of the office fifteen minutes later, and I didn't see her again until the faculty development training at the beginning of the next school year. The training was one large, three-hour session on cross-departmental collaborations. We couldn't schedule an adjunct-only session, though we did still get paid sixty dollars for the day. Miranda and I passed notes back and forth about how we were going to spend the money:

> I'm going to buy clothes from the designer racks at the thrift store on Cerrillos.

> I'm going to get a fancy cocktail instead of a well drink when I go to Tiny's for karaoke.

> I'm going to pay off the rest of my student debt. Ha ha! Not!!

During the lunch break, while stirring the powdered creamer into her coffee, Miranda told me about her anonymous persona on Twitter, where she got out all her anger about debt and degrees.

"I have a bunch of followers," she said. "Don't tell anyone."

"I hate social media, so no worries."

I told her I was working with Carmen to change things for adjuncts on campus through the faculty senate. I invited her to the next meeting, telling her about my conversation with Joe Berry, that he suggested we show Monty there were more of us who were pissed.

Miranda said yes.

CHAPTER EIGHTEEN

Campus Equity Week

In September 2013, an op-ed in the *Pittsburgh Post-Gazette* titled "Death of an Adjunct" broke adjunct social media. It was about an adjunct professor at Duquesne University in Ohio named Margaret Mary Vojtko who lost her position after teaching there for twenty-five years. The Duquesne University administrators claimed that they didn't fire her, that she just wasn't rehired. There's more to the story, they claimed. They claimed that Margaret Mary was a difficult woman. With a shitty income and no health care, and still working multiple jobs in her eighties, Margaret Mary was also battling cancer. To pay her medical bills, she had to stop paying her utilities. During the cold Ohio winter, she slept in her campus office for warmth until the university had her removed by campus police. Margaret Mary passed away while a lawyer for the United Steelworkers, the union that was organizing faculty at Duquesne, was helping her file an age- and disability-discrimination complaint. The labor lawyer was the one who wrote the op-ed.

Miranda said Margaret Mary's story was her wake-up call to get more involved with adjunct activism. Once a teenage mother with an abusive husband, Miranda had lived in a run-down trailer park in rural New Mexico. Higher education had been her path out of poverty, but, as she said often, it was now her path back into poverty. The academic career she had dreamed of was nonexistent. Instead, she was terrified to be impoverished and homeless in her eighties. It was a realistic fear. According to the Integrated Postsecondary Education Data System, *Inside Higher Ed*, and the AAUP, tenure positions declined by 80 percent between 1990 and 2010, while the number of contingent faculty grew by 115 percent. During that same time period, more people earned graduate degrees, growing from approximately 106,000 to 160,000 awarded. So did the number of women earning graduate degrees, growing from 38 percent in 1990 to 51 percent in 2010. However, the number of female college faculty hired into tenure-track positions only grew by 11 percent.

The Steelworkers' op-ed piece did its job. More contingent faculty spoke out on social media, blogs, and op-eds about how contingent work impacted their lives. Happy to see others getting pissed off, I was reminded again that most of the people who planned to be professors held expectations of the system working in their favor, rather than desires to tear it all down. For me, Margaret Mary's death was another reminder that connecting with people along one point of identification didn't mean we shared other beliefs, values, and experiences.

Outrage on adjunct social media over Margaret Mary's death included anger at the Catholic church for not taking care of their own. I had no idea why they thought an institution teeming with pedo-philes would care about this eighty-something woman. I suppose she could have been a lesbian living a closeted life, but that didn't come up anywhere I was looking. I noted the concern about housing was that she couldn't pay her mortgage, and I wondered how she had been able to buy her house in the first place.

❦

In October, Carmen set up a meeting with the VP of the Orwellian-sounding Office of Institutional Effectiveness, to discuss increasing adjunct pay beyond the 2 percent math fix. I was slightly hungover that day, and extremely bored by the impossible-to-follow institutional-speak, until the VP said, "I hear what you're saying, but think about this. I'm also an adjunct. In business management. I don't feel disrespected. So, you see? You aren't representing all points of view."

I glared at this entitled thirty-something man, a decade younger than me, who had worked at the New Mexico Department of Higher Education before he got this stupidly titled job. I'm pretty sure I said, "You've got to be kidding." I'm absolutely sure nothing concrete came from the meeting.

"Carmen," I said as we walked down the concrete-gray painted hall-way away from the Office of Institutional Effectiveness, "we need to stop having these meetings and do more organizing."

"Okay, I trust you," she said.

There were two national adjunct-run advocacy organizations, the Coalition of Contingent Academic Labor and the New Faculty Majority.

They had put out a joint call to organize Campus Equity Week, a nation-wide week of actions to bring attention to adjunct faculty working conditions. I emailed the contact listed on the Campus Equity Week website. He, Craig, called me back a few days later. Craig was an adjunct and a labor organizer, and talking to him was as therapeutic as talking to Jason and Joe. The labor movement was different from other activism I had done. I couldn't put my finger on it. I tried not to think too much about all the men I was trusting.

Craig advised keeping it simple, to just set up an info table somewhere visible on campus. A table would bring attention to our issues while literally putting New Mexico on the adjunct-activist map posted on the website. I thought it was too simple. What about films, and speakers, and even self-defense classes on boundary-setting and grounding exercises that could shift the job-induced trauma? I was wound up. The chaotic rush of an immediate deadline for too many things on my list could propel me into an organizing high as intense on my system as drugs. Fortunately, Craig kept advising to keep it simple. He said the goal wasn't just campus-based, it was part of the broader labor movement. The win was bursting through the bubble of silence surrounding our struggles as workers.

I told Carmen what Craig said. Carmen agreed. She reminded me we only had a week to prepare. She also thought formal approval from faculty senate would be protection if the table ruffled the administration's feathers. I thought we should avoid Monty and the senate and have the student clubs we advised reserve tables for us. We did both. The Spanish and LGBTQ+ clubs reserved tables and made a sign-up sheet for tabling shifts that they posted in the student club office. Students helped us put up posters we downloaded from the Campus Equity Week website. We got the senate to pass a motion to officially participate in Campus Equity Week. Monty didn't argue, but he did abstain from the vote. And no one in senate signed up for a tabling shift.

We emailed the adjuncts on our non-campus email list, asking for help preparing materials and to meet in the adjunct office the Saturday before CEW, as it was called. Miranda signed up. And Georgia! Our working group doubled in size from two to four, meeting the goal Joe Berry had advised. Miranda wrote a short piece that captured why, in early organizing, large numbers aren't as important as building camaraderie. It was never published. Until now...

> Miranda got an email from Jessica asking if she wanted to be involved in Campus Equity Week, to which she responded yes, absolutely. Up until recently Miranda still had delusions of professional advancement, but not after reading the recent press on the life and death of Margaret Mary Vojtko. At that moment Miranda understood that her career was, by design, a dead end. Her only protests until Campus Equity Week had been through an angry and anonymous Twitter identity, so she was happy to be interacting with a real activist for the first time.
>
> When Miranda rounded the corner of the hallway that Saturday to meet Jessica at the adjunct faculty office, she was startled to see Jessica and the other adjunct Faculty Senate rep sitting on the cold tile floor surrounded by their bags of colorful paper and posterboard. The office door was closed.
>
> "It's locked," Jessica said.
>
> "Did you call security?" Miranda asked.
>
> "Twenty times. No answer."
>
> The three women waited, discussing the trouble brewing with the newly hired president of the college and continuing to call security until a new FT hire in the English Department, a twenty-three-year-old with a newly minted MFA, bounced by them decked out in J. Crew. (She was hired by her friends in the department who overlooked all other applicants, including several qualified adjuncts who had taught at the college for years.) The girl looked at the three adjuncts with genuine shock.
>
> "Are you unable to get into your office?" The adjuncts nodded. "You can use my office if you want."
>
> "No thanks," they said in unison.

Waiting for security to unlock the office, we sat on the floor of the concrete-gray painted hallway. We got to know more about each other than we had been able to during the brief breaks and long meetings that happened on work hours. We kept chatting once we were in the office appropriating state funds to make banners out of copy paper, glue, markers, and file folders. We designed simple posters that said, "The national average pay for adjunct faculty is $2,700 per class per semester. It is $1,950 at Santa Fe Community College." We used address labels to make stickers that said *Adjunct* and *I support Adjunct Faculty* in a curly red font. We got into a heated debate over what demand to make with a petition. Miranda wanted to demand people walk out of classes during CEW. Carmen was worried we'd get people fired, and I didn't think anyone would agree to that level of activism on a politically apathetic campus. Georgia quietly asked what we thought we could get if we walked out. We weren't ready to organize that sort of action. We thought about demanding something institutionally possible, like a third adjunct rep to the faculty senate, which would only cost the college $150. One person could benefit from the added pennies, but we agreed the ask was meaningless in terms of the material changes we needed as a whole. We settled on an adjunct-only meeting outside of the faculty senate. It would be a follow-up action to the table that we could track numbers for. The goal would be to double our numbers again.

The two tables the students had reserved for us had been delivered to the main hallway by facilities. Our office supply decor and propaganda resulted in a respectable, grade-school-bake-sale-looking table with sign-up sheets for the meeting, our email list, and even flyers for the next faculty senate meeting. We stood back to admire our accomplishment.

"Let's take a picture," Miranda said.

Georgia didn't want to be photographed, so she took the picture on Miranda's phone. It's one of my favorite moments captured in New Mexico. Carmen is leaning easily, one hand resting on the table and a broad smile on her face. I look pleased with myself, my arms folded across my hoodie, which is turned inside out to hide the beer logo. Miranda is standing between us, looking not quite confident but very proud. The picture captures our joy. It captures our connection built through challenging power. And it captures the moment just before the complications of social media took over.

"I posted it to Facebook!" Miranda said.

"You did what?" I didn't exactly ask.

Miranda was a decade younger than me. For her, social media was a given. For me, I felt like the inside of my veins were being exposed, burning my skin raw. I slid down the wall and hugged my knees to my chest. It felt like I'd been outed as something I wasn't. I felt shards of fear, sure I'd lose my job. Miranda watched me with confusion. She knew I was tough and outspoken; she didn't know what to make of my meltdown.

She asked if I wanted her to take it down. Then she said, "Oh, wait. It's already reposted to the Campus Equity Week page."

I was still freaked out, but now I was curious and my ego was piqued. I had done a lot riskier actions. How did a picture on social media of a naively decorated table in an empty campus hallway wield so much power that I felt physically afraid? The four of us walked over to the adjunct office to look at Facebook together on a computer. The post was captioned "First pictures coming in. Congrats New Mexico!" Underneath were several positive comments tagging Miranda, Carmen, and me. With each click, I saw my tenuous, threadbare job security morph into the protection of exposure. I felt the pull of something bigger than my individual fear. That pull reconnected me to the moment and to my friends in the room. We realized our tabling was a success before it was even officially an action.

The picture of us traveled far enough across the internet that Al Jazeera used it to promote a live Twitter event about precarious faculty. I shared my Al Jazeera credibility on my own Facebook page, now hoping the college would try to fire me. I was no longer simply another "difficult woman"; I had public backing for my point of view, including from friends around the country who cheered me on through comments about their struggles as adjunct professors. That simple action catalyzed more than I could have imagined, including a realization that I didn't need to hide out in the prickly-floored desert feeling ashamed I didn't have tenure.

❦

In the middle of Campus Equity Week, Von and I had to prove to the college that we were a couple so I could be added to his health care plan. I had been on Obamacare since the early rollout, part of the group with preexisting conditions who also hadn't been insured for at least six months. Easiest application criteria I'd ever met. But now, I could have my employer pay for my insurance through Von's full-time job with the same employer. We just had to prove we had a binding relationship. Our lease and electric bill with a notarized and signed affidavit would do it. The assistant director of financial aid, who was a notary, stamped the approval.

"Health care was always the only reason we'd end up making it legal," I told her.

She smiled at me uncomfortably.

Von asked her to say a few words, using his dry humor to poke at her further.

She half smiled more uncomfortably.

We put the documents in an envelope and kissed. I went back to the adjunct office to prep for class, and Von went back to dining services to prep tomorrow's lunch.

Obamacare—the Affordable Care Act—was an ongoing topic of discussion on adjunct social media. Congress was embattled over the details of the employer mandate, a concession to insurance companies. Organizations that had more than fifty workers and chose not to insure their full-time employees, defined by the IRS as thirty hours or more per week at one place of employment, were mandated to pay a tax penalty. Without a federal standard for counting adjunct faculty classroom-prep and grading hours, higher education institutions could report fewer full-time employees, another way to balance budgets on the backs of adjuncts while continuing to exclude us from health care coverage. The New Faculty Majority took on the fight, testifying at an IRS hearing, which resulted in a 1:1.25 teaching-to-course-prep ratio.

Fighting to standardize fifteen minutes of prep time for every hour in the classroom was as equally bad math as fighting for a 2 percent raise in my mind. It lowballed the reality of work outside the classroom, continuing institutionalized wage theft. Those who thought through admin-think argued that the simple ratio would allow contingent faculty to teach a higher number of classes on one campus, ideally earning more money. The 1:1.25 "win" was short-term. Administrators' next move was to impose restrictions on the number of courses adjunct faculty could teach. This resulted in immediate cuts to individual contingent faculty's income, further shrinking full-time contingent positions while expanding the numbers of part-timers. Mandatory employer-covered health care could have been a game changer. Instead, it became a political sports ball between politicians, lobbyists, lawyers, and college administrators. They all helped make CEOs of private insurance companies more money while classroom educators became more impoverished, more stressed, more sick.

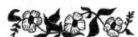

I learned about the employer mandate in one of the online adjunct-activist groups I was in. Before Von and I had our celebratory notarization, I was putting together the necessary paperwork trail to prove I worked at least thirty hours per week. I planned to be first in line to have the college pay for my insurance. In April, I went to HR to find out what I needed to translate my work week—teaching, being on faculty senate, advising a student club, and serving on the President's Diversity Advisory Committee—into hours. HR had no idea about the employer mandate. Neither did my department chair or college dean, my direct supervisors. "Let me know what you find out," each of them said.

I went to the new president's office. A different new president. The one who'd told me to get married had barely lasted a year. The revolving door of college presidents' hiring/firing scandals has been spinning for years. The new president, President Pete, said he had an open-door policy. I opened it, asking, "Are you going to have to cut classes for those of us working full-time?"

"We don't know yet," he answered.

In July, when I was on a special contract to move the Volunteer in the Community class to an online learning platform, I went back to HR. This time, I was representing a number of other adjunct faculty who also worked full-time between teaching and various contracts for committee work and special projects. The one person working in the HR office over the summer, a payroll technician, understood my question. She showed me a list that highlighted, in pink, about two dozen of us considered full-time by the school's own calculations.

"Does this mean I'll be included in ACA coverage?" I asked.

"It looks like it," she said.

I took in a full, deep breath.

I emailed the other faculty on the list, saying they should make an appointment and get a direct confirmation of their status.

In September, at the beginning of the fall semester, none of us had received formal information about our ACA status. I asked my department chair and college dean, again. Neither knew about the list. "Let me know what you find out," each of them said, again.

I had to take a break from banging my head against the wall. It aggravated my IBD.

Then the Margaret Mary article was published.

Carmen and I tried to get the faculty senate to advocate on our behalf. The number of adjuncts affected by this was comparable to one-third of full-time faculty. Monty said that wasn't a big enough number. I went home and cried, again.

In October, during Campus Equity Week, I went back to HR. The payroll technician who had been helpful had been a temp and wasn't working there anymore. The HR director said to come back the following week. I did and she showed me the list I had seen three months earlier, except this time my name, highlighted in pink, was crossed off. So were the other adjuncts' names who had been waiting for confirmation. My heart sank, and my guts braced. Then my guts braced, and my heart sank. According to the math, my three classes added up to twenty-one hours of work a week. I asked how that was possible when full-time faculty only taught one more class than I did. She said it was different math. She said full-time and part-time faculty hours are calculated differently since part-timers only teach.

"But I don't only teach," I said. "I serve on faculty senate, on the President's Diversity Advisory Committee, and as advisor to the LGBTQ student club."

She said that work didn't count toward the ACA, that it was volunteer work. She said not to worry because President Pete was cleaning things up next semester, that he was putting an end to volunteer work.

I left her office thinking how chickenshit my chair and dean were to let a random administrator be the one to tell me that I was going to lose a big chunk of my job. I was sure they knew that the extra contracts I relied on, which the HR director called "volunteer work," were being cut, that the new classes I had been asked to teach by other departments were being taken off the table, and that there had been a decision to keep me and my colleagues from qualifying for health care. If I hadn't been knocking on every door to find out, no one would have told me. I would have shown up to campus to sign my usual contracts and find out then and there that things had changed. Maybe my supervisors didn't know, but that was on them for doing the bare minimum of their job and not considering the impact on people they claimed to care about. I went to the adjunct office to tell the others. Then I went home to cry and drink.

In November, President Pete came to a faculty senate meeting to answer questions about the ACA rollout. He had just sent out an email explaining there was a cap on the number of courses we could teach, but not explaining that the cap was being put in place to keep about two dozen of us below the IRS definition of full-time. The messaging, which Monty was helping spread, was that they were "simply" being more diligent in complying with the college bylaws. I had questions.

Monty avoided calling on me until the new faculty senate vice president told him to.

"President Pete," I said, "we couldn't find the policy you're referencing."

"It's in the bylaws, Jessica," President Pete answered.

"Carmen and I read through those. The policy says we can teach up to twenty-two credits a school year."

"No. That's not right," he said. "It's nine credits a semester."

Carmen handed me the bylaws, open to the page.

"It's right here on page 47. Section 5.3.2. It's the only mention of course caps for adjunct faculty."

"Well, I may be wrong about where the policy is, but we need to be compliant. We made the budget before Congress settled the employer mandate details, when we were reeling from the audit we went through. We already made major cuts across departments. We weren't expecting a large new expenditure."

He answered so honestly, I didn't have a response. I was struggling to wrap my brain around the negligent budget planners who didn't consider that the Affordable Care Act would impact the college, which was one of the largest employers in the area. My face must have said something to that effect, because President Pete gave an embarrassed little laugh and said, "Look. If I was in charge, we'd all have universal health care."

Monty took advantage of my silence to remind people this was a Q and A, not an open discussion.

I was in my head for the rest of the meeting. I couldn't figure out who was in charge and who should let affected faculty know that they weren't getting health care and that in less than two months their income was being cut. President Pete finally got up and shook Monty's hand, ending the meeting. He passed by me and waved as he left the room. I followed him into the hallway.

"Pete, wait," I said, done with formalities. "Will you send an email to adjunct faculty making very clear what is going to happen next semester?"

"Do you think I should do that?" he asked.

"Yes. People are in limbo. They don't know what's going on."

"Okay. I can do that. Thank you, Jessica."

I stood in the hallway only breathing in, until Carmen came out and gave me a hug.

I went home and cried and updated my resume. And apologized to Von. We were fighting all the time.

CHAPTER NINETEEN

Gender Studies Class

Ava had moved to Santa Fe from Seattle for a job at a nonprofit organization I didn't get. She also taught two gender studies classes at the local art college. We had a lot in common and met regularly at the café across from the movie theaters.

"When was the last time we saw each other?" Ava asked as I sat down with my almond milk chai. She was wearing a tailored mahogany-brown suit that gorgeously complemented her creamy skin and burgundy hair. I had on a gray Harley-Davidson hoodie and black leggings that I'd pulled out of one of the ignored piles of laundry Von and I were fighting over.

"The semester had just started," I said.

"Oh my god. I have so much to tell you."

Two of her female students had been raped by the same person, another student. A young man. Another of her female students was in a physically violent relationship. Another young man. Disclosure of gender violence was typical in gender studies classes. Ava's students were starting a "Grrrls to the Front" campus club against rape. They asked Ava to be their advisor.

"Look, you'll love this," Ava said. She picked up her phone to show me a picture of a hot-pink flyer wheat-pasted to a lamppost on campus. The bright-yellow letters read: *justice for survivors on campus = missing.* "I love my students," Ava said.

Ava had signed the necessary paperwork to be the club's advisor and dropped it off at Student Affairs. A few days later, the director of Student Affairs called her, asking her to come in for a meeting. "You know that's never good," Ava said, taking a drink from her mug.

The director said that, because no rapes had been reported, the club was a breach of policy. When Ava said that didn't make any sense, the director replied that Ava should have reported the rapes, that she shouldn't take on things that weren't her job. Ava asked how she could help the students. The director again said no rapes had been reported so there was nothing to do. Ava again said that didn't make any sense. The director told Ava that the student whose name was on the paperwork for the club had a domestic violence complaint against her by the boyfriend she had accused. And the director said that the boyfriend just happened to be the director's nephew.

"Can you believe this fucking town?" Ava said. "That woman breached confidentiality while bragging about nepotism or whatever it is that she's doing to protect her nephew."

Then Ava said that there was more.

She said one of her male students, the white cishet one offended by not being able to use racial and gender slurs indiscriminately (who's in every gender studies class in every college across the country), said freedom of speech includes the freedom to carry a gun into the classroom.

"The problem, Jessica, besides everything, is that he implied he had a gun on him. In the classroom. It was terrifying." Ava described visibly shaken students. She described smoothing her dress over and over, calmly bringing the lecture to a close, and ending class twenty minutes early—but not sure if that was the right thing to do, safety-wise.

The "Grrrls to the Front" stayed back. They didn't want to leave Ava alone in case the angry young man was hovering outside the open classroom door. And he was. He walked back in, one hand behind his back.

"Jessica, something came over me. Not 'something,' the Home Alive class." Ava had taken one when she was a grad student at U-Dub, long after I'd left the collective. She described walking up to her student, placing her hand on his arm, and guiding him back out the door. "I shut that fucking door, Jessica, and somehow remembered to click the thing so it locked." Ava said they were still catching their breath, and the "Grrrls to the Front" were asking her if that was an appropriate time to call the cops, when security arrived. She figured another student had called them. "Jessica, I just wanted to go home to Pudding Cat. I did not want to teach any more lessons that night." She did send an email to her department chair to report the incident before she took two Xanax.

"Only two?" I asked. "That shit called for a few more."

"I woke up to an email from my chair asking me to come meet her on campus as soon as possible. Good, right? I called my mom's caregiver and went to the meeting. Oh, Jessica. Why do we do this shit?"

Ava was hoping to get permission to take the active-shooter training they only provided to tenured faculty, but the meeting was about Ava's role in the anti-rape group. Her chair hadn't read the email about the gun incident. The chair asked Ava about some emails to other faculty, including one about a Take Back the Night rally. She asked Ava to send lecture notes from a class held two weeks earlier. Ava was so stunned that she forgot to ask how to drop the student with the gun from her class. She taught her classes and sent an email with her question that night.

Ava didn't get a response. She had to teach several class sessions with no guidance about how to procedurally address the gun issue, support the students who had been threatened, or support the student who had made the threat. Then, three weeks later, on a Friday at 7 p.m., Ava's chair sent an email informing her that her classes for the next semester didn't have enough enrollment. Ava had been fired.

I stared into my cup of cold chai thinking about the faculty member I'd met last semester who had spent every Monday and Wednesday in the adjunct office preparing their classes and chatting with everyone like coworkers in a regular job. The following semester, their classes were given to some dean's son who had just finished his master's degree. I never saw that person again. I thought about my musician friend who had developed a certificate of study program in sound engineering. His chair, his dean, the provost, everyone, had promised him a full-time position as soon as they could fund it. A decade later, they funded the position and hired someone else. During my year of magical teaching, I designed a History of Video Art class. I was flattered when one of the fancy tenured faculty wanted a copy of the syllabus. The following year, when I was an adjunct instead of visiting faculty, he proposed my class to the department as his own.

I met the resigned anger in Ava's eyes with my own weary gaze.

I should contact the art college. There's obviously a gender studies class available.

I didn't say that out loud, but it's the kind of thought that flashes through one's head when fucking each other over is normalized.

CHAPTER TWENTY

Grief's Tentacles

Death hovered close.

Jennifer OD'd and died. Leon let me know, although they had separated years earlier. We had been so close until Jennifer fell so far back into her addiction that I had to hold her an arm's length away. I left most of my guilt at the pink and black and leopard-print altar set up in the art gallery where her memorial was held, but I still have trouble expressing all the ways I miss her and mourn for her.

Lisa—not Lisa from Chicago, but a sound engineer and musician I knew back in the Seattle days—crashed her motorcycle and died the same year Jennifer OD'd. Lisa took me on one of the few sweet, chivalrous dates I've experienced. We went to a fancy, expensive restaurant. I wore an olive-green camouflage miniskirt and blue button-down men's shirt with a patch over the chest pocket that said *Fuck*. Lisa wore dark denim overalls and an oversized cowboy hat. I have a snapshot in my head of her teaching me about all the different forks laid out on the white linen tablecloth.

Keven, who I knew from the LA trans community, died less than a year after Lisa, succumbing to complications of ALS. Flashes of barbecues at his apartment complex are mingled with memories of him photographing parts of my MFA thesis.

Terry, Leon's best friend, died the same month Keven did. Leon let me know that Terry had crashed her motorcycle. The last time I saw Terry had been at Jennifer's memorial.

Susan died a month later. She had been out of the adjunct office and in the hospital for weeks, an unidentified illness knocking her down. And then briefly, for one day, the Goddess was in again, back at her desk. "Jessica, I want you to know I really appreciate you and being friends with you," she said as I jumped up and down, happy to see her. We hugged and

I rushed off to class, feeling doom in her words. I thought about what I'd say back to her the next time I saw her. There wasn't a next time.

Grief's tentacles wound through old traumas, tripping open PTSD floodgates. I cut words out of the *Santa Fe Reporter*, the free weekly newspaper. I cut out words I could feel. I cut out words with letters that I liked. There were words printed in red ink I cut out when I had a pile of too many printed in black ink. Then blue and green ones when I had too many in red. My kidnapped emotions communicated through the colors and shapes that I arranged into poorly punctuated sentences glued down on food packaging that wasn't accepted by the local recycling center. These Dada-esque ransom notes were poetry for my dead friends, chaotic cadences screaming through my fractured thinking, an attempt to make patterns out of my grief.

The next year, in January, Cindy, a friend from the Highways Performance Space community in Santa Monica, died. I ritualistically dusted the piece of art hanging on my bedroom wall that Von and I had bought from her, a cross made out of two-by-fours, painted traffic-cone orange with a prayer along the center post: *If I should die before I wake please make sure to remove the porn from under the bed before mom finds it, especially the gay bondage stuff.*

Michele, who I met in Santa Fe when I still lived in LA and got close to in both cities, died in the spring. She was in remission from breast cancer, and then she wasn't. In LA, I drove her to chemo appointments and listened to her thoughts on death. She went into remission and became more hopeful. In Santa Fe, we wrote together, witnessed each other sink into and heal from childhood sexual violence. Then we had a complicated falling out during the Prop 8 fight for same-sex marriage. She took an unexpected homophobic stance more naive than I could deal with in my frustration over a conservative, classist, antifeminist campaign catalyzed by estate tax rights for wealthy white lesbians. We didn't talk for eight months too long. The cancer came back in the estrogen cells throughout her whole body. I heard she was in and out of the hospital again. I called. She said, "I can't have heavy conversations about the world, I need to heal." I said, "I love you. I just want to support you however you need." We got to have another year of friendship before she was gone.

Puppy, our cat, died six weeks later, on my birthday weekend. Her death howls were the soundtrack to an already uncomfortable visit with my mom and stepdad.

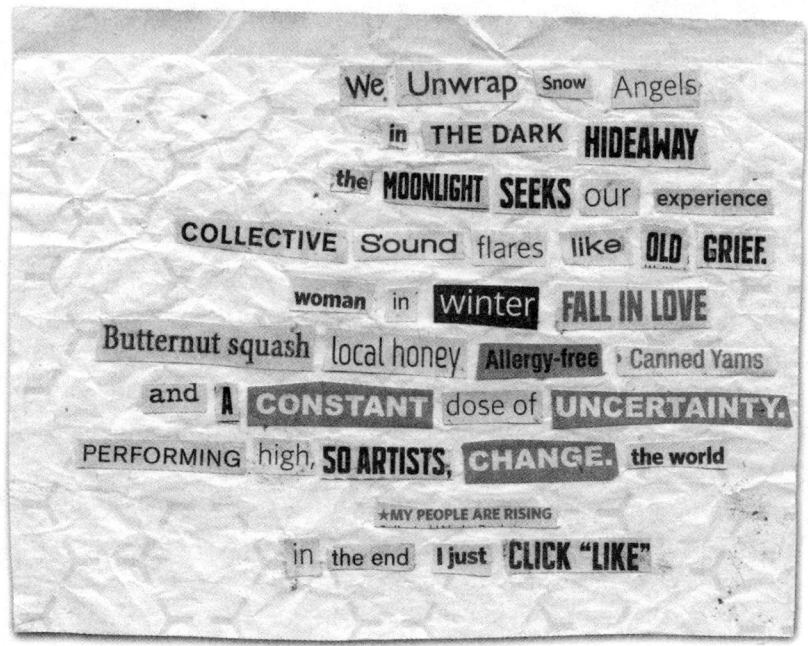

Random Note: *We Unwrap Snow Angels*, **newsprint on foil burger wrapper**

Fear coursed through me all the time. The surface of my body dried out while my internal system was on fire. Near-constant IBD flares showed up as precancerous cells.

I closed my eyes and felt the pull of heroin. It'd been two decades since I'd used, and I still missed snorting the white powder that let me float off into a silence so loud I could puke all over myself without shame on a stranger's stoop on the Lower East Side of New York. I still missed the West Coast brown liquid that would wash away the thoughts I didn't want while I lay on a dirty couch in a dank Seattle apartment full of other kids running away from pain. All I wanted was the false memory of blissful nothingness.

CHAPTER TWENTY-ONE

Depressed and Demoralized

In December, after losing all hope for employer-covered health care, I read an article in *The New York Times* about a former adjunct professor who became a union organizer with the Service Employees International Union. *That's a nice story but nothing is that simple*, I thought while looking up the SEIU website. They were hiring in Seattle, Boston, St. Louis, and the Bay Area. I read more about SEIU and found out they had the first lesbian president of any major union in the country. Meh. President Pete was gay. So was my boss at the vanity nonprofit where I supplemented my teaching on a 1099 contract facilitating educational leadership programs. Both jobs were cutting me at the same time. So much for queer solidarity.

Being depressed and demoralized is not a great state for a job search, especially a never-ending one. My last round had been hell. I had called friends of friends who were house painters, video editors, diversity consultants. No one could afford to hire. I searched *education*, *community*, *program management*, *art* on employment sites and sent resumes out cold, resulting in more insulting interviews.

"You understand this is thirteen dollars an hour," the Planned Parenthood of the Rockies told me.

"Is there room to negotiate?" I asked.

"No. I'm sorry. That's our budget."

The rape crisis center's executive director said the job paid eleven dollars an hour.

"Is there room to negotiate?" I asked.

"No. But if it helps, I've had more people apply to this job than any other in recent years, all with graduate degrees." It didn't help.

I researched more about SEIU. The jobs were for organizers on their new higher-ed campaign unionizing adjunct faculty. I asked Von what he thought about moving again. He said he'd always wanted to live in the

Bay Area. He said he'd be fine living in Seattle, though he was worried my past would haunt me.

I asked Jason, the AAUP organizer, what he thought.

"How old are you?" Jason asked. "I mean, we're around the same age, right? It was a hard job when I was in my twenties: ten-hour or more days, no sleep, a lot of drinking and fast food. Weight gain I just finally lost."

I couldn't deal with gaining any more weight. Besides, Crosby, Von's ex, and some other LA friends were coming to visit. I decided to turn in my grades and not worry about my employment until after the new year.

On January 2, I asked Jason and Joe Berry and Craig, the Campus Equity Week organizer, to be references. They all said yes right away. It was the first time all my references were cis white men. On January 4, I called a friend of Zoë's from the labor choir in Seattle who was a director in a Washington state SEIU local. He said he'd put in a good word for me. On January 5, I pressed send on my application. It was a Sunday night. Monday morning, January 6, I got a call to set up a preliminary interview. It's the interview where the woman said I sounded "mature," the one that went really well. Tears of anxiety flowed out of me during the few days I impatiently waited to find out if I would get a second interview. I put my angst into writing a letter to the editor of the *Albuquerque Journal.* They had published an article on adjunct faculty in which they interviewed a man in his sixties who'd retired from a lucrative career and was teaching to "give back." The other person interviewed in the article was a man in his sixties with a full-time administration job where he taught. He said, "The extra money is like lunch money." I hated them both. I hated the paper. I wrote:

> In response to the article "Part-timers face 'double standard,'" it is not reasonable to consider that a "double standard" is acceptable for any profession. Simply because some unknown percentage of the group has other secure employment does not mean it is okay to de-professionalize the entire group.
>
> Expecting people who have invested time and money in earning graduate degrees to use their expertise in "teaching positions [that] provide little in the way of pay and no employee benefits" is unethical and creates a two-tiered system where budgets are cut on

the back of one of the fastest growing, most educated, precarious labor pools in the US.

What message does this send students taking on exorbitant debt to earn their degrees, especially in a state that consistently rates among the highest for functionally illiterate adults and the lowest for high school graduation and college matriculation?

Would you expect a dentist to work for "lunch money" because they love what they do? Why is it acceptable to expect college professors to teach for less than minimum wage and no benefits because they have a satisfying profession intellectually? What does it say about us as a nation if we expect the majority of the professoriate to be working for "lunch money"?

This article is painfully biased against addressing a key labor issue that is destroying the higher education system in our country. Shame on the *Albuquerque Journal* for minimizing the economic reality and lived struggles of a large part of New Mexico's workforce.

❧

The letter didn't get published.

I got the second interview.

I tore apart a decaffeinated Earl Grey tea bag package and sent an art signal into the universe.

❧

The second interview was a group interview. My guts were so trashed I couldn't hear them trying to remind me about the time I had applied for a job with Alaska Airlines when I lived in Seattle. I knew people with visible piercings and tattoos who worked as flight attendants for the Seattle-based company, so I'd filled out an online application. At the time, online applications were a new phenomenon used mostly for corporate jobs. I got a reply from Alaska Airlines with an invitation to a group interview. Whatever aesthetic individuality the company allowed, a group interview was a sign that I had to be willing to be an interchangeable pawn in a corporate system. I wasn't. I didn't go to the interview. Twenty years later, hiring processes, the economy, and my choices were different.

SEIU expected me to purchase my own plane ticket to Oakland and then submit receipts for reimbursement—just like the college in

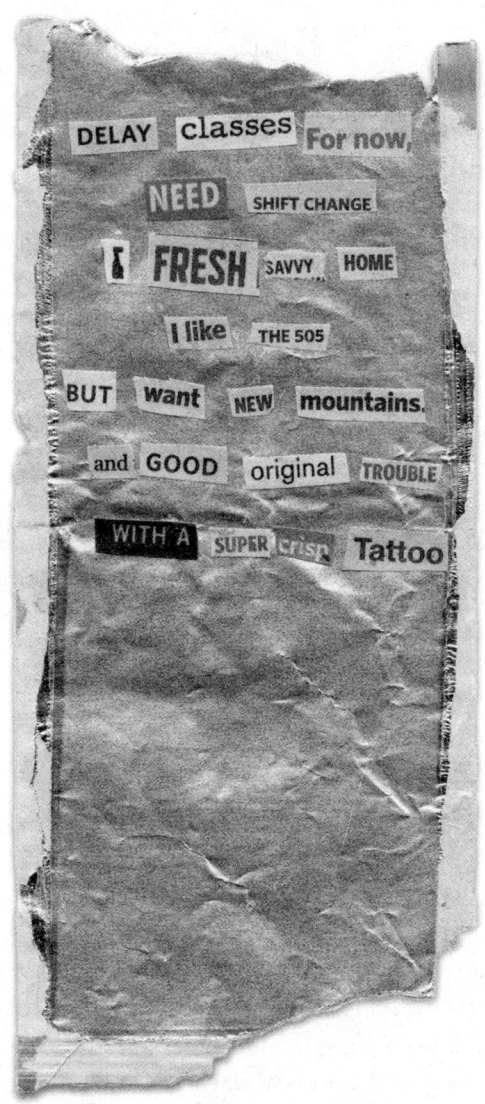

Random Note: *Delay Classes for Now*, newsprint on tea wrapper

New Jersey had. *Why do I need to perform middle-class stability for a job in the labor movement?* I wondered while simultaneously ignoring the red flag. Von and I still didn't have credit, let alone credit cards, since the bankruptcy. I bought a plane ticket using my debit card with all of my fingers crossed during a month I wasn't receiving a paycheck. I made arrangements to stay with Mich, who was living in Oakland. I arranged to borrow an ex's truck the day of the interview. Then I looked up what "business casual" meant, which is what I was advised to wear in the information I was sent. I chose three different outfits, which I modeled for Mich when I got to her place. We chose the purple dress with a zipper front and pockets, black tights, and calf-high black boots.

A small group of people were huddled outside the locked door to the SEIU office when I arrived. A few minutes passed before someone let us in and then told us to wait with a slightly larger group of people in the front lobby. There were about twenty-five of us, total. Eventually we were led to a large meeting room, where we had to sign in and wear a name tag. We were told to sit around the conference tables that were set up in a U-shape in the middle of the room. As I settled onto my metal folding chair, I saw that there were five people with clipboards sitting on a row of folding chairs along a wall. They observed us, obviously making notes, until everyone was seated. Then a really tall woman greeted us, saying we should expect to be there for five hours. I managed not to scream.

Except for three of the people with clipboards, everyone in the room was evidently younger than me. I still managed not to scream.

The tall woman went over the agenda written out on a flip chart stationed in the open part of the U. It felt like an Activism 101 meeting, except the group of people were dressed for a professional job.

We had to go around the table, say our names, and say a historical figure we'd like to have dinner with. I managed not to answer, *Are you fucking kidding me?*

We had to go around the table again and name someone in our lives who inspired us. I couldn't think of anyone and don't have any memory of how I answered, because I was so thrown off by all the people who said their mother or father inspired them.

Then we had to role-play.

I wanted to die.

When it was over, we were given an expense form to fill out for travel reimbursement. I had brought a folder for the interview panel with my resume, the unpublished letter to the *Albuquerque Journal*, and an *Inside Higher Ed* interview Miranda and I had done together about our experiences as adjuncts. I walked over to the group of people with clipboards to introduce myself and hand one of them the folder. They were grabbing their luggage and running out of the room, their body language very clearly telegraphing they were not having a conversation with me or any other interviewee. I left my folder in the pile of expense forms. I drove the borrowed vehicle back through the unfamiliar city to my friend's house, where I broke down crying.

I flew home the next day and alternated between sleeping and crying while lying on the couch and hoping to get a call from SEIU offering me a job while dreading what that would mean. I never considered not taking the job. I didn't have any other possibilities, or the will to continue a job search. The backup plan was Von and me moving in with his sister's family in LA. Which made me start a backup backup plan to move in with Zoë and her partner Jehn, up in Seattle, which added to Von and me fighting all the time.

After three days, I was convinced I didn't have the job.

On day four, I got the call and had a job in Oakland as long as I passed a background check and a fingerprint scan. It was a worrisome caveat, but I didn't say anything. I relished not feeling like a total loser who only knew how to make bad decisions. I felt kind of, sort of, almost happy.

※ ❀ ❁ ❀ ※

The salary was $36,600. "Whether we send you to the campaign in the Bay Area or St. Louis," the hiring manager said on the phone. I heard a warning in her tone that I didn't understand as I was adding and subtracting: $36,600 was $20,000 more than I made at the community college and $8,000 more than I had made my last year at the Claremont Colleges. This salary was about the same as I'd made through my contracts at the educational leadership program over the past two years, except I ended up owing the IRS $10,000 in taxes I was ignoring because I couldn't afford to pay. Sounded fine to me, as I looked out at the semi-rural, cactus-filled, and parched New Mexican landscape.

The hiring manager said there was no room to negotiate my salary with the international because it had been determined by the staff union collective bargaining agreement. I heard another type of warning in her tone, but I was busy trying not to let her know I didn't understand the sentence she'd just said. Eventually, my coworkers in my union for SEIU staff taught me that "the international" was the national SEIU run by elected members and paid staff. I was being hired by that entity while being placed at a union local in the Bay Area. The local had its own elected members and paid staff as well as its own budget. The goal was to get hired by the local, which paid more than the international.

The thing I eventually realized about the hiring manager's tone when she gave me information about my salary was that she was feeding me an anti-staff-union message, planting seeds against the union that represented me to the international for salary and other negotiations. She made it sound like the staff union chose the salary amount. What I learned later is that the bosses set the salaries and then the unions fight for as much of a raise as they can pressure out of the bosses.

What I knew when I was first hired by SEIU was that unions were a solution most adjunct-activists believed would change our working conditions. I wanted to be in a position to make that change. In 2014, post–Great Recession, neoliberal universities needed a massive organizing institution to counter the thickening economic crises. And as a perimenopausal, tired-ass queer, I wanted the health care, sick days, vacation days, pension contributions, and union contract that came with the SEIU job. I'd almost never had any of those things in my three decades of working. The air reaching my clenched nervous system through the deep breaths I took in overrode the warning signals my knotted guts sent to my heart and brain about how far astray I was wandering from my art and from my anticapitalist and antiauthoritarian beliefs.

There was no time to think. SEIU wanted me to start in two weeks. I said I needed two months to leave my job, pack up my house, and move to another state. We negotiated six weeks so that I would be in attendance at a three-day campaign training in LA. I had to stop considering all the variables in my life and jump into action. Suddenly, everything felt urgent.

I gave notice at the community college. It was a month into the spring semester. "We'll miss you," my department chair said. Then, while I was still in the room, she picked up the phone and called another adjunct professor to take over my classes. They were filled before the door could close behind me.

We gave notice to our landlord. Von needed to stay in Santa Fe until the end of the semester to finish his culinary degree. We had to pack up around things he and the cats would need for several months, around things I needed to bring with me immediately but in a temporary living situation, and around things Von would bring me when I found a place for us to live before he and the cats arrived. We tried to get our deposit back early to help with the move. The landlord said she needed to keep it to repaint the walls we had painted in colors that she had approved.

I went to one last faculty senate meeting, because Jason from the AAUP was attending. Monty invited him to speak about unionizing. I finally told Monty his lack of solidarity was the main barrier for adjunct faculty to organize with full-time faculty. Then we had an uncomfortable lunch, made by Von, in the cafeteria with Jason, Carmen, and two other senate members. President Pete came up to the table and shook my hand, thanking me for my work and wishing me luck with the SEIU job. It was a political move mixed with a touch of genuineness I appreciated once I saw the look on Monty's face.

Carmen was moving on from the community college as well; her husband had accepted a job out of state. She stopped by the house on the ranch a few days before she and her family left town. We hugged good-bye, teary as we talked about the changes we had accomplished together. Miranda came over and helped me bubble-wrap and box up the art in between video chats with other adjunct-activists across the country. We got on calls with SEIU organizers and longtime labor activists, all older men, who gave me a lot of information about generational and political tensions in adjunct labor organizing. We chatted with a couple of older women, who mentored me in my transition into the labor movement. And we got involved with a more intergenerational group that did anonymous culture jamming against different college administrators who had insulted adjunct faculty on social media. It was silly but cathartic.

Some of my Random Notes were part of an art exhibit where lines of poetry were painted onto plate-glass windows around town with textured snow paint. Unplanned but appropriately, my piece was installed at a temporary employment agency. The week before I left, I read my pieces at two different exhibit events.

Von and I drove up to the Rio Grande Gorge Bridge in Taos the day before I left for Oakland. It was one of our favorite places because of the stunning beauty—and because the bridge was the location for the scene in *Natural Born Killers* where the two main characters slice their hands and merge their blood, promising to kill for each other forever. *Natural Born Killers* was the film we'd both chosen a romantic scene from without consulting each other for a trans community Valentine's Day party our first year dating. It's when I knew he was my person. Eleven years later, we fought the entire ninety-minute drive because I wanted to slice our hands and he didn't. We cried together, looking out at the staggering landscape. I was scared of leaving; he was scared of the motion the

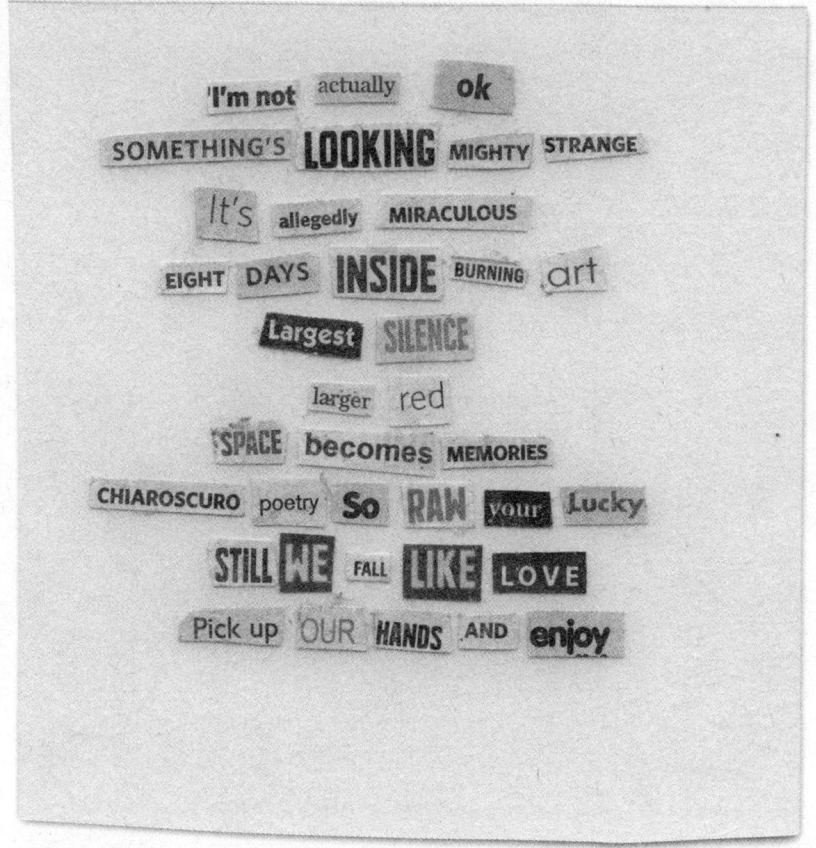

Random Note: *Pick Up Our Hands and Enjoy*, newsprint on heat shrink plastic

suspension bridge made while I purposefully jumped up and down to make it sway. Then we scattered dried rose petals I had saved from our death altar.

I had no idea what was coming next.

I didn't feel ready to leave.

It was time to go.

PART THREE

(DIS)EMBODIED

[OAKLAND AND

SACRAMENTO]

CHAPTER TWENTY-TWO

The People Who Brought You the Weekend

I unpacked my one suitcase and small backpack in the hotel room overlooking the basin between Oakland and Alameda. It was peaceful, calm. The other side of the hotel butted up against the long lines of trucks on the 880 freeway adding to the dark smog in the air. The bent metal highway barriers marked violent crashes that occurred near the Fruitvale station, where Oscar Grant had been murdered by BART police. I felt like maybe I belonged here in between the beauty and the violence.

Oakland's history was fascinatingly present. One of the cooks making the hotel breakfast buffet was a former Black Panther. A demonstration against the ills of capitalism happened almost every day of the week. Antioch friends, friends from different queer communities, safe exes, and some adjunct-activist friends all lived nearby, having been pushed out of San Francisco during the first and second dot-com booms.

Some days I felt awed by my new job as an organizer-in-training, not at all bothered that most of my new coworkers were closer in age to my former students than to me. Morning check-ins were held in the union office, which was the same place where the obnoxious group interview had happened. Sitting around conference tables with both new and seasoned organizers felt like I had joined the inner sanctum of the contingent faculty movement I had been looking for. Everyone freely expressed their shock and anger about the daily reality of contingent faculty's struggles and spoke about faculty senate leaders and college administrators as the enemy I had felt they were on my worst days of teaching.

"You're not an adjunct anymore," one supervisor told me during my first week, after I had offered what I thought was helpful advice on reading the class schedules being used to find individual faculty. I looked at her questioningly, and she said, "You said 'we.' Don't say 'we.' You're an organizer now." I had trouble accepting this instantly granted title. It seemed like it should take longer than a couple of days to be considered a professional union organizer. On the other hand, four years of college, five years of graduate school, and nine years of teaching still hadn't been enough to be fully considered a professor in academia. So, cool. I was an organizer.

My assignment was small, private, nonprofit liberal arts and visual arts colleges in San Francisco, Oakland, and towns north and east of the Bay. I'd meet my coworkers on a campus or drive around the entirety of the Bay Area doing house visits, talking to adjunct faculty about unionizing. Our assigned task was to get them to sign a union authorization card—the first step toward a union election. Every conversation took at least an hour, even though we were supposed to do it in twenty minutes. Like me, most contingent faculty had a lot to say about their debilitating economic struggles, and union organizers were the first people they met who both cared and got it. These were the conversations I'd wanted to have with my colleagues in New Mexico. I found it healing.

"You aren't a therapist," a different supervisor said during a one-on-one debrief. "Don't linger in the conversation. Get in and get out. This is organizing. We're offering a solution, not processing feelings. Get the card signed." She was queer, but I had trouble connecting with her. Or maybe it was that she had trouble connecting with me. She was genuinely perplexed when I explained that artists, and academics in the humanities, were conceptual, analytic thinkers, that telling someone like me to follow prescriptive steps doesn't work. We—I mean "they"—wanted to understand the process of forming a union from every angle. We—I mean "they"—usually weren't going to sign a union authorization card on the first ask. When an adjunct professor said they needed to do their own research, they meant it. It wasn't the anti-union brush-off seasoned organizers assumed (and this was a few years before "doing your own research" was code for falling down a QAnon-inspired rabbit hole). Adjunct faculty would want to read the *New York Times* and *Inside Higher Ed* articles in the packet we gave them. They'd want to see who they knew on the flyer with pictures and quotes from other adjuncts who signed and then give them a call to talk through what it meant to sign the card. They'd want to look up the website and anything else they could about SEIU, which wasn't known as an education union. They'd want to figure out if being part of a service employees union would further deprofessionalize their job as a professor. Research and not teaching, I explained, is what one learns to do in graduate school. Also, I knew how isolated adjunct faculty felt in their jobs. It could take a couple conversations to believe a union would make a difference. Multiple conversations to get a signed card should be factored into the campaign plan. According to my supervisor, my input wasn't useful. What we had to do was meet the goals for getting the necessary number of cards signed, determined by the supervisor's supervisor, as quickly as possible. Get in, get the card signed, get out.

One-on-one debriefs weren't my favorite thing about my new job. My favorite thing was being part of a team. I had never been on a team, except for horrendous experiences in grade school gym class. While I still didn't like wearing matching T-shirts, which I had to do for union actions, I had appreciation for my coworker relationships that were similar to the roommate relationships I'd once had. Instead of having to figure out the material and political aspects of the job on my own, I had the solidarity of not only working for a union but also being in a union with my coworkers. I worked for SEIU, but I was a member of CWA, Communications Workers of America. My team was willing to get into it with each other about the contract issues and negotiations with our SEIU bosses, and then work out bad feelings over meals or drinks. We learned details of the different worlds we went home to. We met each other's partners, pets, kids, and parents. We hung out at each other's homes. We backed each other up. We cared about each other.

My organizing team was particularly badass. We won more union elections in one year than most longtime organizers did in a career. Mills College was first. Then the San Francisco Art Institute. Then Saint Mary's College in Moraga and Dominican University in San Rafael and, finally, California College of the Arts, where I spent most of my time.

There was a time when I imagined the story arc of this book would mimic Leslie Feinberg's *Stone Butch Blues*. That book, which you should read if you haven't, is a fictionalized account of working-class butch/femme life pre-Stonewall up through the early years of the gay liberation movement. Informed by Feinberg's lived experiences, the main character, Jess, endures decades of gendered violence they wear like a protective cloak against more trauma. Eventually, the cloak hardens into walls, becoming a barrier against love and intimacy. The walls start to crumble only when Jess is safe enough in their own skin to experience healing. Their survival is dependent on their belief and immersion in collective liberation. It's a cathartic, devastating, yet inspiring story that ends in a hopeful, deep exhale.

For a minute, my new job felt like that exhale. I thought I was writing a story that built up into release. I was releasing the mythology I had created around being a formerly battered homeless woman who became a college professor for a new narrative I was going to craft inside the labor movement. It was a story of fighting back as a union organizer and, like Jess, healing old wounds in a righteous fight for dignity and respect.

But, of course, that isn't what happened.

※❦※

The first Saturday that I didn't have to work, I went to my ex's house, the one whose truck I'd borrowed the day of the SEIU interview, to cry. I lay on MJ's blue microfiber couch, tears streaming down my face while they nursed their nine-month-old across the room on the matching loveseat.

"You know that saying, right?" MJ asked. "Unions: the people who brought you the weekend and then took it away." I could always count on them to know the exact amount of snark needed. They grinned at me with the warmth of someone who had held me close while I fought against myself.

※❦※

I had to memorize an organizing conversation script that I was tested on daily: during morning team meetings, in afternoon one-on-ones on the phone with a supervisor, in the evening debrief with a different supervisor. I regularly failed at reciting the script line for line, resulting in humiliating reprimands in front of my coworkers.

Every few days, a new coworker wasn't at the morning meeting. "They're in Sacramento," one of our supervisors would say ominously with no other details. Then the coworker would never come back. I vowed never to go to Sacramento.

I had to keep my phone on 24/7, answer no matter what time it was, and not question working ten-to-twelve-hour days, six or seven days a week. I envied younger coworkers who could afford to leave the job on principle.

Some of my new coworkers who jumped from political campaign to political campaign, union local to union local, taught me that, in case I didn't pass probation, I should use the vision and dental insurance that kicked in immediately. It was so common to not pass probation in these jobs that the insurance conditions were a negotiated benefit in our union contract. Other coworkers taught me how to fill out the weekly work plans, a type of paperwork I hadn't had to do in my three decades of working. Not getting the work plans in was grounds for not passing probation. I learned to take cigarette breaks with my coworkers—even though I didn't smoke—so we could talk away from the constant surveillance of our supervisors, who weaponized our solidarity against us.

Tears perpetually sat on the edges of my eyelashes, not dropping. It was too depressing to cry.

Alone in my hotel room, I wrote:

It breaks my heart to remain underutilized.

Some part of me likes just doing. No part of me likes the hierarchy.

The problem is I don't feel attached to anything. Completely uprooted. The only reason I am here is because of my paycheck.

Years of anticapitalist politics and actions, years of letting art and politics lead, and I am only grounded by a paycheck. I miss the classroom. I miss the values I have around art and politics being a given. I miss trusting people. I miss my dreams and hopes.

They are gone for a paycheck to pay back the government for my dashed dreams.

I missed Von. I missed the cats. Our worlds were so far apart that the phone calls, texts, and video chats were unsatisfying.

My lack of control over my schedule was exactly what I didn't want my work life to be. Inevitably, the health care regimen I had followed the six months before I moved—an extremely limited diet of whole foods that reconstructed my gut flora and lowered my inflammation, and therefore my risk of colon cancer—was out the window. I ate vending machine dinners made up of dairy-full candy bars and glutenous chips.

I drank excessive amounts of Dark and Stormys, a cocktail made up of rum and ginger beer.

On another drunken night, I wrote:

> I pull the covers back, crawl under one leg at a time. I sigh with that sweet sensation of finally being able to rest. Rest my mind, rest my body, rest. On the edge of that sweet sensation is a razor-sharp pain. It cuts my heart and I can't take a breath. It is longing. It is lonely. It is change. It is not having my kitties, the sweet part. It is not having my honey, the sensation part.
>
> It is sensation because I am in tune to his body, his being. I am always aware of where he is. When he will call. When the car will pull up. Now it is all fucked up. I tore us apart.
>
> I tore the family apart.

✿❦✿❦✿

"Jessica, you need to find a place to live. You can't stay at the hotel indefinitely," one of my supervisors said, a month into the job. I added a housing search to my impossible schedule, quickly learning that the $36,600 salary that had sounded like security in New Mexico wasn't anywhere near a livable wage in the Bay Area.

I looked at a one-bedroom apartment in Oakland between MLK Way and Adeline Street. I walked up the wooden stairway into the back door of the apartment, avoiding a massive gap in the floorboards. Omar, the architect/owner, called the empty space "the kitchen." There weren't any appliances. There wasn't drywall over the exposed lath. The big bay windows in the other rooms were beautiful. There was a ton of sunlight. Unfortunately, there were no doors between any of the rooms and there wasn't a toilet in the bathroom.

"Should I come back when you're done?" I asked.

"No. We're taking applications now," he said.

I filled the application out in my hotel room and emailed it back. *You didn't send us your credit report or bank account information*, he replied. I didn't imagine those parts of the application were actually required. I paid thirty-five dollars for a credit report that included my bankruptcy and sent my bank account information to a stranger. I didn't hear back.

I emailed him to follow up. He replied, *Your credit score is under 700. It says very clearly on the application we don't consider applicants with a score under 700.* I didn't imagine that part of the application was real either.

I went to open houses where there were lines of young tech workers streaming in and out. I'd check water pressure while a white tech bro handed over cash to jump the application line. I saw a gorgeous apartment miles away from public transportation where I did my best to bond with Jihoon, the young, gay landlord who worked in Silicon Valley. He thought I was funny but wasn't convinced the cats wouldn't ruin the new carpet he'd put in. Also, he couldn't get over my income and didn't buy my lie about Von already having a job. "Do you have a parent who can cosign the lease?" he asked me more than once.

I called more ads and followed the advice of the butch-sounding person I spoke to who recommended I drive through the neighborhood before I make an appointment. The triplex was tucked behind a cemetery, on a bus line that went to the BART train, and close to MJ and their family. I made an appointment to see it. The landlords were a butch/femme couple who welcomed animals as family members. They were willing to ignore the bankruptcy and low credit rating. "We're Black. We get it," the butch said. I signed the lease. The next week, I checked out of the hotel. Von sent me an air mattress and lamp. MJ's family supplied me with curtains, another lamp, a camping chair, a side table, bedding, and a two-month supply of toilet paper.

❦❦❦

"We have to do house visits this weekend," one supervisor told me when I asked for time off to go back to Santa Fe to finish my move.

"I don't know when you can take time off, maybe next week," another supervisor said.

"We need all hands on deck," she said the next week.

Von and I couldn't plan when to reserve a moving truck, when to tell his friend to take time off work to help him drive the truck to Oakland. I didn't know when to buy a plane ticket.

"What about Memorial Day weekend?" I asked. "We have Memorial Day off, right?"

"Probably. Don't buy a ticket yet," one of my supervisors said.

"It's going to be too expensive for me to purchase soon," I said.

"SEIU will pay for it. It's part of your relocation," she said.

I was slightly less annoyed.

On Memorial Day, Von picked me up at the Albuquerque airport wearing his Charlize-Theron-as-Aileen-Wuornos T-shirt, an anniversary present I had given him. At the house on the ranch, Coco Glamora, who came into the family after Puppy died, rubbed against my legs while Sadie Viva leapt up on the arm of the couch and stretched toward me for kisses. I couldn't stop giggling.

Miranda came over the next day to help me finish packing the house. We strategized adjunct organizing while sweeping glitter and scraps of newspaper out of the corners of my studio. She posted pictures of us on social media with the caption "Mirandica back together again!"

Von and I fought most of the five days I was in town.

We decided I should take Sadie Viva and Coco Glamora back to Oakland with me. I'd be less lonely, and he'd be less worried I was setting up a life without him.

We bought the required harnesses and leashes and squeezed both cats into one airline-approved animal travel case. Waiting to board the plane in Albuquerque, I reached into the case to rub the antianxiety tincture from the holistic vet into their fur. Sadie hissed. Coco's green eyes were giant black marbles.

On the plane, I took an aisle seat then stored the carrying case in front of the middle one to prevent anyone from sitting there. A dude in an expensive-looking jacket pointed at the window seat. I pointed to the few inches of the cat carrying case sticking out. He shrugged and climbed over it, leaned his head against the window, and fell asleep. Periodically, the cats' case shook and swayed. Tufts of fur flew out and rolled down the aisle of the plane like tumbleweeds. When I heard howling, I opened the zipper a tiny bit to pet them. Sadie bit me for the first and only time in her life.

✿❀❁❃❉

Von arrived in Oakland a month later. I was working all the time. We couldn't explore the Bay Area or settle into our new home together. I was never around to help Von get situated. We fought all the time.

Von got a job as a cook at the Levi Strauss headquarters in San Francisco's Financial District. He had to catch a bus to the Fruitvale BART station at 5 a.m., in the dark. The bus was unreliable, so he often had to walk a few more blocks in the early morning darkness to catch a

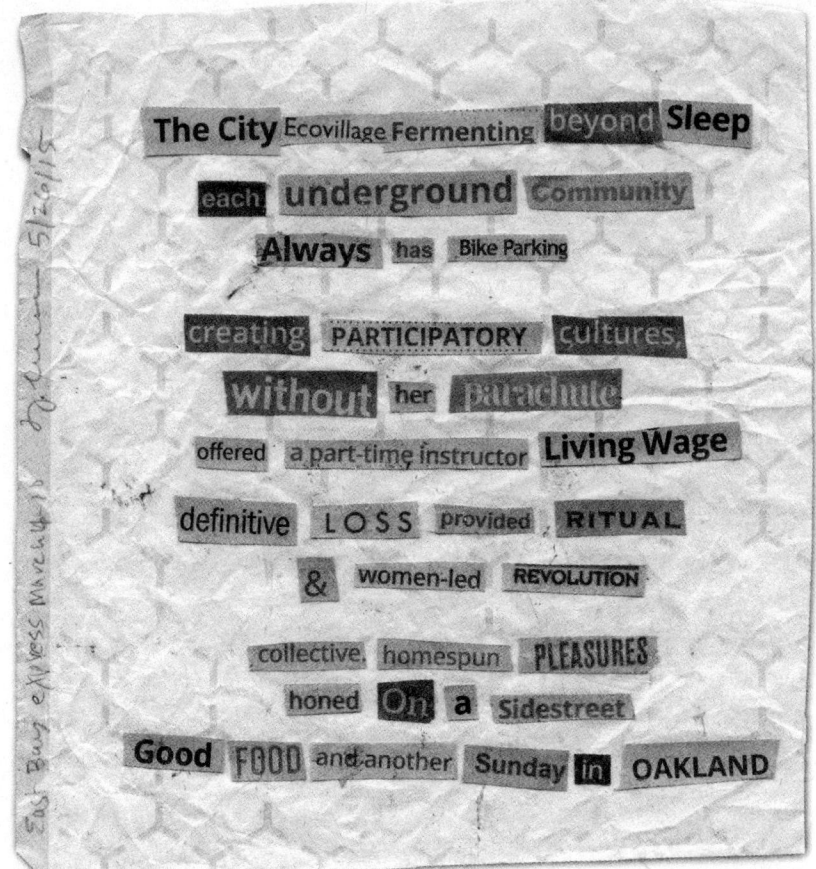

The City Ecovillage Fermenting beyond Sleep

each underground Community

Always has Bike Parking

creating PARTICIPATORY cultures,

without her parachute

offered a part-time instructor Living Wage

definitive LOSS provided RITUAL

& women-led REVOLUTION

collective homespun PLEASURES

honed On a Sidestreet

Good FOOD and another Sunday in OAKLAND

Random Note: *Another Sunday in Oakland*, **newsprint on foil sandwich wrapper**

bus on a busier street. Levi's advertised free shuttles from the Financial District BART station to their headquarters as a perk for their employees. Except the shuttles didn't start early enough or go late enough for the cooks, maintenance crew, and groundskeepers working first shift or last shift. Von's psyche and body were frayed from constant exposure to the worst parts of the extremes of the Bay Area post-recession economy. The excitement he'd felt about moving to the storied queer city was subsumed by the stares he endured from the tech bros that had replaced the San Francisco queers.

I was scared Von would be queer-bashed getting to and from work. I was scared my death on the freeway was inevitable driving between house visits, especially if I turned the steering wheel sharply into oncoming traffic, a constant urge I had to fight. I was scared I wouldn't pass probation and there was no answer for *What then?*

I collected copies of the *East Bay Express*, the free weekly paper.

I cut out words and glued them onto the inside of a clean foil burger wrapper that Von had snagged from his job.

CHAPTER TWENTY-THREE

Mirandica

I think I fucked up again, I texted to Miranda while I lay on my couch after another twelve-hour day, trying not to disturb Von, who had to wake up in three hours to take a bus, a train, and a trolley to work.

Hell no! You're a hero to all the adjuncts! she texted back. Miranda was always awake, no matter what time I was done with work. *I'm going to quit my job and come out there!*

Lol. I wish, I texted.

The next day, Miranda texted me her fantasy about us organizing together in the Bay Area. She'd live in the tiny room across from our bathroom that we'd set up as an art space but never had time to be in. She'd send out radical missives on social media while I organized on campuses. We'd burn down higher ed, rebuilding it into a site of just employment and free education.

Lol. I wish, I texted again.

A week later she texted, *Should I bring my vacuum cleaner?*

Sure! We don't have one! I texted back as I drove to another address on my list. The local had culled the list from poorly kept HR records, voter registration records, and social media pages. The addresses weren't vetted and may or may not have been where the adjunct faculty currently lived. The list was all I had to go on to meet my daily signed-card goals. Fantasizing with Miranda was a fun distraction from the near impossibility of my task and stuffing all my feelings with more and more gut-expanding, inflammation-producing fried-food nuggets.

What about my animals? I don't want to leave Murry and Ajax in Santa Fe, she texted, referring to her fluffy black-and-white cat and her sweet, calm dog.

Duh, I replied.

OK, I'll be there January 10th! Miranda texted.

Lol. I wish, I texted back.

For real! I quit! I'm driving out to live with you!

Wait. What? For how long? I replied.

Forever! she replied. *Mirandica lives!*

I wasn't ready for that.

Von and I were barely getting by financially, barely past every little annoyance blowing up into a huge fight. There was no way having another person in the house was a good idea. Especially someone who didn't have a job or savings and needed our financial and emotional support. Except one of our relationship agreements was that we would always open our home to friends in need of a place to stay, honoring our own experiences of homelessness. Ready or not, we didn't say no. Miranda was on her way.

At first it was fun. Miranda and I went to solidarity rallies between SEIU's fast-food worker and adjunct faculty campaigns. Miranda came to the metro area meetings where adjunct faculty from around the Bay Area at different stages of organizing supported each other. She came to art and literary events Von didn't want to go to with me, and she went to restaurants where I couldn't eat with Von. Then the honeymoon phase ended.

Miranda regularly misgendered Von in public, not understanding the insult or safety issues. Worse, according to Von, she drank all his coffee without replacing it. We asked her to talk about sharing household responsibilities, including financial. She avoided the conversation, spending most of her time alone in her room. She blew off a meeting we'd scheduled so she could go on a date with an untrustworthy, sexist asshole she met through my job. That pushed my buttons and my willingness to keep giving her space. It pushed all of Von's buttons. Our home was our haven from the straight world. He didn't want to reschedule, he wanted her out. My stress from our barely-getting-by life was exacerbated by my passive-aggressive pissed-off partner and my passive-aggressive ignorant friend refusing to talk.

The small-town quirkiness I had appreciated about Miranda in Santa Fe became glaring annoyances in Oakland that I responded to poorly. I put unspoken expectations on her she couldn't meet. She'd take her dog for a walk and come back loudly describing our Black and Yemeni neighbors through stereotypes. I didn't have patience for 101 conversations in my own home. I didn't say anything most of the time, which was a different exhaustion.

Miranda was scared of driving in a city but more scared of taking public transportation. She couldn't figure out how to get groceries or go on job interviews without help, so she didn't. While Von and I were gone for twelve to fifteen hours a day getting to and from the jobs rapidly destroying our already fragile sense of hope, Miranda and her pets took over the house in which we hadn't yet had time to unpack and hang our art. Sadie and Coco spent their days hiding in the bedroom, avoiding Ajax and Murry and the furballs Miranda didn't sweep up.

I wish it didn't get so messy.

Through my own pain, I couldn't see how much pain Miranda was in. She kept pushing boundaries; I kept seething without explaining why.

Her neediness shut me down.

My anger shut her down.

We had an explosive fight two months after she moved in that ended with her stuffing her belongings into garbage bags and driving off with Ajax in the middle of the night, leaving Murry behind. Sadie's health was declining, and Murry still in the house wasn't okay. We did our best to find a home for him in the little time we had not working, until weeks had gone by and we had no choice but to surrender him to a shelter. We called every day to make sure he wasn't going to be put down, spending five days constantly debating possibilities of how to keep him. We were completely gutted, even after we got word that he had been adopted.

It was hard to feel the lighter air in the house.

I was tired of grieving so many relationships.

The morning after we won the union election at the California College of the Arts, I woke up hungover from the victory celebration, stretching with joy for not having to work on a Saturday. Enjoying the slow-moving morning of unscheduled time, I pulled up the movie of *The World According to Garp* on the laptop. It was one of Von's favorite books, and he'd been rereading it. I had tried to listen to it in the car during my work-day but couldn't give it enough concentration between traffic, following GPS, getting calls from one of my many supervisors, and crying to one of my coworkers. I decided to surprise him while he was at work and rewatch the movie. I made scrambled eggs with ghee and drank several cups of chai, which made it take longer to get through the movie, since I had to pee a bunch of times.

On one trip to the bathroom, I remembered to turn on my phone. There were twelve messages from family in Chicago. We still didn't speak with any regularity. I assumed it was death. I just wasn't ready. I put the phone back down on the hallway chest and submerged myself in the last twenty minutes of *The World According to Garp*.

The first person I could get a hold of was my cousin, who had to tell me my stepfather had died. It was sudden and unexpected. He didn't feel well, went to the hospital, and died from pulmonary blood clots while in emergency care. My mother was understandably a mess, in shock and terrified to be alone. I surprised myself by getting a flight to Chicago right away. I put in for bereavement time, ignoring the warnings I'd heard from other organizers about people who were let go because they took time off for funerals. I performed normalcy, pretended to be grieving for a dead parent I didn't miss, and was rewarded with time to mourn.

I flew back to Chicago more times over the next several months than I had in decades. My mom didn't know how to manage the smoke-and-mirrors finances my stepfather had created to keep a veneer of middle-class life. My brother and mom were having screaming matches over everything, then calling me to complain about the other. I liked being the hero; it was a new role for me with the family.

Of course, old chaos was present. The guy who had been renting a room in my family's house for a long time, who had become a drinking buddy of my stepfather's, hadn't paid rent for at least a year. The last time I had visited, I traded my benzos for his oxys. Then, in the middle of the night when I got up to pee, I ran into him creeping around the hallway. He staggered and leaned in too close to me, using desperate body postures I was familiar with from bar culture and last-call attempts to hook up. Hypervigilance set in for the rest of that visit. I couldn't sleep or look the dude in the eye, though I was always aware of where he was. With my stepfather's death, it seemed like the perfect time to get another creepy drunk man out of my mom's house.

"He doesn't drink anymore," my mom responded when I said he wasn't a healthy human and shouldn't live in her house.

"He'll hang out with Mom, watch TV with her, keep an eye on her," my brother explained when he arranged for the guy to keep staying there rent-free. Hero or not, my safety still wasn't a factor in the family system.

I understood my brother was overwhelmed. Our mother was placing all the emotional needs she got fulfilled by men onto him. He was willing to figure out her finances but didn't have the capacity for her growing daily demands to assuage her loneliness and fear. I felt for him. She had taken to lashing out physically, angry at him for not being my stepfather. She even tried to push me down the basement stairs during one of my post-death visits. Since my brother was the one who had to deal with things in person, and because of a lot of therapy, I was willing to agree to what he thought was best.

In one more film-noirish twist, my mother made a demand of the renter guy to stay up with her every night watching movies until her antianxiety meds kicked in and she fell asleep. She demanded he accompany her to her bedroom before he went up to his. It didn't go well when he started a new relationship. My mom was pissed. She made his rent-free status contingent on not spending nights or weekends with his girlfriend.

My brother reported these developments to me over dinner and drinks with him and my sister-in-law when I was in town. He had been doing his own therapy and was able to admit seeing some of the family dynamics I had always seen. He stopped upholding family narratives for a while, able to accept the framework of abuse I offered. We bonded as adult siblings for the first time as he was forced to deal with his anger at our mom and I was forced to see her as a complicated and hurt woman. Without my stepfather between us all, I could ease up on my defenses. It was a freeing death.

✿❦❧✿

My legs were jelly. My brain was flipping around, looking for reason. The email subject line was "RIP Marc Sanford." I needed it to be spam that in some sick coincidence had my former Seattle roommate's name on it. A joke about my friend who'd helped me learn to read LA maps, who I'd caught up with last year. He was happy, married, a stepparent, running his own cabinet-making business. With shallow breath, I clicked the message, hoping to get a virus.

Nope. Marc was dead. He'd been murdered on a weekend getaway with his wife.

They were crossing the street when a man in a mental health crisis, driving an SUV, purposefully mowed them down. As he had just done to another person when he'd torn through a thrift store parking lot a few blocks away. Articles said the man's parents had been trying to get him services before he went on a killing rampage, beating his father and family dogs to death with a baseball bat, almost beating his mother to death, setting the house on fire, and then tearing across town in the family vehicle.

Marc's partner survived. Obviously, she was pissed. Her life had been turned upside down. And she was beautifully tough and gracious in her pain when I visited her, holding the trauma of nearly dying, of her partner being killed, in the complex roots of systemic violence. As a health care worker, she was intimately familiar with the failed mental health system. She had to deal with hospital administrators using budget cuts as excuses for staffing shortages, then contracting out unionized jobs to temp agencies that didn't provide proper training to workers. The laws passed, as checks and balances were meaningless politicking. No one had flagged this person's attempt to buy a gun or his refusal to take his meds just before he had his murderous breakdown.

Marc's death flattened me. I didn't feel as gracious as his partner, though I tried to follow her lead. I was mad about feeling helpless inside of the growing, inescapable, never-ending fog of violence. I needed to curl up under a blanket and mourn. Instead, my job required me to stay braced for a fight. Whether it was convincing someone to sign a union authorization card or convincing people to maintain lines in the sand we had drawn against the boss, my job was to uphold false binaries. I'd drive back and forth across the Bay Bridge, overwhelmed by the glittering wealth washing over proliferating tent cities. My grief was barely tempered by news analysis about other workers like me who were earning what should be middle-class salaries but couldn't survive.

Marc's death shook me enough to recognize I was way too far away from my creative core. When I couldn't stop imagining turning my steering wheel and slamming into the car next to me, I realized I had to a find a creative outlet before I became a story Von had to tell. *Fuck it.* The short essays about being an adjunct professor who became a labor organizer I'd been writing, they should be a book.

❧❦❧

Ariel, the protagonist in Ariel Gore's novel *We Were Witches*, sees the shape of a penis when her writing instructor draws Freytag's Pyramid on the board during a lesson on narrative structure. Rising action into a climax. Falling action into a resolution. Ariel (the character) wonders what happens if your arc doesn't rise like a penis, if your writing career (I'll add: art career) doesn't follow cishetpatriarchal norms. Ariel (the character and the author) writes an inverted storyline shaped like a V.

You know, vaginal.

Ariel (the author), in a manuscript writing workshop I took with her, gave us an assignment to draw the shape of our story arc. I made a messy collage that didn't have an identifiable shape. It reminded me of the time my therapist in Seattle asked me to close my eyes and imagine the gender of the person I saw myself with in the future, a man or a woman—the understood choices in language at the time. I closed my eyes and didn't see an identifiable gender. Genitalia have never defined my destiny.

Stories about resiliency in the face of trauma, conquering adversity, rising out of the ashes—these stories value independence and individuality over interdependence and collectivity. The story I've been trying to tell for so long is neither penile nor vaginal; it's intestinal. It twists and turns, tucks inside of itself and wraps around, gets stuck and unstuck, takes in, expels out, connects to nourishment, energy, mood, immunity, and pleasure. It can be uncomfortable, embarrassing, and funny. It's longer than expected. The end isn't obvious unless you're willing to poke around and find it.

Come home as soon as you can, Von texted. *Sadie.*

All through 2016, as her eyesight worsened, her hearing lessened, her energy waned, and her senior moments were constant, I made Sadie promise not to leave me. I couldn't handle losing her the year MAGA politics took over everything. The best cat ever, she waited until 2017.

When Von texted me, I was working an election for union officers at the local's largest San Francisco chapter. The chapter had a history of contested elections. It was tense. I didn't care. I had to get home. I texted the person supervising the election, who also had a cat she loved more than any human. I told her my cat was in the dying process.

She replied, *I'll find someone to cover your shift. Don't leave yet. I'll text you soon.*

An hour later, Von called. "Really, come home now," he said.

I texted my supervisor, *I have to get home now.*

She replied, *I don't have anyone to cover you.*

I texted, *My cat is dying.*

She replied, *DO. NOT. LEAVE.*

Moving numbly, I told my coworker that I had a family emergency. I gave them my member list and got my car from the parking lot. I drove through jelly, the cars in front of me blurred. I couldn't see the Bay Bridge as I crossed it. I must have remembered to call my staff union rep, fearful of retaliation for having something in my life more vital than work, because a coworker and cat mama friend knocked on the door five minutes after I got home. Von and I tended to Sadie while my union sibling calmed down the elections supervisor over the phone and found people to cover my election shifts for the next few days.

I held Sadie all night. I held her while the mobile vet injected her with death drugs. I held her stiffening body, tears falling. Grief and fear. Loss and pain. I cried for a time I couldn't remember. A time when I didn't always feel broken and terrified.

The election went smoothly.

That supervisor put me on her shit list.

I stopped feeling anything good.

A rep position was available. I applied for it. Anything to get out of the organizing department. Fascinatingly, only two years into this career, I was an extremely experienced candidate who got the job. Instead of organizing new unions for adjunct faculty teaching at private colleges, I represented already unionized public health workers. Organizing was part of the job, but instead of focusing on winning a first union election, the main objective was enforcing the existing union contract for workers at San Francisco General Hospital* who ran meals between the cafeteria and patients' rooms, who stored organs in freezers for transplants, and who filled prescriptions.

My rep position included social services workers in the Tenderloin, a historic queer neighborhood, and a neighborhood where drug use and sex work happened openly. Single-room-occupancy hotels, liquor stores,

---

* San Francisco General Hospital, or SFGH, has a storied history in the early HIV/AIDS crisis, developing compassionate care models in the face of homophobic responses to the epidemic. While I was a union rep there, Mark Zuckerberg and Priscilla Chan, his doctor wife who'd once worked at SFGH, gave the hospital a $75 million donation. SFGH officially changed its name to Zuckerberg San Francisco General Hospital and Trauma Center, or ZSFG. Ick.

and strip clubs dominated the area that has inspired noir literature and where the pre-Stonewall, trans-women-led Compton's Cafeteria riot occurred. It was hard not to be in awe and on edge walking through the syringe-littered, piss-smelling, densely populated streets where San Francisco's most marginalized residents did their best to survive by all means necessary. It was harder not to be shocked by the shiny new businesses that served the thousands of Twitter employees working at the nearby newly built headquarters. At ground zero of the post–Great Recession widening wealth gap, the grievances were about racist policies at the social service agencies and going on medical leave because of increasingly stressful workloads.

I won a case for a Black nurse whose son had been murdered. The crime had been all over the media. A coworker was loudly talking about the murder on the nurse's first day back after a six-month medical leave. She had a panic attack and ran to the bathroom without following protocol for leaving her station. Her supervisor gave her a disciplinary warning and then discipline when it happened again. She and I held the hospital to account for their Black Lives Matter rhetoric, demanding they apply their messaging to policies. We won her case.

I won another case for a queer, Black social worker whose partner had a heart attack and died in front of her in the middle of a fight. While she was on medical leave, healing, one of her clients died. She went to the single-room-occupancy hotel where he had lived to mourn with his neighbors. Another worker reported seeing her at the SRO. The labor relations manager who heard grievances, a gay Latino man who had been at the hospital since the height of the AIDS epidemic, obtained security camera footage to prove the social worker had been socializing at the SRO during her medical leave. I wanted to get along with this guy and be able to negotiate solutions together, but he was dickishly patronizing. I moved her case through to a higher level with more neutral grievance officers.

These two cases were how I learned about medical leaves and the possibility of getting a break from work to grieve and heal while still being paid.

My supervisor in the rep department, who had been part of South African antiapartheid uprisings, had an ex who was an academic. This supervisor understood the consequences for college faculty lacking job security better than my organizing department supervisors. He told me that when he'd been a rep and been covered by the staff union contract, it had sabbatical-type leaves that he thought should be brought back. He may have been lying to me to gain my trust, but he seemed genuinely interested that I was writing a book about having been an adjunct professor who now worked in the labor movement. "That's exactly what the sabbaticals should be for," he said. I strategized how to get his support for a leave when I was accepted into a two-month residency in New Mexico at the Santa Fe Art Institute.

I searched for an opening for a conversation with him in between members' job crises and the labor movement crisis of *Janus*, an impending anti-union Supreme Court ruling that would allow union members representation without having to pay union dues. The opening didn't happen with my supervisor. I wasn't going to miss the opportunity to have free housing in Santa Fe while I wrote and made art. I found the opening with my therapist, who agreed I needed a break from work. She wrote the medical recommendation, and I signed up for state disability to make up the rest of my salary for the month. I held a bake sale to help cover costs, selling vegan cannabis treats Von had made. I arranged to be at the residency in October and January, giving me time to figure out how to pay rent and bills for the second month.

Von drove out to Santa Fe with me. We drove up to the ski basin to see the aspens change colors and ate at our favorite Ayurvedic restaurant. He visited his best friend and then he flew home, leaving the car with me. The first three days, I attended a weekend writing retreat Ariel (the author) hosted at her Santa Fe home. I wrote with the community of queer, feminist writers drawn to Ariel while setting up my room and studio at the residency. I bought a pass for a parks district swimming pool on Alta Vista, across from the vet where I used to take Sadie. I wrote and made art and swam every day. It felt like a dream.

❀❀❀

"Jessica. Miranda's dead." Leanne, an adjunct-activist I knew from social media had called to make sure I knew, to find out if I knew, what had happened.

I didn't.

I was spending time at the community college and cafés where Miranda and I had become friends. I was writing about our friendship and activism, our falling-out and slow rebuilding of trust, sinking into the spectrum of emotions I had about her. Dead? No. Uh-uh.

My phone rang again. It was Jason from AAUP. "What the fuck, Jess?" Jason and Miranda had kept up the fight against Monty after I moved to Oakland.

"I don't know, I don't know," was all I could say.

I called Von. He had also just seen the fundraiser Miranda's daughter had posted to social media that had spurred the calls and messages. Her daughter needed money to get Miranda's body from Boston, where she'd died, to scatter her ashes on the California Central Coast. It was Miranda's favorite place she'd ever lived. She had told me stories about being a small child enchanted with the lapping ocean waves, the rocky coast an escape from her parents' fighting.

I heaved with sobs, choked on my shallow breath.

I slipped out of my residency room and into my car, drove over to the pool and swam for my life. I felt the weightlessness of the water cradling me as I dipped down, held my breath, pushed my body forward. I came up out of the water gulping big deep breaths. I went back down into the quiet blue, my tears blending with the salinized warmth. I felt every inch of life meeting every inch of death, Miranda's face in front of me when I looked ahead to the wall marking the end of a lap, the point to reach and then turn around again, to keep going without thought. I felt the grief pulling me down, severing me from other human beings once again.

What the fuck, Miranda?

❧

She'd left our house and driven up to Portland to stay with a friend. Then she drove up to Seattle for an organizer job on the SEIU higher ed campaign. We texted about her excitement on the campaign, but never about what had happened between us. I had learned she didn't have the capacity to delve into and shift difficult emotions through processing conversations. I was willing to move on without settling what happened, but I didn't fully trust the friendship, never really took my defenses down with her again. I don't feel guilty about that decision; I feel wrecked about all the brokenness that got in our way.

Miranda told me about a male supervisor in Seattle who was sexually harassing another adjunct-activist, that he was known for harassing female staff and members. She told me she had spoken out about it and was disciplined. She was taken off the adjunct union campaign and sent

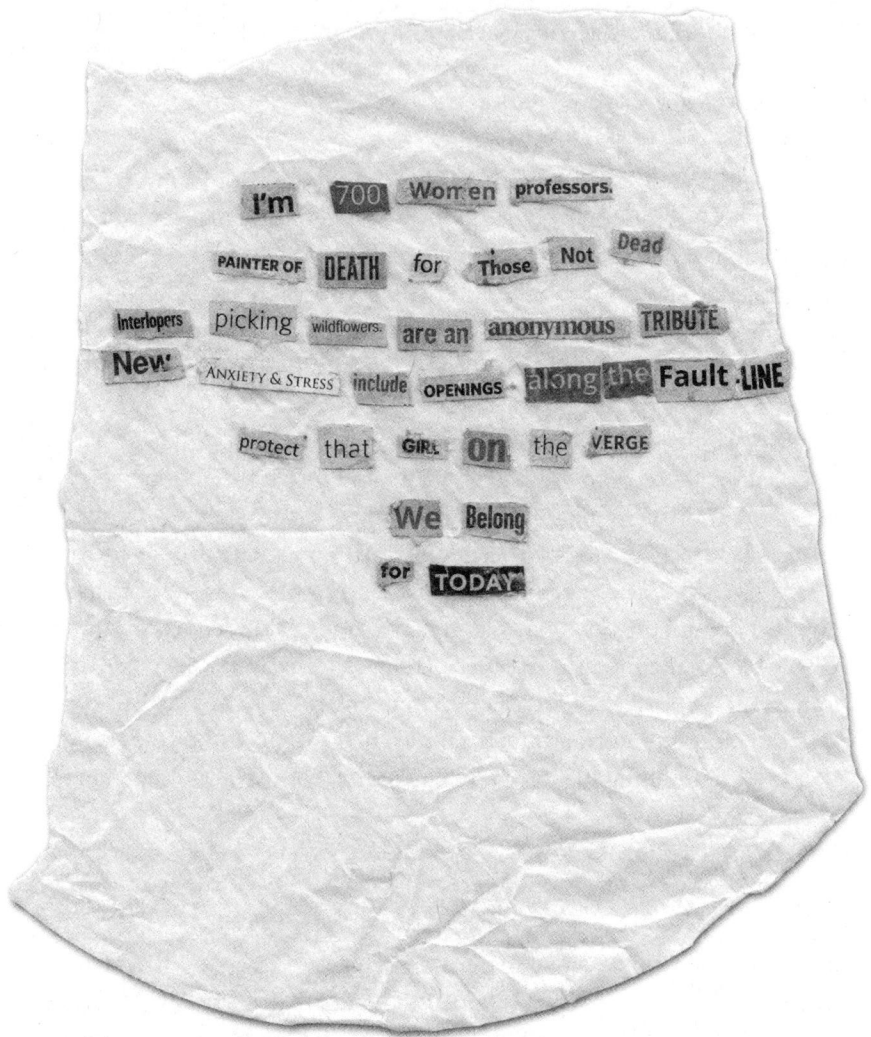

Random Note: *700 Women Professors*, newsprint on tissue-paper packaging

to the equivalent of Sacramento. I was proud of Miranda for speaking out, reminded of our shared values and shared anger, the things we had first connected over.

She called me when she was let go. She said she couldn't give me details because she had to sign a nondisclosure agreement to get severance pay. Her voice was audibly terrified. She sounded confused, paranoid that she was being tracked by SEIU. She may not have been wrong to be so fearful, but she had lost all anchoring to the reality she'd built her life around. Higher education had failed her. The labor movement had devastated her. Her physical and mental health were deteriorating. Without health care, she used whatever she could to medicate the diagnosed and undiagnosed demons crowding her head. Miranda drove out to Boston to live with another friend and never found her footing again. A new health crisis landed her in a hospital. She had new, exorbitant medical debt on top of her old, exorbitant student debt. She reached out for help, stopped, then died.

CHAPTER TWENTY-FOUR

Another Job Search

Two days after Miranda died, #metoo went viral. I lay on my bed in my room at the residency reading social media posts. I sat at the table in my studio cutting out and gluing down words while listening to podcasts with people finally, freely talking about well-known predatory, abusive assholes. SEIU's sexual harassment cover-ups made the news. The lesbian president had been protecting one of her top male leaders. Someone I'd briefly worked with married the dude in a last-ditch effort to squash the story days before the news broke. She had been blatantly sleeping her way into promotions with the power cadre of untrustworthy dyke leadership when I knew her. She tweeted "love wins," alongside pictures of her het shotgun wedding. Her nonsensical politics perfectly summed up SEIU's unprincipled leadership.

I had knots in my chest thinking about all the uncomfortable, tangible undercurrents of sex and power at that workplace. A supervisor once chastised me for something I had said in a meeting she wasn't at, getting her knowledge from a coworker she was sleeping with. That coworker would be given the best driving route on the days he fed the supervisor information she could use against one of us. Another supervisor had gotten a former rep pregnant. Everyone knew. He got a promotion; she was forced to leave. At another SEIU local, another adjunct friend working on the higher ed campaign called out yet another predatory supervisor known for violent outbursts. My friend was removed from the campaign, sent to a Southern California equivalent of Sacramento. The supervisor they called out later transferred to the Oakland office. I told trusted supervisors about a member's misogynistic behavior toward me, about my discomfort with a member who told stories about getting blow jobs in the back of a building we were mapping, about a member accused of assault that none of us wanted to be alone with. Every one of my trusted supervisors said, "Toughen up. It's just union culture."

I looked out my window at the desert, at the cholla cacti and Sandia Mountains I had left almost four years ago, remembering how I'd hoped that a job with financial stability would also bring emotional stability. I knew I would have to leave my job.

I swam every day before I left the residency. Submerging my whole body in water was the only thing that calmed my nervous system. I cut words out of the *Santa Fe Reporter*, the class schedule at the community college, grocery store circulars, art house film schedules. I digitized the tiny Random Notes and had them printed as big as possible, as big as my grief. I wrote words for this book that may or may not be the ones you're reading.

Von flew out so we could drive back to Oakland together. We stopped at the Grand Canyon. Snow flurries blew past us. I leaned into the wind seven thousand feet above sea level watching raptors hunt and osprey fly in communal formations, separating to chase each other in twos, threes, and fours, then join back together with the rest.

I didn't know how I'd face another job search.

❦

A certified letter from SEIU arrived in the mail the day after I got home from the residency. I didn't pass the probationary period for the rep job. I'd have to return to the organizing department. Technically, it was illegal to change my assignment while I was on a disability leave. Technically, there wasn't a clear probationary period for the rep position. Technicalities didn't matter once the union wanted to get rid of me. They were experts at making workers feel scared and alone. It's the very condition we tell workers a union will change.

My coworker who helped me get through Sadie's death had gone through the same thing two months earlier. We'd both been visible activists during our staff union contract negotiations. We'd leveraged our real relationships with member-leaders and had them wear buttons that said *No Hypocrisy at 1021* during a member convening. When the organizing director wrote up a different coworker for wearing one of our red CWA staff union T-shirts to a May Day demonstration instead of a purple SEIU T-shirt, we made a poster that said *SEIU 1021 Targets Workers*. At the next organizing department meeting, the director ominously stated that everyone had to be 100 percent with SEIU or we should plan to lose our jobs. Our bosses were pissed.

They couldn't outright fire me, because I had passed my original probation, so they made up a policy saying there was a six-month probationary period for the rep position. They were building a case for dismissal by putting disciplinary notes in my HR file. To make sure I got the message, my new work assignment was a one-hundred-miles-a-day round-trip drive to a remote campaign in Sacramento.

Every morning before work, I swam at the outdoor parks department pool. I submerged my body in the warm water and emerged into the cold air, wrapping my swim jacket around me to stay warm in cloudy forty-five-degree Oakland weather. At work, I smiled and performed my duties as well as I always had, surprising my immediate supervisor. In honor of Miranda, I made an exit plan and a promise to myself not to let the labor movement destroy me.

✿❀✿❀✿

Aisha died when I got back from the residency. She was another SEIU organizer I'd bonded with over our disappointment with the labor movement's hypocrisy. Aisha had a lot of union horror stories she was working on letting go of as she also dealt with breast cancer.

When her mother could watch her youngest kid, Aisha would hang out at our house and pet the kitties while exploring different weed strains with Von, looking for the best one for her pain. Her mom, who I was closer to in age, joined us when she could. She was a big fan of Von's cannabis baking.

During the 2016 presidential election, Aisha and I partnered up for precinct walking as much as possible. She and I would clandestinely pick up her daughter from school and then go to her mom's house before we went door knocking. Our immediate supervisors, Black women with children, wouldn't allow Aisha—a single Black mother—the time she needed to deal with childcare. The supervisor above those two, a Black woman who had survived breast cancer, made it unnecessarily difficult for Aisha to schedule her cancer treatments during work hours. All of these supervisors ignored Aisha's requests not to work with the person who had been disciplined for sexually harassing her at her last job and was leading the precinct walking out of the Central Labor Council office. Unprincipled as usual, our supervisors wrote up Aisha for bringing her kid to work on a Saturday, a Saturday that had been scheduled last minute. When there was a second mandatory, last-minute Saturday shift and Aisha had to bring her daughter to work a second time, they let her go. Though what they said was that she didn't pass probation. It was heartless.

Aisha and her family still came over to our house regularly after she was fired. Then I was hanging out with her in different hospitals. And then in her hospice bed. And then she was gone.

We moved out of the dyke-owned place after Von opened the front door to go to work one day and stepped out onto nothing, barely catching himself before he fell into an open space where our front steps were supposed to be. It was the last straw of two years of constant construction the landlords were doing to flip the property. Building debris was always scattered around the walkways. We rarely had warning when a construction crew would be on the property, so we lost a lot of plants and porch art. Our new place was just around two corners, closer to the liquor store and across from the pretty greenway and stream running behind the row of houses on High Street. The new landlord was an artist who only charged us $800 cash to move in. He didn't ask to see our hand-to-mouth bank balance or ask us to pay for another embarrassing credit check. So we ignored the strange unpermitted structure where he lived in the back yard and the obvious illegality of the rental. We ignored the dog shit in the yard that he never cleaned up, the mushrooms growing on the side of the bathtub from a leak behind the bathroom wall he wouldn't fix, and the black mold in the cracked bottle-glass windows.

We paid the new slumlord $400 a month more than the last one. During the two years we lived in that moldy, dark house, while my job at SEIU morphed into a nightmare, Von ended up getting injured on his job as a cook at UC Berkeley. He went out on workers' comp, like most of his coworkers had to do at some point. The university purposefully understaffed the kitchen that turned out nine hundred meals a shift, deciding it was cheaper to pay out for workers' comp than to have a safe working environment. We were ready to leave Oakland.

We taped a piece of chart paper to the wall as if outlining a campaign. The first thing we did was list out the pluses and minuses of our current situation:

+ J makes twice as much as the salary we moved for 3½ years ago.
– Our rent is 50% more in Oakland than in Santa Fe, and rising.
– V will be on workers' comp for an unknown number of months.
+ V's union contract will protect his job and provide for disability while he recovers.
+ We have more stable income and health care than ever before.
– The cost of living in the Bay Area puts us further in debt every month.
– Sadie died here.
– Trump is president.
+ Activism is effective in the Bay Area.
– We are miserable.

On another piece of chart paper, we wrote out our dreams:

Art and writing come first.
Leave the country.
Stop working.
End capitalism, colonialism, racism, misogyny, trans/homophobia, cisheteropatriarchy.

It was the same dream I'd had as far back as I could remember, the same dream we had together for as long as we'd been together. We looked over the charts every night after I got home from work, sitting on the couch petting Coco and Gracie, our foster-fail kitty that had recently joined our family. We brainstormed how to have health care and make money, how to go toward a future we wanted instead of running away as fast as we could from another hellacious situation.

We were dreaming of living in Spain when two different friends in the labor movement called to tell me about rep jobs in other higher education unions. I filled out the applications just in case.

I got hired.

My guts twisted and churned through familiar paths while Von and I packed our things to move to my new job.

In Sacramento.

CHAPTER TWENTY-FIVE

Held Hostage Inside a World I Wanted to Destroy

It's been almost six months since I've had a period. Another six months and I'll officially be menopausal. Fingers crossed. Crossing my fingers is about all I can do these days.

❦❦❦

The first year of COVID, I couldn't write anything. Nothing mattered. Time was confusing. Death kept happening.

Teresia, a friend in New Mexico, died from COVID, leaving behind two young kids.

My dad's wife died after a decade-long Alzheimer's decline.

Leah died. Leah, an artist to her core who shared her mom, Cleo, with me when I needed a mentor to apply to graduate school. She lived on her own terms in ways I wish I was brave enough to do.

During the second year of COVID, my anxiety was at an all-time high. I had to take extra precautions because my IBD meds made me immunocompromised. I watched from a safe distance physically, while feeling eons of collective emotional unsafety as new generations of activists poured into the streets responding to the racist police murders of Breonna Taylor, George Floyd, and so many more names to say. Mass shooting after mass shooting by white supremacists shook awake my old fears from the night Bryce shot off the gun. Back then, no one talked about the consequences of angry young men having access to assault rifles, whatever side of the political spectrum they were on. Back then, there weren't any studies pointing to the lethal nexus of broken men who commit domestic abuse and are extremely distrustful of the government. I sank into it, processing the past while living a much less romantic version of the dystopic future that had seemed so much further away.

Diviana, a friend from the Highways Performance Space community, OD'd. She was sixty. Her death was a reminder that queer femmes don't always escape the past, no matter how hard we try.

I managed to leave the house about once a month. I'd make my trip to the drugstore, an outing of great significance, singing loudly to Sia or Janelle or Patti as I drove. I'd call Zoë or Mich and then I'd go into the store and search for the pee pads and curl cream that weren't always on the shelves because: *Supply chain. Abundance of caution.* If it wasn't the drugstore, it was getting my hair done by Jaime, who could do safe visits alone in her salon with our masks on. These visits were a release within the wreckage. Jaime and I collaborated on intricate cuts and color. She'd cut my bangs hyper short and ragged when I asked her to "make them look like a chipmunk chewed them off." She'd razor-clip half my hair with a number three guard to highlight the silvery roots. My top layers of long, salt-and-pepper hair were dyed black except for the bottom inch, which was a deep red to make my hair look like a brush dipped into paint. In the summer, while the fires burned, I decided to fade the black into different colors of a sunset.

"I got the call," Von said as I walked in the door and took off my mask. "Also, your hair looks nice."

"What call?" I asked, washing my hands for twenty seconds in the kitchen sink.

"The Crosby call," he said. "She's dead."

Crosby, Von's ex.

The Walmart name tag.

The queer girl in femme drag.

The woman who never let go of Von and was always a factor in our lives, who was always loved by Von in a way that pulled him into her addiction more than our relationship could sometimes handle.

Crosby had one goal in the past two years: to drink herself to death. She achieved it.

There's no end to death or grief.

There can be healing if we live long enough.

I'm so glad I'm not a professor today.

Higher education is a different place than it was when I created the fantasy of *Formerly homeless woman becomes college professor*. It was never a benign institution. Those don't exist. But it did once provide teaching jobs with a stable income, health care, a retirement plan, often a union, and a lot of other perks if one was willing to keep the system churning along. Even if one did challenge parts of the system, tenure was a protection. That kind of security, that kind of stability, allows for a lot of breathing room to continually push the political and aesthetic edges of culture. Which is exactly why far-right, religious conservatives have gone after higher ed (another statement even truer as this book goes to publication than when I first wrote that sentence).

I graduated from high school in the Reagan era, the beginning of the shift into neoliberalism. By the time I got to college, the AIDS epidemic was full-blown. Policymakers debated isolating gay men into something akin to Japanese incarceration camps. I had an internship at the New Museum in New York in 1988. I was immersed in art openings and artist talks, in town halls held in galleries where people shaping the art world also shaped the intellectual left. I met people bringing the New York ACT UP chapter into form, including the artist who designed the pink triangle that still represents HIV/AIDS activism to this day. An image of the space where the talk took place floats through my mind, along with snippets of how Gran Fury, the ACT UP artists' collective, used design and advertising principles rather than fine art principles to create the impactful image. They wanted shock value when they inverted the pink triangle that queers living under the Nazi regime were forced to wear. When I walked into my shifts at the New Museum library, I would pass Gran Fury's *Let the Record Show*, a temporary window installation that's now a historical art piece. Another artist collective, Group Material, hosted a series of talks at the New Museum called "Democracy." I heard people speak who don't mean much to anyone today, many who are long gone, but were instrumental in creating the categories of "artist-activist" and "culture worker." They introduced me to thinking of art and education as intertwined hubs, as a space where artists worked collaboratively toward transformative social change.

Almost two decades later along this intestinal path, I was a graduate student at UC Irvine, studying with some of the people who had been a part of the "Democracy" series, who'd had essays in the book series that came out of the project. I was teaching a visual culture course, an artist-activist on my way to being an art professor. The course was a requirement for undergraduate art students, a studio class where they could work in any medium, making art based on art theory and art history readings. I loved putting together syllabi based on what I thought they should know going into the world, whether or not they ever made art again. One of my students was an openly born-again Christian. She was back in school, completing the degree she had dropped out of when she'd gotten pregnant and married, around the same time I was in New York. This student engaged thoughtfully in the class, expressing both her discomfort and curiosity with Robert Mapplethorpe's fetishistic photographs of gay male kink. She intelligently considered the reasons behind Yolanda López's feminist reinterpretation of the Virgen de Guadalupe, Renee Cox's *Hottentot Venus*, Cindy Sherman's monstrous self-portraits. She was moved by Félix González-Torres's poetic images of grief over his partner's AIDS-related death, moved that González-Torres had also died of an AIDS-related death.

The day it was this student's turn to do her site-specific performance, she set up a single chair in the middle of the classroom. She asked me to sit on the chair, which I did. She asked if she could blindfold me. I hesitantly said yes. She had the class observe from the outside as she stood in front of me and read from a piece of paper she was holding. She expressed fears that had been triggered for her by the images we had viewed in class, intermingled with biblical quotes.

My skin crawled.

I had trouble taking deep breaths in.

I felt like I was being held hostage inside a world I wanted to destroy.

It was hard not to cry.

It was hard not to interrupt what I understood as dangerous beliefs.

My student ended her recital with the question I used to start every class discussion: "What do you think?"

It was a skillful recreation of how she experienced learning from me. At the end of the semester, she got an A. I got a heartfelt thank-you note.

Today, a student with those beliefs would have been trained to go to my bosses—the university administration—and report the unsafe learning environment they felt they were in. Those bosses would have done a performative investigation that would have resulted in disciplinary measures against me. The autonomy I had in the classroom, as a graduate student and as an adjunct professor who believed in education as a liberatory experience, allowed me to set up the classroom as a temporary experimental-learning zone. There, I facilitated knowledge exchange that gave space to differences and allowed for collective, emergent, transformative adventures. That autonomy has been lost to a carceral culture of surveillance and punishment.

Working in faculty unions, my colleagues and I repped numerous professors being disciplined for showing images much tamer than what I used to show. Many of my union colleagues would call those faculty members idiots for thinking those visual materials were appropriate in a college classroom. The reps agreed with the students making complaints and the administrators doling out punishment that the materials were offensive. Never mind that the instructor was trained in the field to make pedagogical choices about educational lessons. It came down to personal offense and a mediated culture where everyone being an expert on everything doesn't create an even playing field, it creates conditions in which the conservative assholes win. No matter how progressive a rep believed their politics were, I saw so many of them get awfully conservative up against queer sexuality, or any other topic where artists were doing what they do: pushing culture to its edges. As you might imagine, the union didn't always effectively mitigate punishment. Of course, faculty members did fuck up. There were plenty of faculty who clumsily stepped into a generational difference about language and meaning that could have been avoided with patience and respect for their students. Instead of battling it out, they could have listened and found meaning in the tension. But the ultimate issue was that university administrators catered to students and the government or parent footing the tuition bill. Faculty were an afterthought, disposable and contingent. Something not worth protecting through tenure and academic freedom. These are ideological decisions administrators began making decades ago, which they hid behind budget lines and the excuse of "just doing their job."

Never one to just do my job, as a union rep I was direct with members. I'd name what they did as racist, transphobic, misogynist, or out of step with changing cultural norms and unnecessary to keep in their syllabi. But then I'd fight for their job.

A grievance win in higher education was rare. The process could take months (unusual) to years (usual). In that time, department chairs, deans, and upper administration could have changed sometimes several times over. Often, a faculty member retired or moved on before a resolution was made. Equally as often, the faculty member became an embittered persona non grata struggling every step of the way for professional advancement. Working in unions made it very clear that punitive measures don't change harmful behaviors. They create death-adjacent grief, trauma with no communal outlet, and highly stressed, chronically ill worker-zombies.

CHAPTER TWENTY-SIX

Women of Her Generation

As I've been writing this book, baristas, warehouse workers, software programmers, rideshare drivers, and student workers fed up with being worker-zombies have won new unions in work sectors once thought impossible to organize. Rolling strikes have been organized by teachers, health care workers, autoworkers, package delivery drivers, writers, actors, and graduate students. It's a common reality to be exhausted from working multiple precarious jobs that don't provide benefits or pay enough for basic needs.

Work Won't Love You Back: How Devotion to Our Jobs Keeps Us Exploited, Exhausted, and Alone by Sarah Jaffe captures the nightmare work has become for most everyone. Focusing on jobs that are culturally feminized work, Jaffe wrote a feminist, punk anthem eviscerating toxic mythologies of love. The example for nonprofit sector exploitation is an anti-union campaign waged by the management of Planned Parenthood of the Rocky Mountains—the same Planned Parenthood where I interviewed for a position at a nonnegotiable thirteen dollars an hour. They hired an expensive union-busting law firm and leveraged the first Trump administration's anti-union policies to try to overturn—unsuccessfully—a fairly won union election.

During the first years of the COVID pandemic, a government safety net provided stimulus checks, student debt pauses, and eviction holds. Health care workers, considered essential, were applauded but not given hazard pay. Burnt out and traumatized, they left their jobs. In 2021, forty-seven million workers quit their jobs. According to the Bureau of Labor Statistics, midcareer professional workers between thirty and forty-five years old were the fastest to resign and reassess work-life balance. With schools and childcare shut down, two million women left the job market, making apparent that raising children is still gendered and unpaid.

The immediate response to being fed up with work was to organize. Between October 2021 and March 2022, the National Labor Relationship Board reported a 57 percent increase in petitions for union elections. Renowned union organizer Jane McAlevey observed, in one of her last articles before she died from cancer at only fifty-nine years old, "The tight labor market signaled by the Great Resignation—when so many workers took individual action, leaving jobs and employers they hated—has converged with other economic and cultural trends to create a unique set of conditions that support union organizing."

I heard McAlevey at a talk for her book *Raising Expectations (and Raising Hell): My Decade Fighting for the Labor Movement.* In the book and during the talk, McAlevey took SEIU to task, critiquing top-level bosses by name. She called out mid-level bosses, many of whom had moved to the top level when I worked there, for being focused on their personal power rather than building a worker-centered movement. I was excited by her forthright criticism. I sashayed up to her to fan-girl, overjoyed at hearing someone call out power as a tangible currency. That talk, and subsequent others, helped me understand that my bosses were indeed hypocrites, taking everything personally and bullying staff because they were threatened by collectivity. I'm sorry I never emailed her, as she warmly invited me to do. I fantasized about gossiping with her, getting more dirt on the horrendous union bosses who made my life miserable.

In the first few pages of *Raising Expectations (and Raising Hell)*, McAlevey describes being pulled off one campaign for another, explaining how treating staff like moving chess pieces keeps hierarchies intact. She says overuse of this disruptive staffing method by decision-makers who are far from being on the ground impacts workers' lives outside of work. This adds to snap judgments informed by implicit biases being commonplace. Relationships are transactional when organizers come and go. The deep relationships needed for organizing are constantly broken, making it more difficult to organize against the boss. But then, McAlevey excuses the disruption to her life because of the importance of the campaign. She was sent to Florida to help with the extended vote count of the 2000 presidential election and led a team collecting affidavits for Gore, from voters whose ballots had been thrown out. I wanted her criticism of the misuse of power to hold. Instead, the story—and the book—end up being about a kinder, gentler approach to the things I found abhorrent working in the labor movement.

The opening scene of the book takes place at the West Palm Beach Hilton, where senior organizers and union management are gathering. I stayed at a lot of Hiltons when I was an organizer, because many of them are unionized. What's not noted is the cost of all the people who flew on last-minute flights, the cost of all the individual rental cars and individual hotel rooms. All paid by union member dues. Unions are 501(c)(5) nonprofit organizations, but many of them spend money like the corporate world they have modeled themselves after. The term *worker* is used rhetorically. The purpose for most labor unions is to build and maintain the middle class as a political bloc to uphold normative middle-class values.

One of the worst values upheld is war. There were "War Rooms," rooms with a nameplate that actually said *War Room*, at both the Oakland and San Francisco offices. It seemed so obviously absurd. I offhandedly, but seriously, told one supervisor I thought we should put a "No" in front of the word "War." I was surprised by their nervous laughter, like I had suggested something radical. I didn't understand how we could transform work culture if we mimicked militarized language, if our values were rooted in violence. If we were overthrowing those holding the power, I'd be all in on the full diversity of tactics. But we were negotiating incremental legal changes while dressed in business casual, using lawyers in suits and all the top hits of white supremacist culture: urgency, paternalism, objectivity, defensiveness, quantity over quality, either/or binaries, the written word.

Union management called us "line staff," a corporate term for hierarchal organizations where management keeps control through "flexible" hiring practices. You know, like the problem for adjunct faculty. Or health care workers, or autoworkers, or government workers, or grocery store workers. Unreasonably long probationary periods meant union management could staff up a campaign, easily get rid of people without due process, and then bring in another round of probationary workers. Management weaponized our fear of losing our jobs into a culture of paranoia, punishing us for disrespecting what they called "the chain of command," without ever explaining all the layers of middle management and who to go to for what. There is absolutely no transparency. Union culture includes the well-known term *rank and file*, referring to union members who aren't in elected leadership positions. *Rank and file* is another military term. It refers to foot soldiers lined up in formation, with the commanding officers giving orders from the outside. The labor movement operates through a hierarchy of well-paid, well-coiffed generals who create wars using elected officers and unintentional mercenary soldiers to keep the rank and file in line and ready for battles.

Hired into a militant bureaucracy for reform, I was hoping to find guidance in McAlevey's book but, unfortunately, kept getting hung up on how she discussed her relationship to staff. She describes *giving* organizers two weeks off for the December holidays "because there would be no more time off, vacation, breaks, or really much other sleep" until the following year. They had just come through a year of intense campaigns but couldn't use their earned paid time off to rest and recuperate. A job with benefits is meaningless if you can't use them. It's one of the reasons people choose to unionize.

McAlevey describes solving a staffing budget problem on an affordable housing campaign by hiring college interns who would be okay without housing. "Unions were becoming cool again and there were college students who actually wanted to spend their summers working for low pay," she writes. Mattresses for the students were set up on the floor of a vacant office in the rented campaign headquarters. There weren't showers or kitchens. The interns had to shower at a nearby YMCA and eat out every meal. These working conditions aren't conducive to staying sharp when learning new skills or having the wherewithal not to center your own needs when knocking on a stranger's door to offer support for their basic needs.

In the book, McAlevey describes union staff like rotten fruit, writing, "Most of the organizers sent [by SEIU national headquarters] were so green as to be nearly useless, and some so bad we sent them back." The metaphor didn't read poetically, especially when sacrifice over well-being gets romanticized as movement-building. She continues, "Charts and diagrams papered the walls. People fell asleep on the floor. It felt like a movement. For me it felt like home." Working until you drop is capitalism's goal for all workers. It's macho, ableist, competitive bullshit.

The behaviors I'm criticizing have been excused as generational, with defenders saying that McAlevey is a woman who had to forge her way in a man's world. News flash: It's still a man's world. I'm holding the women of her generation who are in labor movement leadership roles accountable because we are, more or less, the same generation. Mimicking masculinist tactics and strategies for decades isn't an inherent aspect of being a certain age; it's an age-old aspect of holding on to power within the existing system. The organizing director at SEIU, the one who demanded staff be unequivocally with the union or leave, she was a couple years younger than me. The supervisor who had survived breast cancer and approved firing Aisha, leaving her without health care in the midst of her breast cancer treatments, she was a couple years older than me. Women directors at the Sacramento union job, who were my generation, wrote me up for not knowing the union president's full schedule when he visited one of my campuses. They extended my probation when I supported Palestinian and Arab members being targeted in their jobs. They weren't interested in trans and queer members' concerns when the university contracted with a telehealth tech company run by evangelical Christians that explicitly promoted Christian counseling for LGBTQ+ students. The same women uplifted TERFy members' leadership on gender education trainings. They taught reps to tell members that the union couldn't help them with claims of sexual harassment, that the issue wasn't covered in the union contract. They prevented members from targeting the university chancellor, who had protected violent and sexually predatory administrators when he went back to a faculty position and joined the union. They spent years representing a faculty member with repeated charges of sleeping with a student and then threatening to kill colleagues who reported him, instead of representing the faculty who had been threatened.

I won't excuse the women of my generation.

Their desire for power is classist, fueled by internalized misogyny intersecting with internalized racism and queerphobia.

As leaders in the labor movement, no matter their sexual orientation, gender presentation, or race, they cause deep ruptures and harm to the workers they supervise and members they represent. Keeping business as usual is not only hypocrisy but also an intentional, counter-revolutionary fight.

The labor movement shouldn't be a model for leftist activist organizations looking to scale up or lead mass mobilizations. Unions as a whole are so deeply embedded into the democratic electoral system and upholding liberalism that the left needs to look elsewhere. Instead, we need to consider that it's time to abolish unions.

PART FOUR

KNOWLEDGE

[WORLDWIDE]

CHAPTER TWENTY-SEVEN

Waiting for an Opening

"Abolition for me is a long-term project and a practice around creating the conditions that would allow for the dismantling of prisons, policing, surveillance and the creation of new institutions that actually work to keep us safe and are not fundamentally oppressive."

That's Mariame Kaba from her book *We Do This 'til We Free Us*. I can open that book to any page and find ideas that help me think about what abolishing unions can mean.

Here's one: "PIC [prison-industrial complex] abolition rejects the expansion in breadth or scope or legitimation of all aspects of the prison-industrial complex—surveillance, policing, and imprisonment of all sorts."

Unions operate on laws governing labor. A union contract defines the laws an employer might break and outlines how to hold them accountable. That's not a bad thing. It is a limited, faulty system developed to be interpreted by experts who are paid to twist it in the favor of whoever has the most power. A union also outlines aspects of the workplace that, when breached by a worker or management, are resolved through punitive measures the union mitigates. Like all legal processes, surveillance, policing, investigation, and manipulation are part and parcel of the grievance system. Like all legal processes, it can take years to reach a compromised and limited solution that will never be justice. Sometimes the process is extended because the entire union staff is assigned to work political elections for weak, compromised politicians or legislation. Workers can lose employment and any benefits that come with employment during the process. It isn't prison, but it is punishing and goes hand in hand with everything that upholds the prison-industrial complex.

Oh, another one: "As an Abolitionist I care about two things: relationships and how we address harm. The reason I'm an abolitionist is because I know that prisons, police, and surveillance cause inordinate harm. If my focus is on ending harm, then I can't be pro deathmaking and harmful institutions. I'm actually trying to eradicate harm, not reproduce it, not reinforce it, not maintain it."

Abolishing unions isn't a call to destroy unions. It's a call to ensure all workers can be free from violence, punishment, and harm at work. Abolishing unions means creating a world where policing and surveillance are not how we address differences and fears, or how we shift the dynamics of power and control. Abolishing unions means my liberation is bound up in yours, even if we don't like each other.

Most labor bosses operate out of fear instead of vision, using solidarity as a weapon instead of a principle.

When another person who's marginalized and minoritized by white supremacist, cishet patriarchal structures comes for me, it's hard not to lose my shit. I hold them to a higher standard than the straight white man's ways because I know we can do better. I understand we're tired; I don't understand doubling down on things just being what they are.

Our imaginations have been stolen from us. We have to liberate them.

I dream of an abolitionist feminist labor movement that transforms the harm of work inside and outside unions. Emergent strategies dance through the dream. adrienne maree brown conjured up these strategies, and I believe they have miles of landscape to travel through to help us move toward abolition.

"There is a conversation that only the people in this room right now can have. Find it." The organizing methods of the labor movement are based on the assumption that people act only in their own self-interest. Decolonize those assumptions by finding your people, building affinity, acting collectively.

"Trust the people. (If you trust the people, they become trustworthy)." All the people. We don't need supervisors, managers, administrators, bosses, or to be led. We need nonhierarchical, catalyzing and collaborative, transitory leadership.

"What you pay attention to grows." It can be paranoia, or it can be trust.

"Small is good, small is all" and "Move at the speed of trust. Focus on critical connections more than critical mass." More ≠ better. Coerced unity ≠ transformative wins.

"There's always enough time for the right work." "Less prep, more presence." We are passed the baton from our elders and we pass it on when we become elders. Shhh. Listen. "Never a failure, always a lesson."

"Change is constant. Be like water." Merge, submerge, emerge.

My dream of abolition includes a self-defense concept I learned through Home Alive: waiting for an opening.

Take a breath in. Deep or not, the action brings oxygen to the brain. Take another breath, feeling as much of the body as possible. Pause. Assess. Create a plan.

In our classes, we'd practice breathing while lying on the ground with a learning partner sitting on top of us, pinning our arms down. We'd practice looking around the room from this position, identifying escape routes and possible weapons. We were waiting for the moment to save ourselves. We talked about how that moment sometimes, even often, appears after horrifying, life-altering violence occurs. If we're still alive, the opening is the breath we take when we access support systems and the breath we take decades later when we realize healing is lifelong. "Waiting for an opening" means developing the patience for the long game while finding the right moments to take or pass one of the many batons flying through the air. One of them is: "The personal is political."

CHAPTER TWENTY-EIGHT

The Edge of the Stage

A few days ago, I got the same text over and over. *Did you see this?* each person asked, sending me a link to an article that says the fuckhead who killed Mia is dead.

I try to remember what I wanted all those years ago, what I thought justice or vengeance might be. I already hated cops and the legal system, knew the violence and danger to Black and Brown and Indigenous people, to poor women, to me. I carried this contradiction, this tension, underneath every conversation about abolition. I hoped for his death. I never imagined he'd die in a global pandemic that disproportionately killed people in prisons. Some things are so real they are impossible to dream up.

The embodiment of fear and terror I've carried with me since Mia's murder is gone.

I think about swimming. In a pool. Reaching a wall, turning around, going back. Reaching another wall, turning around, going back.

Repetitive.

Meditative.

Merge, submerge, emerge.

I think about floating in a lake. An undertow tickling the ever-present edges of danger. Keep breathing, keep twisting. I hear Mia's voice: "C'mon, girl. Keep going." I hear her singing: "Don't like to be a violent woman, but sometimes I fucking have to."

Von is in the other room making dinner, the cats in their thirteenth hour of sleep for the day. I'm sitting at my desk writing. A pencil drawing I made when I was four is taped to the wall in front of me. A shining sun in the top left corner, five smiling figures, arms entwined or swinging wide, a field of flowers underneath them. At the top of the page, in my childish scrawl, it says, "My sister is dancing with me." I didn't have a sister then.

More lyrics of Mia's float through my head as if I were at a Gits show yesterday, drinking and feeling and loving and hurting. Mia sings: "This twisted world can sometimes seem like it's caving in around me.... Just keep your twisting, keep your twisting, I'll keep breathing, I keep breathing."

Vibrantly alive in my memories, Zar and Sadie sit like gargoyles on the edge of the stage. My throng of sisters sing along with Mia from the pit. Jennifer and Leah sweat on each other, jostling each other. Michele skips in circles. Aisha and Miranda pass a joint back and forth. I jump on the stage next to Mia, between Sadie and Zar. Feeling the purest pain, I dive off into the purest joy. Zoë and Mich catch me.

Acknowledgments

Reading acknowledgments feels like reading a secret note that fell out of the writer's pocket. I love reading them and enjoyed writing this. If you thought you might see your name but don't, just know you are here. Menopause.

Thank you to Mattilda Bernstein Sycamore for being there every single time I needed you as a writing mentor, even when that wasn't what we had planned. Thank you to Raechal Anne Jolie, Ariel Gore, Jessica Hoffman, and Anya Achtenberg for guiding and mentoring me through this year's long endeavor. Thank you to Daria Yudasefsky and Susie Bright for critical support at just the right times. Thank you to Charlie Allison and Sarah Lyn Rogers for editing this up to the finish line, and to Wade Ostrowski for lifting it on over. Thank you to Joey, Courtney, Stephanie, Steven, Dan, Ramsey, and all the other PM Press folks for making this, like, an actual book.

Thank you to Jessica Beard, Katie Tastrom, Dana Garza, James Tracy, Josh Fernandez, Steve Moriarity, Samdie Ajari, Patricio, Jinha, the Howard Zinn Bookfair Coordinating Committee, the Literary Kitchen writers, and the *make/shift* magazine community for being the radical writers I've grown, and keep growing, with.

Thank you to IJAN for being my political home, the Sacramento Palestinian liberation activist community, JVP Sacramento, and Queers for Palestine Sacramento for being needed comrades at different points since Israel ramped up the US-funded occupation into a US-funded genocide. Thank you to Dean, Danielle, Theo, Genevieve, Sarah A, Bee, Rev. Alex, Rain, Maggie, and Patricia for getting me through many of the darker moments of doubt.

Thank you to CFA, CHESU, SEIU 1021, and CWA 3404 union siblings, especially Michelle, Fili, Leti, Lindsay (and Andrea!), Nicola,

Luna, Marlyn, Cecil, Nicki, Daniel, Noga, David, Rob, Carol, Alisa, Hugh, and, obviously, Mary.

Thank you to all the founding members of Home Alive, and to everyone who participated in and carried the organization through the seventeen years of its various manifestations.

Thank you to all my Antioch people, to those of you on campus between 1985 and 1989, to those of you I got to know in Santa Fe between 2009 and 2014, and especially to Sarah Meyer and Danielle Giudice Wallis. Thank you to Lisa Kezios for the thread that extends further back than Antioch (and Mariska too!). Thank you to Katie Kadwell, Amy Robinson, and Shira Goodnight for each showing up again, when you did. Thank you to Lando for always being there as a brother. Thank you to Devin and Dylan for Shitting Glitter and moving to Sacramento.

Thank you to Sadie Viva Chiquita and all the other animals and humans who are too numerous to list out, who gave so much love and laughter and purring, and were here for too brief a time.

Thank you to Steve for teaching me how to fight for myself and what I believe in. Thank you to Sanna for teaching me art can be the bottom line. Thank you to (Morry) and Judy, and Mort and (Lia), for filling in some of the missing pieces. Thank you to (Mars) and (Cirla) for doing what you did for Sanna and Steve. Thank you to Clint for unknowingly ending some cycles. Thank you to Mick, Ellen, Jason, Sterling, Kaela, Kelly, Chris, Cheryl, Bridget, Erica and family, and Davin, Jake, and Tyler for the different concepts of what it means to be relatives.

Thank you to Mary Ann, (Don), Mary, Alex, Rosa, Bryan, Aimee, Kassie, Erik, Monica, Bame, Moises, Troy, and Kathy for so easily accepting me into your family.

Thank you to Pauli for teaching me what it means to want to nurture, love, and protect another human being unconditionally.

Thank you to Zoë and Mich for picking me up and brushing me off since the First Gulf War, for sticking around and doing it over and over, still. Thank you to Linda and Jehn for being part of this chosen family.

Thank you, Von. This book wouldn't exist without you. You feed me even when I don't realize I'm hungry. You feed Coco Glamora and Grace Bean, who are always hungry. You love us all and make a safe home for our fractured, traumatized nervous systems. You make it worth it to keep trying.

About the Author

Jessica Lawless is an artist and one of the cofounders of the self-defense collective Home Alive. Her artwork has been shown in galleries across the US, included in international anarchist and queer film festivals, and censored by a Catholic university. She was a regular contributor to *make/shift* magazine and periodically contributes to the *Anarchist Review of Books*. Jessica wrote the introduction to *Lady Lazarus: Confronting* 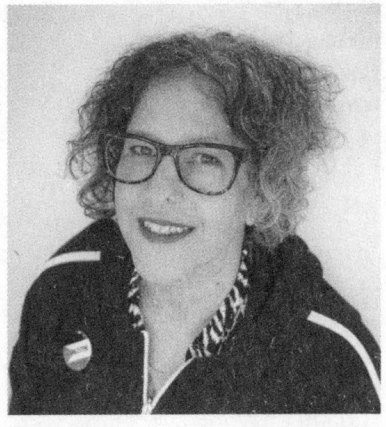 *Lydia Lunch*, contributed a chapter to *Resolutions 3: Global Networks of Video*, and had pieces in the anthologies *Feminisms in Motion: Voices for Justice, Liberation, and Transformation* and *Places Like Home*. A former adjunct professor and labor organizer, she lives in Sacramento, California, with her partner, Von, and their two toothless cats.

ABOUT PM PRESS

PM Press is an independent, radical publisher of critically
necessary books for our tumultuous times. Our aim is to
deliver bold political ideas and vital stories to all walks
of life and arm the dreamers to demand the impossible.
Founded in 2007 by a small group of people with decades
of publishing, media, and organizing experience, we have
sold millions of copies of our books, most often one at a time, face to face. We're
old enough to know what we're doing and young enough to know what's at
stake. Join us to create a better world.

PM Press
PO Box 23912
Oakland, CA 94623
www.pmpress.org

PM Press in Europe
europe@pmpress.org
www.pmpress.org.uk

FRIENDS OF PM PRESS

These are indisputably momentous times—the financial
system is melting down globally and the Empire is
stumbling. Now more than ever there is a vital need for
radical ideas.

In the many years since its founding—and on a mere
shoestring—PM Press has risen to the formidable challenge of publishing
and distributing knowledge and entertainment for the struggles ahead. With
hundreds of releases to date, we have published an impressive and stimulating
array of literature, art, music, politics, and culture. Using every available
medium, we've succeeded in connecting those hungry for ideas and information
to those putting them into practice.

Friends of PM allows you to directly help impact, amplify, and revitalize the
discourse and actions of radical writers, filmmakers, and artists. It provides us
with a stable foundation from which we can build upon our early successes and
provides a much-needed subsidy for the materials that can't necessarily pay
their own way. You can help make that happen—and receive every new title
automatically delivered to your door once a month—by joining as a Friend of PM
Press. And, we'll throw in a free T-shirt when you sign up.

Here are your options:

- **$30 a month** Get all books and pamphlets plus a 50% discount on all
  webstore purchases

- **$40 a month** Get all PM Press releases (including CDs and DVDs) plus a
  50% discount on all webstore purchases

- **$100 a month** Superstar—Everything plus PM merchandise, free downloads,
  and a 50% discount on all webstore purchases

For those who can't afford $30 or more a month, we have **Sustainer Rates** at
$15, $10, and $5. Sustainers get a free PM Press T-shirt and a 50% discount on
all purchases from our website.

Your Visa or Mastercard will be billed once a month,
until you tell us to stop. Or until our efforts succeed
in bringing the revolution around. Or the financial
meltdown of Capital makes plastic redundant.
Whichever comes first.

The Hands That Crafted the Bomb: The Making of a Lifelong Antifascist

Josh Fernandez

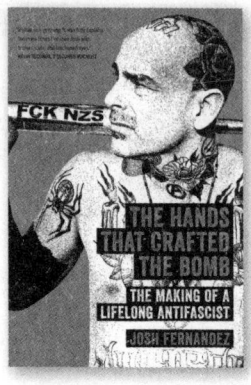

ISBN: 979-8-88744-023-1
$22.95   256 pages

Josh Fernandez is a community college professor in Northern California who finds himself under investigation for "soliciting students for potentially dangerous activities" after starting an antifascist club on campus.

As Fernandez spends the year defending his job, he reflects on a life lived in protest of the status quo, swept up in chaos and rage, from his childhood in Boston dealing with a mentally ill father and a new family to a move to Davis, California, where, in the basement shows of the early '90s, Nazi boneheads proliferated the music scene, looking for heads to crack. His crew's first attempts at an antifascist group fall short when a member dies in a knife fight.

A born antiauthoritarian, filled with an untamable rage, Fernandez rails against the system and aggressively chooses the path of most resistance. This leads to long spates of living in his car, strung out on drugs, and robbing the whiteboys coming home from the clubs at night. He eventually realizes that his rage needs an outlet and finds relief for his existential dread in the form of running. And fighting Nazis. Fernandez cobbles together a life for himself as a writing professor, a facilitator of a self-defense collective, a boots-on-the-ground participant in antifa work, and a proud father of two children he unapologetically raises to question authority.

"Fernandez is scathing on the corporate-minded liberals who talk about equity and diversity, antiracism, and gay rights but can't deal with people actually defending themselves or challenging authority. What he offers instead isn't heroics or militant slogans or even measured analysis—it's the messy story of a 'fucked-up person' trying to 'channel rage into something less destructive,' a guy who tends to run face-first into danger but also has the good sense to run away screaming when confronted with a knife-wielding racist. Fernandez's account of violence, trauma, and loneliness is hard to read in places, but there's an underlying sweetness here, a hopefulness about flawed people helping each other out, a sense that if we can get past the lies, we can remake this world together."
—Matthew N. Lyons, author of *Insurgent Supremacists: The U.S. Far Right's Challenge to State and Empire*

Queercore: How to Punk a Revolution: An Oral History

Edited by Liam Warfield, Walter Crasshole, and Yony Leyser with an Introduction by Anna Joy Springer and Lynn Breedlove

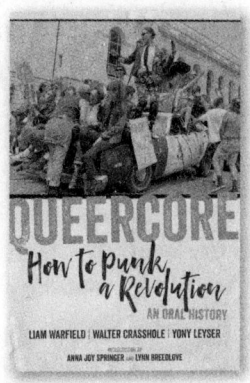

ISBN: 978-1-62963-796-9
$20.00   208 pages

Queercore: How to Punk a Revolution: An Oral History is the very first comprehensive overview of a movement that defied both the music underground and the LGBT mainstream community.

Through exclusive interviews with protagonists like Bruce LaBruce, G.B. Jones, Jayne County, Kathleen Hanna of Bikini Kill and Le Tigre, film director and author John Waters, Lynn Breedlove of Tribe 8, Jon Ginoli of Pansy Division, and many more, alongside a treasure trove of never-before-seen photographs and reprinted zines from the time, *Queercore* traces the history of a scene originally "fabricated" in the bedrooms and coffee shops of Toronto and San Francisco by a few young, queer punks to its emergence as a relevant and real revolution. *Queercore* is a down-to-details firsthand account of the movement explored by the people that lived it—from punk's early queer elements, to the moment that Toronto kids decided they needed to create a scene that didn't exist, to Pansy Division's infiltration of the mainstream, and the emergence of riot grrrl—as well as the clothes, zines, art, film, and music that made this movement an exciting middle finger to complacent gay and straight society. *Queercore* will stand as both a testament to radically gay politics and culture and an important reference for those who wish to better understand this explosive movement.

"Finally, a book that centers on the wild, innovative, and fearless contributions queers made to punk rock, creating a punker-than-punk subculture beneath the subculture, queercore. Gossipy and inspiring, a historical document and a call to arms during a time when the entire planet could use a dose of queer, creative rage."
—Michelle Tea, author of *Valencia*

"I knew at an early age I didn't want to be part of a church, I wanted to be part of a circus. It's documents such as this book that give hope for our future. Anarchists, the queer community, the roots of punk, the Situationists, and all the other influential artistic guts eventually had to intersect. Queercore is completely logical, relevant, and badass."
—Justin Pearson, The Locust, Three One G

Be Gay, Do Crime: Everyday Acts of Queer Resistance and Rebellion

Edited by Zane McNeill, Riley Clare Valentine, and Blu Buchanan with a Foreword by Cindy Barukh Milstein and an Introduction by Working Class History

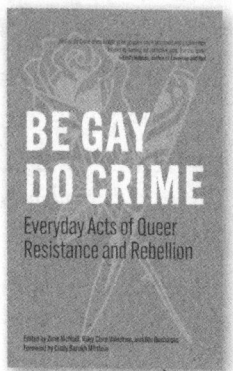

ISBN: 979-8-88744-130-6 (paperback)
      979-8-88744-143-6 (hardcover)
$24.95 / $49.95   304 pages

Sometimes it pays to be gay and do crime.

As communities are boldly rising to challenge capitalism, white supremacy, and authoritarianism, *Be Gay, Do Crime: Everyday Acts of Queer Resistance and Rebellion* is your ultimate guide to LGBTQ+ resilience and rebellion. Packed with daily snapshots of radical queer history, this book celebrates the bold, the brave, and the beautifully defiant moments that have shaped the fight for justice.

Ever wonder why the Stonewall protests became an uprising or what the earliest acts of queer resistance looked like? How about the ways queer communities have organized against oppression across the globe? *Be Gay, Do Crime* dives into these stories and so many more—from fierce acts of resistance to joyful victories—bringing to life the rich, diverse history of LGBTQ+ liberation.

By situating readers within a larger pattern of struggle, these everyday acts counter the erasure of queer people from history and serve as a reminder that our struggles are part of a broader fight against systemic violence and dehumanization.

But, this isn't just a history book; it's a rallying cry. Flip to any page, soak up some inspiration, and join the legacy of resistance.

"The history of queer people is marked by resistance and resilience against significant hostility and harassment from those in power. Be Gay, Do Crime explores the strategic use of arrests and police violence as tools to suppress individuals who bravely refused to go back into the closet. This almanac highlights incredible acts of defiance in the face of power and shows us all on whose shoulders we stand."
—Erin Reed, transgender activist and journalist

"Day by day, the collective vigilance of queer people in the US and around the world has led us on paths toward liberation. This book of days names the names—some renowned and many forgotten—and celebrates quotidian victories, one day at a time. This daybook is a keeper!"
—Rahne Alexander, intermedia artist and writer from Baltimore